hell bound

New Gothic Art

hell bound

FRANCESCA GAVIN

LAURENCE KING PUBLISHING

LAURENCE KING

Published in 2008 by
Laurence King Publishing Ltd
361–373 City Road
London EC1V 1LR
United Kingdom

t: 020 7841 6900
f: 020 7841 6910
e-mail: enquiries@laurenceking.co.uk
www.laurenceking.co.uk

A catalogue for this book is available from the
British Library.

ISBN: 9781856695633

Design: Studio8 Design

Cover image: Ken Kagami, *Red Bicycle*, 2007. Mixed
media and cotton, 18 x 27 x 40 cm. Courtesy the artist
and gallery.sora., Tokyo

Inside cover illustration: French

Introduction
Francesca Gavin

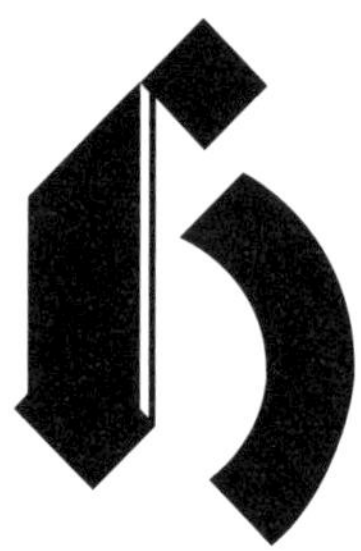as anybody seen the Devil? Mephistopheles does not have a clear-cut image anymore. The iconic personification of evil has disintegrated and become absorbed into all other aspects of modern life. Hell is no longer simply a destination after death. It is within the landscape and the architecture, within our own bodies, within communities, within technology. Hell is humanity itself.

In the past decade there has been an increasing number of artworks that play with the imagery of horror, death, torture and violence: a gothic blackness. Why now? The cliché that horror is an expression of millennial anxiety – the 'fin de siècle' syndrome – doesn't fit. The idea that as a century or millennium comes to a close we panic about the end of the world, and this spills out into a culture of horror, is inappropriate. The year 2000 has come and gone and the taste for the gothic is increasing. Nor does this theory explain the penchant for horror imagery in the 1940s, 1960s and 1980s. We are far enough into the twenty-first century for it to be founded on something else.

One argument is that the gothic is a response to what Michael Moore coined 'the culture of fear' in his film on America and guns, *Bowling for Columbine*. He suggests that teenage ultra-violence is partly a response to the contemporary media's sensationalist reportage of crime and violence. It could be claimed that horror in contemporary art is another step in this violent cycle. Shootings are carried out in response to a culture of materialism and fear. Art is created in response to the shootings. There's nothing new about that idea. The Marquis de Sade argues in his examination of the novel, *Idée sur les Romans*, that gothic literature 'was the inevitable result of the revolutionary shocks which all of Europe has suffered'. He established the idea that the manifestation of horror in creativity was a response to a world desensitized to violence. Charles Baudelaire complained about the sensationalist aspect of the media in the 1860s, calling newspapers a 'tissue of horrors' and an 'orgy of universal atrocities'.

Arguably the media has always been preoccupied with shocking imagery and violent narrative. 'Being a spectator of calamities taking place in another country is a quintessential modern experience,' as Susan Sontag put it in her book *Regarding the Pain of Others*. Positive news has always been in the minority (except when an instrument of propaganda). The media is a reflection of the ideology of everyday society. Slovenian philosopher and cultural critic Slavoj Žižek observes in Alfonzo Cuarón's documentary *The Possibility of Hope* that the main mode of politics today is fear – of immigration, of a strong state, of taxation. People in the modern world are mobilized through fear and pleasure.

What are we so afraid of? Anything that transgresses the safe, cultural codes of 'civilization'; anything that crosses between reality and fantasy, social laws and taboos, the rational and irrational. Much of the art in this book is a manifestation of contemporary fears – of death itself, of the war in Iraq, of serial killers, paedophiles, guns and gang culture, apocalyptic fears about environmental disaster and global warming. There is a lot to be afraid of these days. Exploring dark imagery or ideas in art arguably helps create a sense of control in a world where we have none. Catherine Spooner argues in the book *Contemporary Gothic* that the 'gothic contains our fears so we can live in safety'. That safety is looking pretty tenuous. This imagery reflects our struggle to have an identity in a society losing its sense of self.

Horror also connects to one of our most primal desires: voyeurism. The imagery of death and evil could be a metaphor for art itself – the uncontrollable desire to look. By looking at violence or horror we become complicit in its creation, part of the cause – hence part of the discomfort in looking. We know that humans are often the cause of terror, not some imaginary outside evil force. We are creating our own nightmares.

These artworks are as much about the creation of art itself as the political or sociological zeitgeist. This is post-pop art, which references imagery of daily life and the media in order to connect to its audience. It was an approach pioneered by Andy Warhol in his screen prints of the electric chair and car crashes. The gothic is a contemporary language that people can connect to on an instinctive level. The artworks that reference horror or the gothic are often not dark or negative. Horror is a language we can use to look at all the other issues in life. These images have been interpreted as Freudian, Marxist, feminist, semiotic, imperialist. The gothic can be whatever you want it to be.

Often expressions of horror are self-referential and poke fun at the genre's fairground imagery. Humour is central to so much of this artwork. Sometimes it verges on hysteria; sometimes it is self-conscious irony; sometimes it is a vehicle for political satire.

It would be facile and incorrect to describe the artists in this book as purely gothic. In many cases it is only part of certain pieces or periods in their careers. It would be wrong to throw everyone who uses black paint into the same creative pigeonhole, but there is a thread of dark imagery or ideas that runs through much contemporary art.

These artists all have very different aims and desires – and many different forms of expression. There are monsters, the grotesque, violated or mutant bodies, the divided self, ghosts, dolls, masks, skulls, disgust and the abject. These are images filled with the colour black, decay and instability. Fear is reflected on to the environment, or on to the self, or on to others. Sometimes the work is nihilistic or anarchic.

Bret Easton Ellis's novel *Lunar Park* is a perfect expression of this wide-open twenty-first-century horror. Here the writer protagonist is haunted by his own literary creations. Terror is projected on to the entire landscape – the house itself he lives in becomes a living, breathing creature of fear. Reality and fantasy blur. This is what makes contemporary horror so effective and intriguing; we question where art stops and real life begins.

james aldridge

It all began with birds. James Aldridge's stylized paintings and graphic cut-out wall pieces reflect a childhood interest in natural history. 'My dad is a keen bird-watcher and I used to copy pictures from his bird books and try to get them right. When I was about nine or ten I got into rearing moths and butterflies with my brother, so I was copying images from entomology books.'

As he grew older this attraction to nature merged with an interest in heavy metal, which he sees as a major influence on the dark atmosphere in his work; it was the darkness not just of the music, but also of the imagery that surrounded it. 'In the last few years I have rediscovered this music and its more extreme, modern-day incarnation. It is really interesting how something that is clichéd, dumb and anti-intellectual can produce such inspired, strange and radical new music. The atmosphere it creates is really important to my images and it is always playing while I work.'

His work explores the paradoxes around popular art forms and cultural prejudice. He aims to take overly familiar images and use them out of context so that they are reinvigorated with a different emotion or energy. 'I'm really interested in pictorial cliché. I'm trying to create an atmosphere in my work from these elements, by placing them in a different context. Some of the reactions to the work are really strange and I think they can give a very good indication about what people expect art to do.'

There is a sense of lost narrative in his work. Instead, Aldridge creates an atmospheric impression. 'I increasingly want to create a sense that something is happening, but you aren't sure what it is. I'm also trying to add a sense of

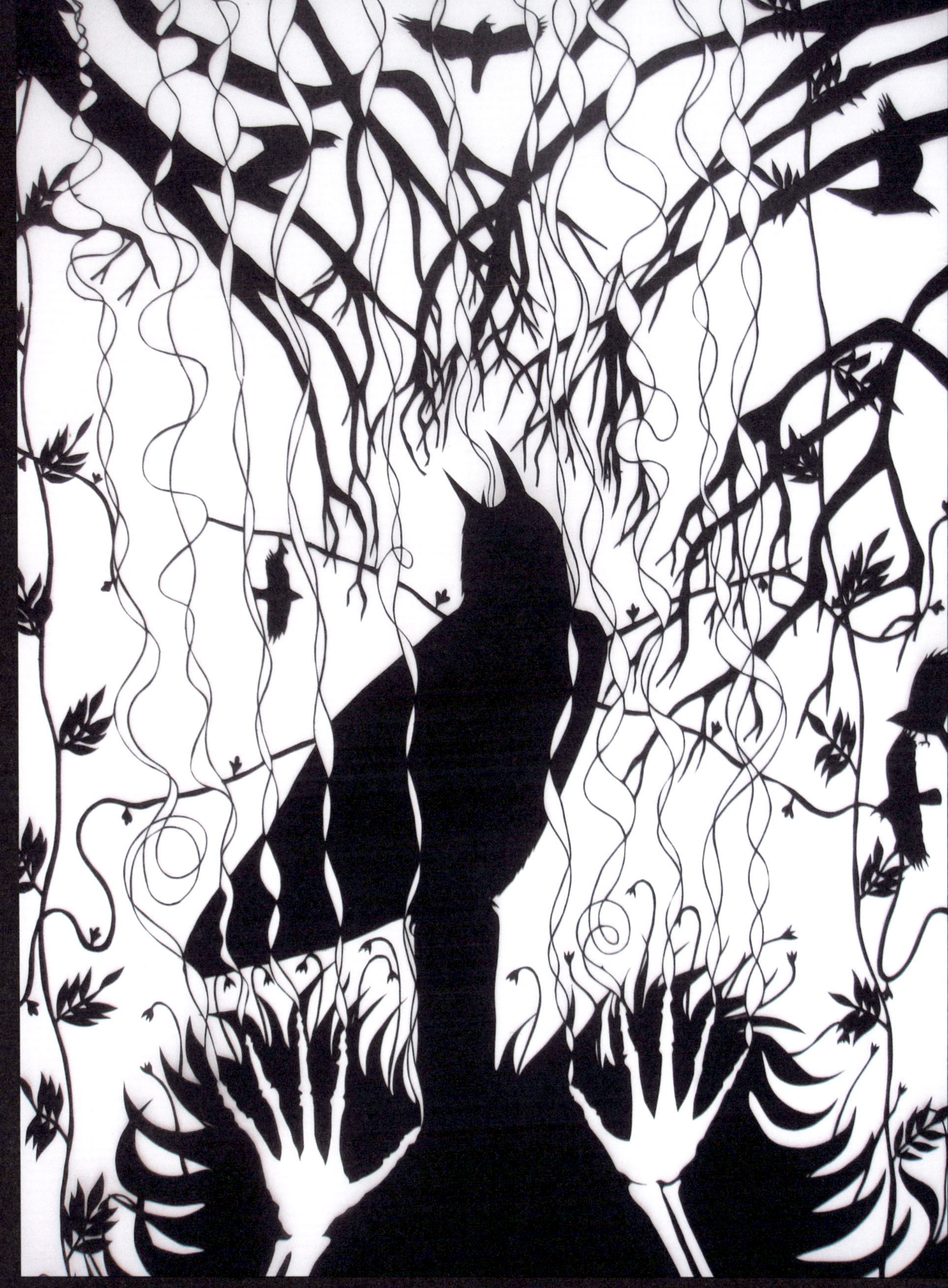

animation, introducing elements such as smoke that create a different space and sense of time.'

He uses silhouettes to depict animals, birds and plants. These are often dark crows and swamp-like landscapes, rather than overtly positive natural images. 'People are generally suspicious of crows. They suggest desolation and bleakness, and I like the contrast with the richer, more decorative elements of my work.' He has made other pieces with vultures, exploring why they are seen as more repulsive than other animals despite their essential role in the natural cycle. Aldridge sees the avian scavengers in his work as somehow placing the viewer in the position of a body dying on a battlefield. The viewer, and humanity itself, is in decay.

Skulls often litter his landscapes. 'The process of decay is part of the cycle of nature and is not necessarily something bad. A bird perching on a bone suggests something altogether more strange than the reality of a situation like that. The idea of decay is unnerving to us because it reminds us of our mortality.' Aldridge uses bones and skulls to suggest a human presence in the work, without having to depict individuals. 'The skull suggests something that has been. When I see a skull or skeleton I can't help thinking about the person it was. It was an individual who has become an object.' Skulls are used symbolically to suggest something negative and mysterious.

Although he depicts nature, Aldridge is not naturalistic in his approach. Instead, the pieces are flat and stylized, with layers of block-like imagery. Alongside paintings, Aldridge creates large paper cut-out installations. Here, instead of adding lines, he eliminates space. The negative spaces around the shapes are removed to reveal an image, so the outcome is never completely known. 'I make them on panels that all fit together and are site specific. Because of their size and fragility, I never know how they are going to look until they are installed. I have to have a very clear mental picture of how the image is evolving.'

The contradiction between beauty and horror in nature is something Aldridge sees as key. It is what gives his dark imagery its impact. The artist is aware that we are surrounded by horror in the media every day. Art, for him, forces you to look at imagery that you want to avoid. 'It's a different thing to be confronted by a static piece of art that you have to engage with. You can't turn it off.' We may not want to confront gothic images in art, but reality is far more disturbing.

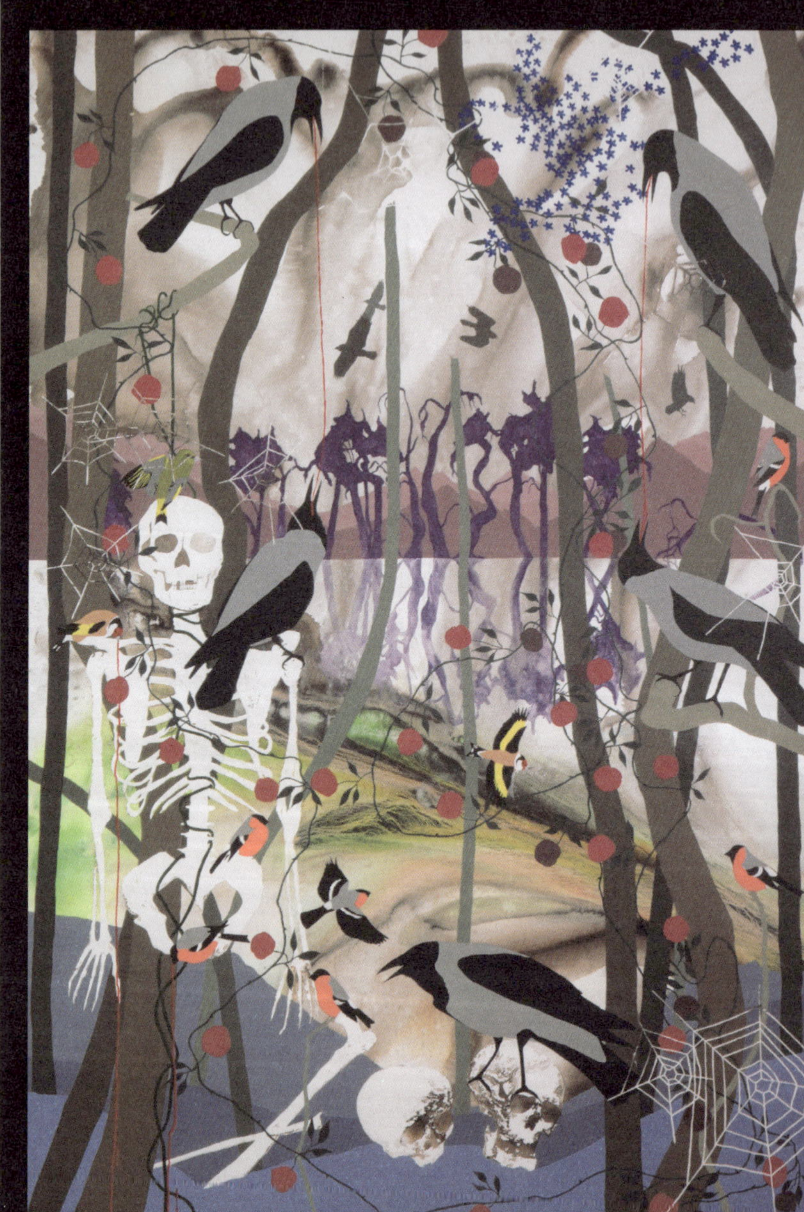

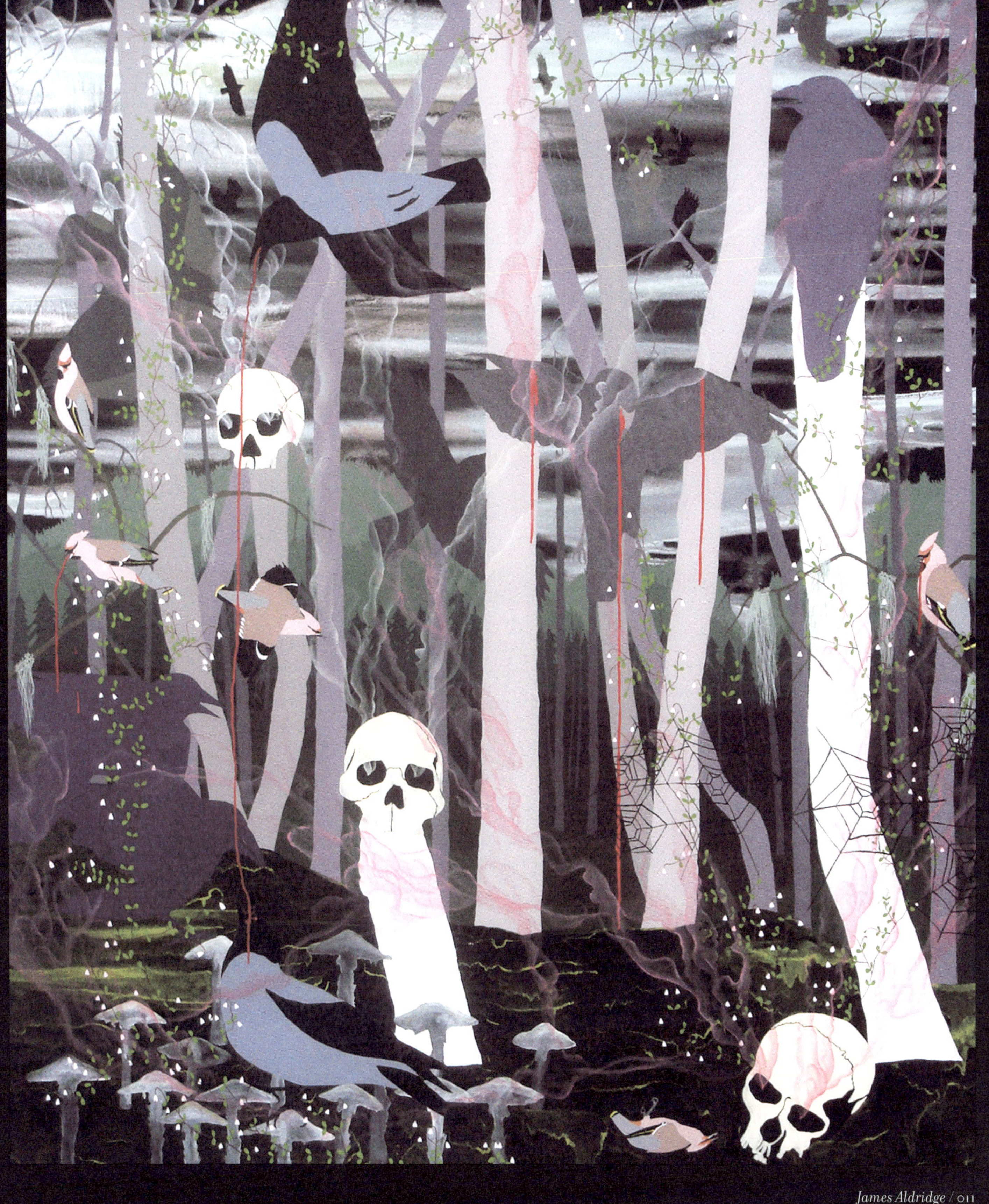

olaf breuning

Olaf Breuning's photographs and installations brilliantly fuse humour with imagery of the monstrous. 'I guess I am a funny person. I like to laugh. Isn't life hard enough?'

Many of his pieces resemble some insane version of *National Geographic* images of unusual tribes around the world. He often depicts strange kinds of tribal 'families' grouped together in a comic line-up or hiding in their 'natural' environments. 'It is always fascinating how a culture tries to find answers for all the big and small questions in life. For me, it is one of the most exciting observations. As a child of the post-modern, my door is wide open to different possibilities of how to manage this life.'

Breuning strives to make these groups of 'others' more menacing. In the installation *Apes*, he surrounded masked, hunched figures with glowing orange lighting and added red demonic eyes. 'At the end we are still primitive. It never will be a "brave new world". There is always an archaic and primitive side to us. Maybe I am romantic about the primitive side of life, but I am still very fascinated by the fact that it will be always a big part of existence – no matter how far we go with technology.'

The artist's online installation – *olafbruening.com* – is an impressive exploration of our relationship with technology. Instead of creating an easy, clickable site, Breuning forces the viewer to interact physically and type in page domain names, in order to follow a kind of visual treasure hunt. 'I bought software to make homepages and it was way too complicated to learn. The only thing I was able to do was to upload one photo. So I had to buy a lot of domains

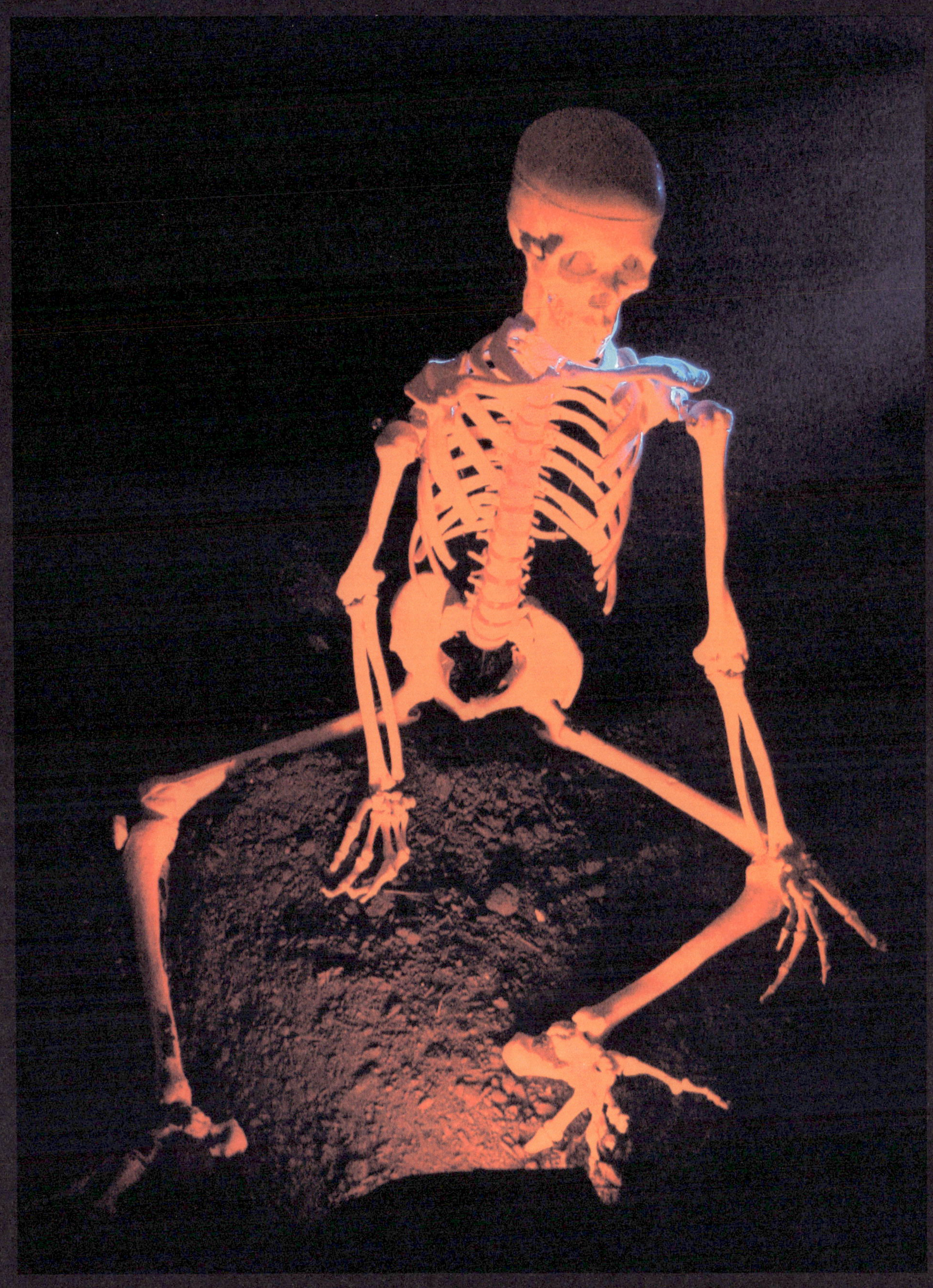

in order to have many pages. Also I liked the idea of letting visitors struggle a little. Nothing comes from nothing.'

Ghosts also 'haunt' his work – their shadows are lined up against a wall, or a crowd of toy ghosts 'scare' the viewer. A larger *Ghosts* installation consists of a long line of life-size ghost characters (with floating balloons for heads under sheets) snaking around a gallery space, the white sheets covered in cartoon-like graphic faces and dripping blood. His depiction of phantoms is consciously comic. He often uses the classic tongue-in-cheek image of ghosts in white sheets. 'That is the only idea I have so far of what a ghost would look like. I like to work with this simple cliché of a ghost.' Here horror is an immediately recognizable language that viewers can relate to and understand.

Breuning's installation *Hello Darkness* fuses death with sex and a dose of psychedelia. He created a space through the smashed wall of a 'library' where people could watch a skeleton having a conversation with a sex doll lying in a coffin. They discussed death and philosophy. 'It was one of the most expensive sex dolls on the market, made out of silicon. She was lying in a sunset-painted coffin having a sing-song with a skeleton. They spoke about life and she was asking the skeleton how it is to be dead. The whole setting was in darkness, there was a blue laser tunnel and a lot of speakers with a very melancholic soundtrack.'

The photographic pieces that are the bulk of Breuning's work are only the remnants of his creative process. His images demonstrate that a lot of effort goes into creating a set or something sculptural to shoot. Breuning does not just capture life – he creates an alternative heightened world that echoes life at its most amusing and inventive. 'I really would like to find some kind of "Olaf Land" where I would only have to put my camera in position and press the button and it would already be there. Since that is not the case, unfortunately, I have to stage the whole scene to get my fantasy going. In order to make my visual diary real, I have to move things around and create the scene physically.'

His fantasy environment questions reality itself – and perhaps, on a deeper level, examines social ideologies and the accepted vision of the other. 'The photos are a kind of documentary. They speak about something that happened. That is what I am interested in – creating something that looks nearly real. A scene which first makes you think "yes, that could be" and, after watching for a while, you see that it is somehow strange and weird. It irritates you and makes you question what you see.'

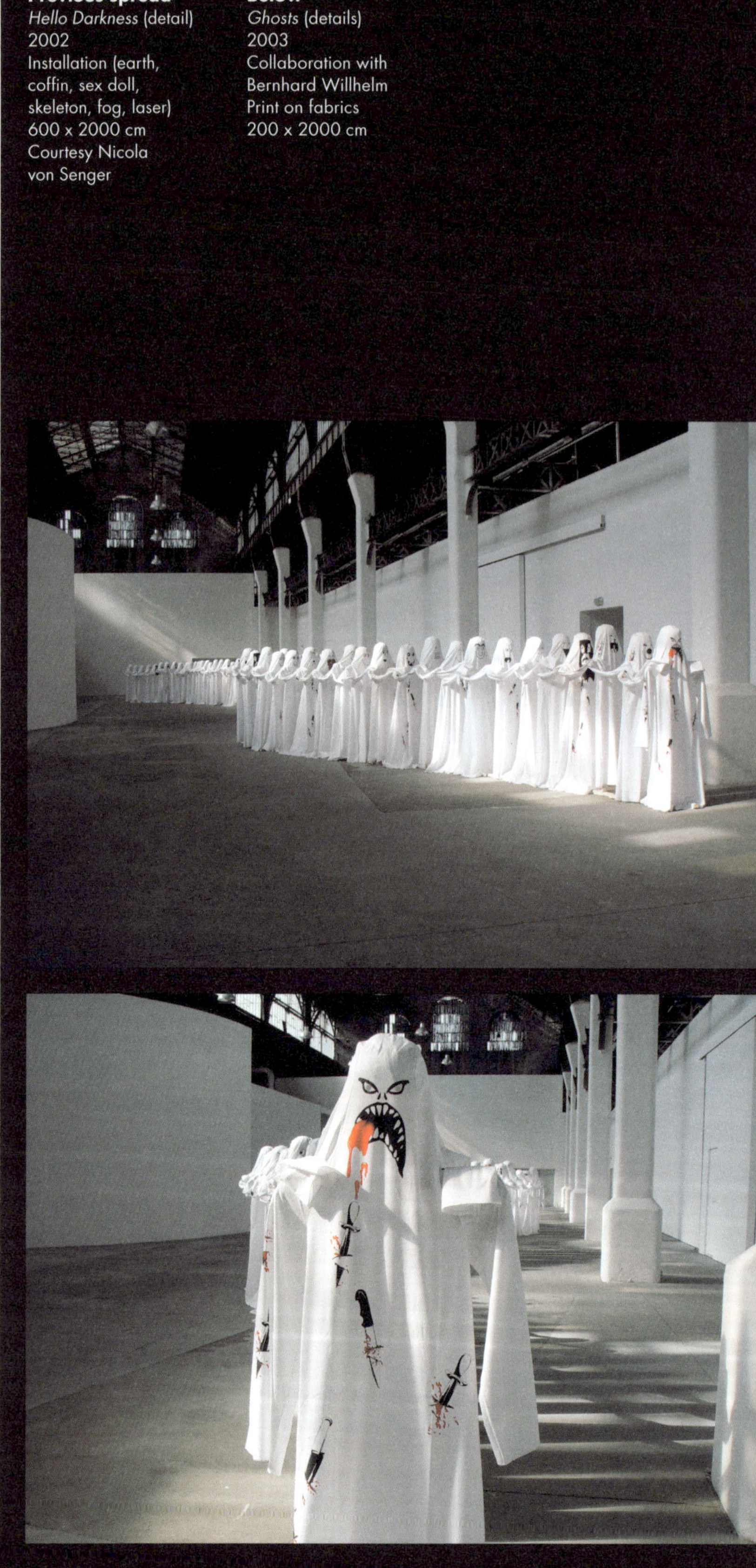

Previous spread
Hello Darkness (detail)
2002
Installation (earth, coffin, sex doll, skeleton, fog, laser)
600 x 2000 cm
Courtesy Nicola von Senger

Below
Ghosts (details)
2003
Collaboration with Bernhard Willhelm
Print on fabrics
200 x 2000 cm

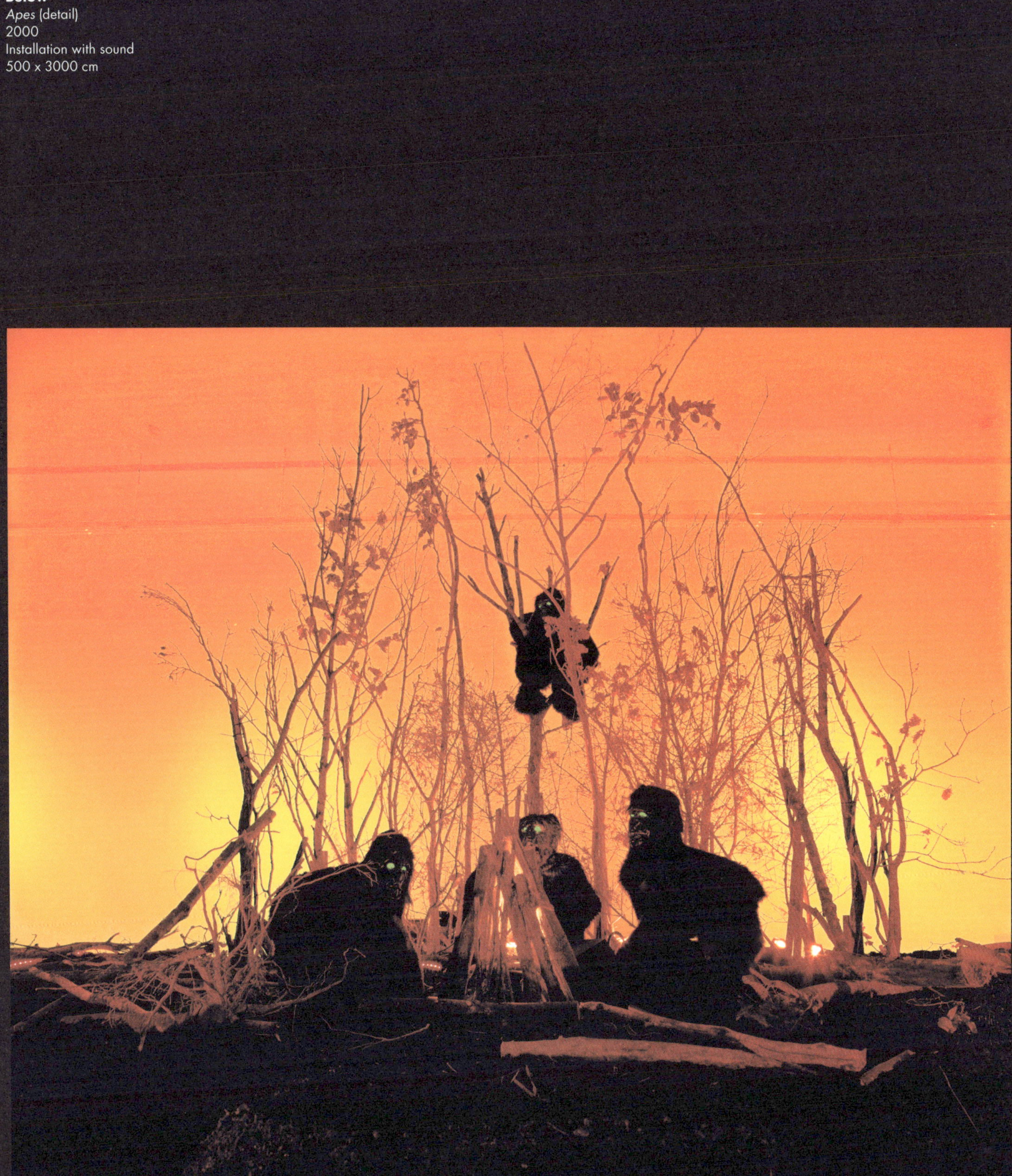

Below
Apes (detail)
2000
Installation with sound
500 x 3000 cm

luke caulfield

t's hard to get a good look at Luke Caulfield's paintings. These lushly painted objects are often boarded up with pieces of wood. Much of his work resembles a pile of badly packed objects in transit. They lean against walls like images held within makeshift prisons. You can't see the work in its entirety — which only makes you want to peer in and look harder.

Caulfield puts this process down to a case of split identity. 'I split the authorship of my paintings up. My alter ego — Hurm Must — boxes those things. I could suggest maybe he does them as some sort of protection or maybe he's pushing people out,' Caulfield explains. 'I just couldn't bear being myself any longer. I found myself very contradictory and extreme in my tastes. It was difficult to understand that, without making someone else. In a way maybe he's the artist, and I'm just the documenter.'

The concept of the alter ego also connects to the artist's interest in comics. Caulfield points out that Marcel Duchamp's alter ego, R Mutt, also came from an English comic. 'I wanted the name of someone who seems quite inarticulate and socially inept.' Inspired by Rorschach Man, from Alan Moore's graphic novel *The Watchmen*, he envisaged a character who was alienated, unkempt and unclear, the 'lowbrow', instinctive side of the artist.

The paintings themselves are filled with images of horror and deformity. There is rawness in these airbrushed or acrylic versions of heavy-metal T-shirts, stories from literature and the Bible, and horror-film characters. Caulfield's monstrous lexicon mostly comes from his own imagination. 'On the whole they

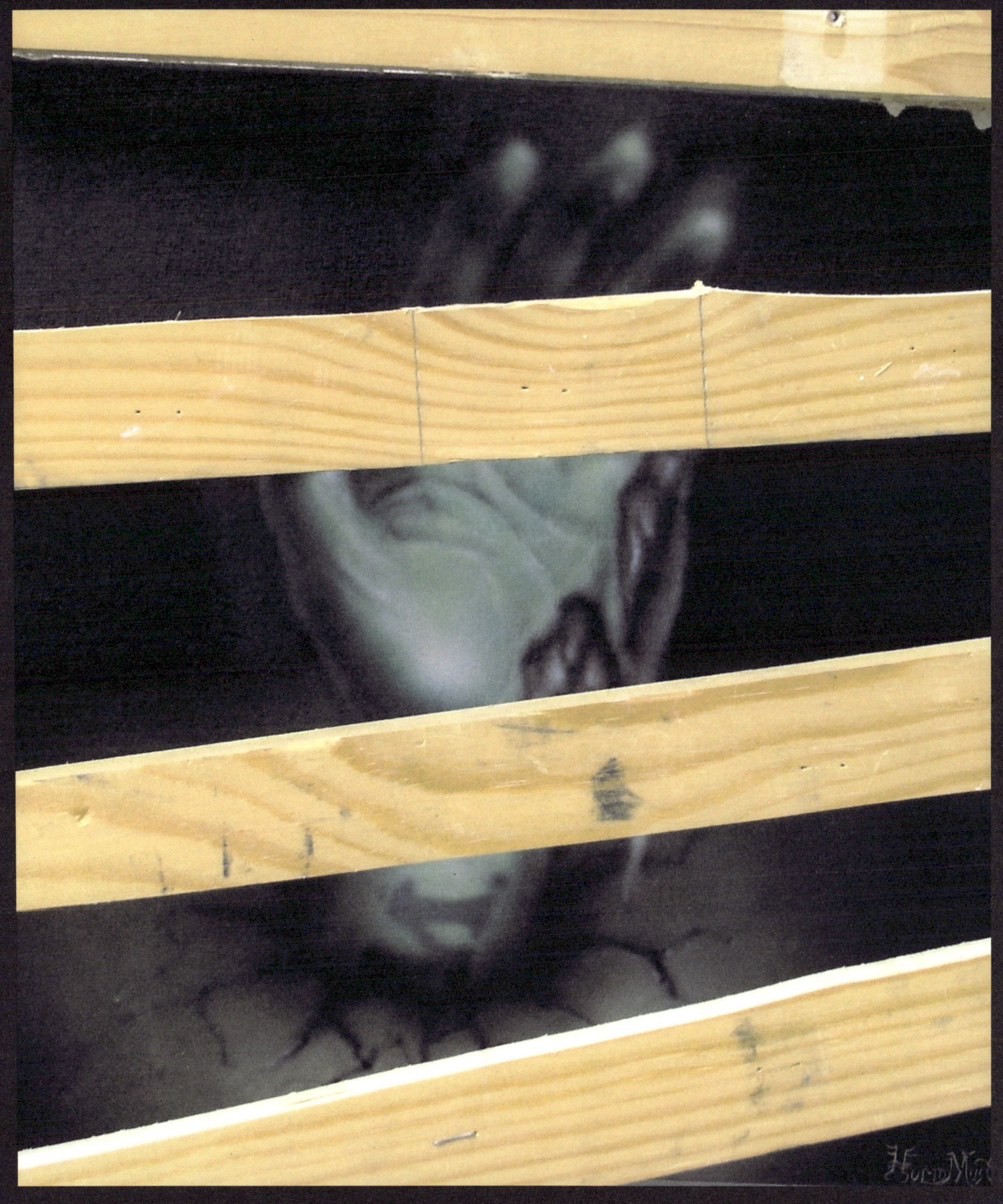

are pretty loose. They often just come out. There is no preparation.' Skulls are a persistent motif. 'We all walk around, and that's how we will look – that's our future face. They are portraits of our future, in a way.'

The artist sees this interest in horror as something that has always been part of him. His great-grandfather, W. W. Jacobs, wrote gothic horror stories, including *The Monkey's Paw*, published in 1901. Terror is in his blood. This fascination with darkness is also intended as a comment on art history; 'blending what we think of as high culture and what we think of as low culture, and putting it in a non-hierarchal form'.

What lies at the root of these dark, atmospheric pieces is often an idea of mirroring or duplication. Caulfield sometimes splits images in half so they resemble intensely worked ink blots. 'The theme of the doppelgänger and the double are really prevalent in horror – *Jekyll and Hyde*, *The Hulk*, *Dracula*, *Picture of Dorian Gray*.' His paintings often have a softness to them – as if viewed through a gauze or fog. The lack of clarity is part of the artist's desire to stop you entering the image, alienating the viewer in some way. 'I like encapsulating something in a time bubble. You never really see the original work of art properly, so in a way it doesn't really exist any more. There's nothing there.'

Part of Caulfield's practice is creating these objects. He also 'documents' these works by painstakingly repeating them in other paintings. Often these second versions place the original in real space or time. 'The documentation is not just the duplication of the image. It is a duplication of the time and space in which the image is in, the materiality.' Much of his work depicts an artwork within an artwork.

There's nothing easy about looking at Caulfield's work. 'I very rarely present something in a straightforward way. I'm interested in the different elements of visual perception and how time works with perception. What is the object and how do you feel about it?' The artist aims to describe the experience of the passing of time. The boxed pieces look as if they are ready to be shipped or removed. 'The work isn't really there or in the documentation. It is somewhere in between. I like that transitory feeling.' The same applies to the 'documentations'. These jewel-like paintings are depicted in non-spaces – in stairwells, sheds, in the white void of an empty room. The artist is not just recording the works. He is documenting the process of looking.

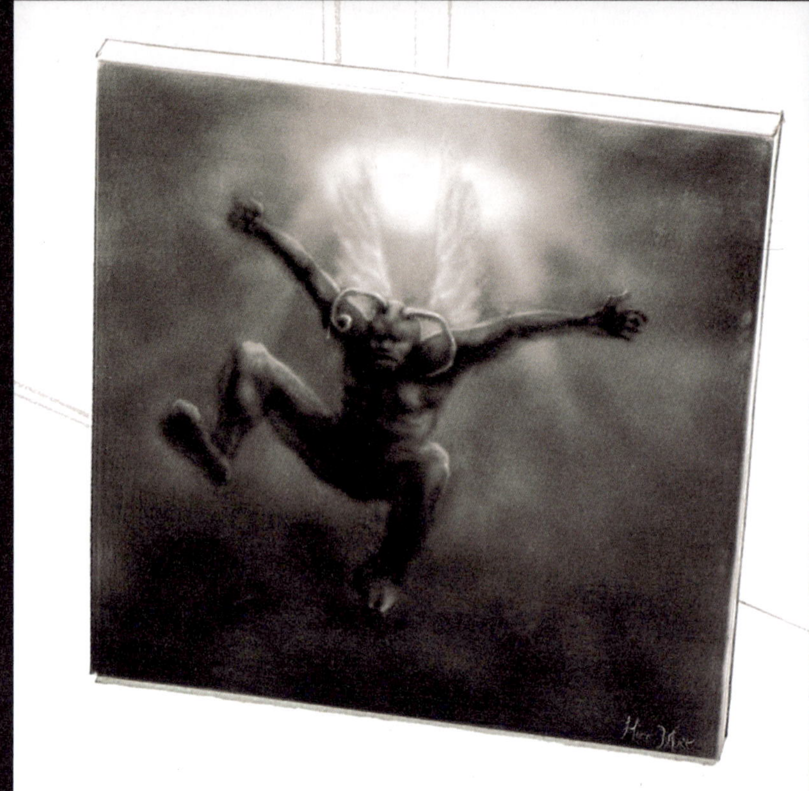

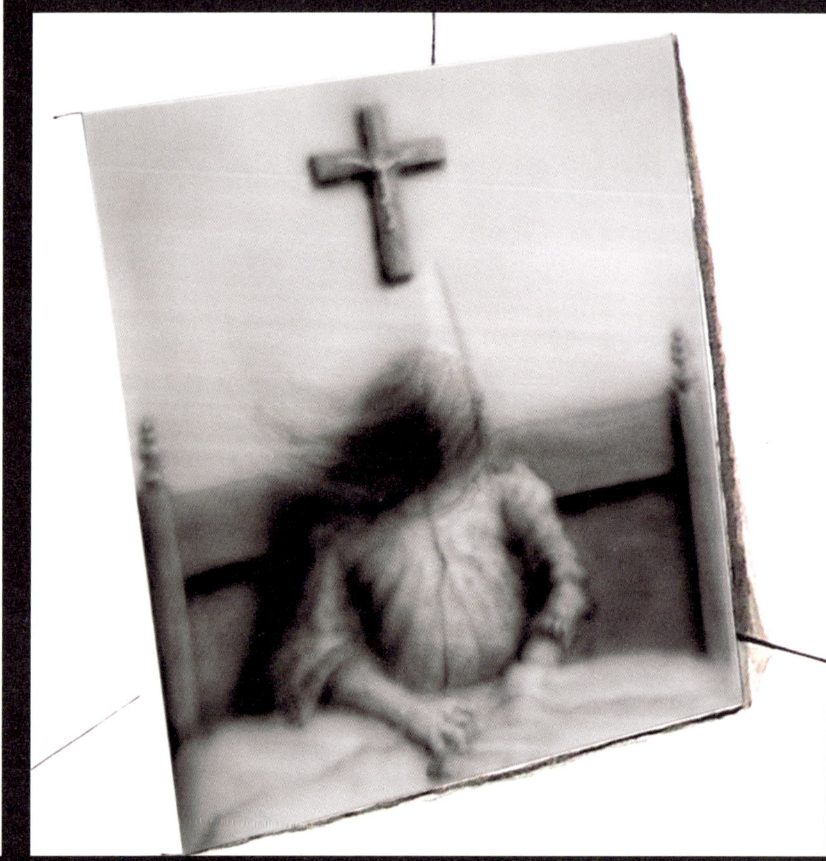

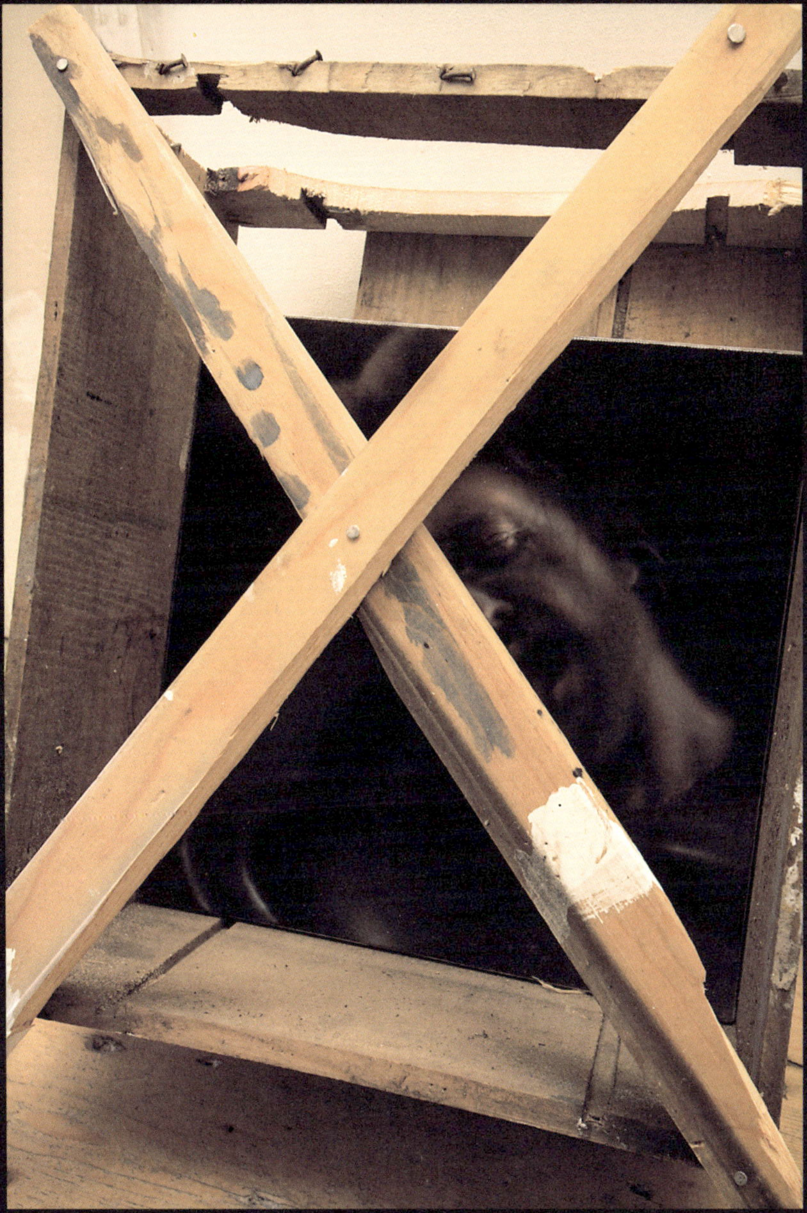

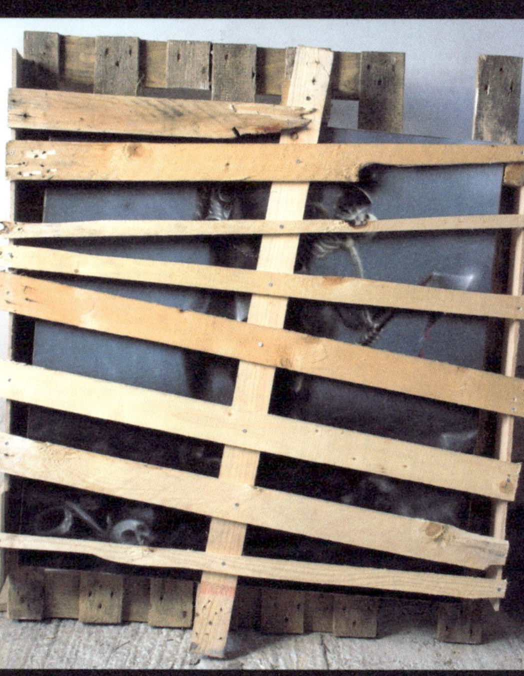

Nuno Cera

If the camera is the eye, then Nuno Cera's camera is a stalker. His films are filled with disturbing tracking shots. Figures are followed around abandoned buildings, glimpsed in the distance – just out of reach. The buildings themselves, as in horror films, become imbued with a sense of terror. 'For me, it is not the gothic and dark imagery that is important, but rather the culture of fear that exists in some urban contexts today.'

Nuno Cera originally studied photography, but in 2002, during a residency in Berlin, he began to create films. 'Initially, I made art to communicate my vision, but recently I've felt the need to represent reality as well as make fiction – to create situations and document them.' Often his work veers between art and documentary, as he uses real spaces as the basis for his films. Empty desolate architectural landscapes fill his works. His early interest in suburbia, non-spaces, peripheral architecture, gas stations and modes of transportation developed in response to Berlin. 'I began discovering abandoned buildings, each with specific stories and distinctive memories. The videos and series of photographs became more specific. I am interested in the connections between the spaces and memory, how I can use an abandoned space, and the architectural remains of the past, to construct a story. Like a photo-video-archaeologist, I use my vision to register, document and communicate these spaces for the future.'

The Prora Complex was Cera's first film using video. 'The Town of Prora was originally intended to be a seaside resort for the Nazi organization "Kraft durch Freude" (KDF) on the island of Rügen.' Cera's quasi-documentary video is about this enormous 'ghost' building that was never

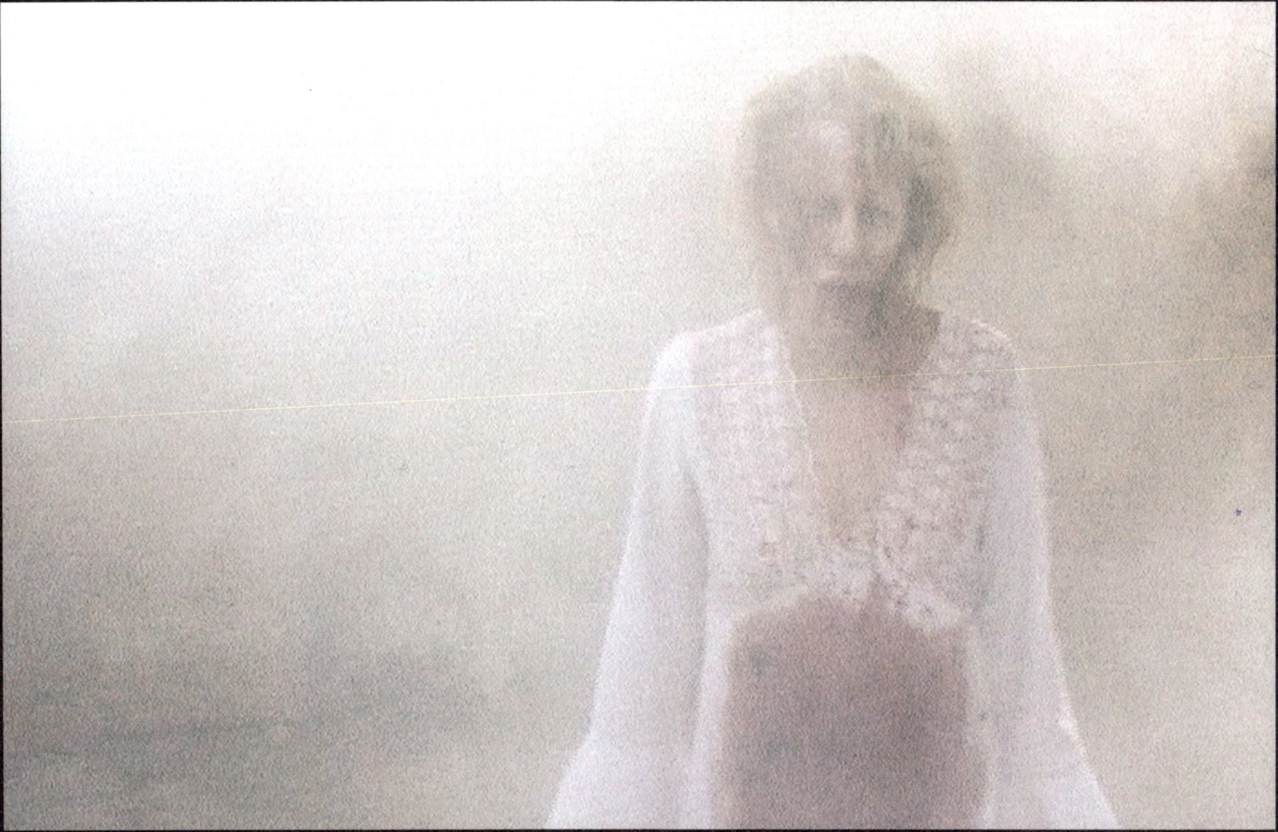

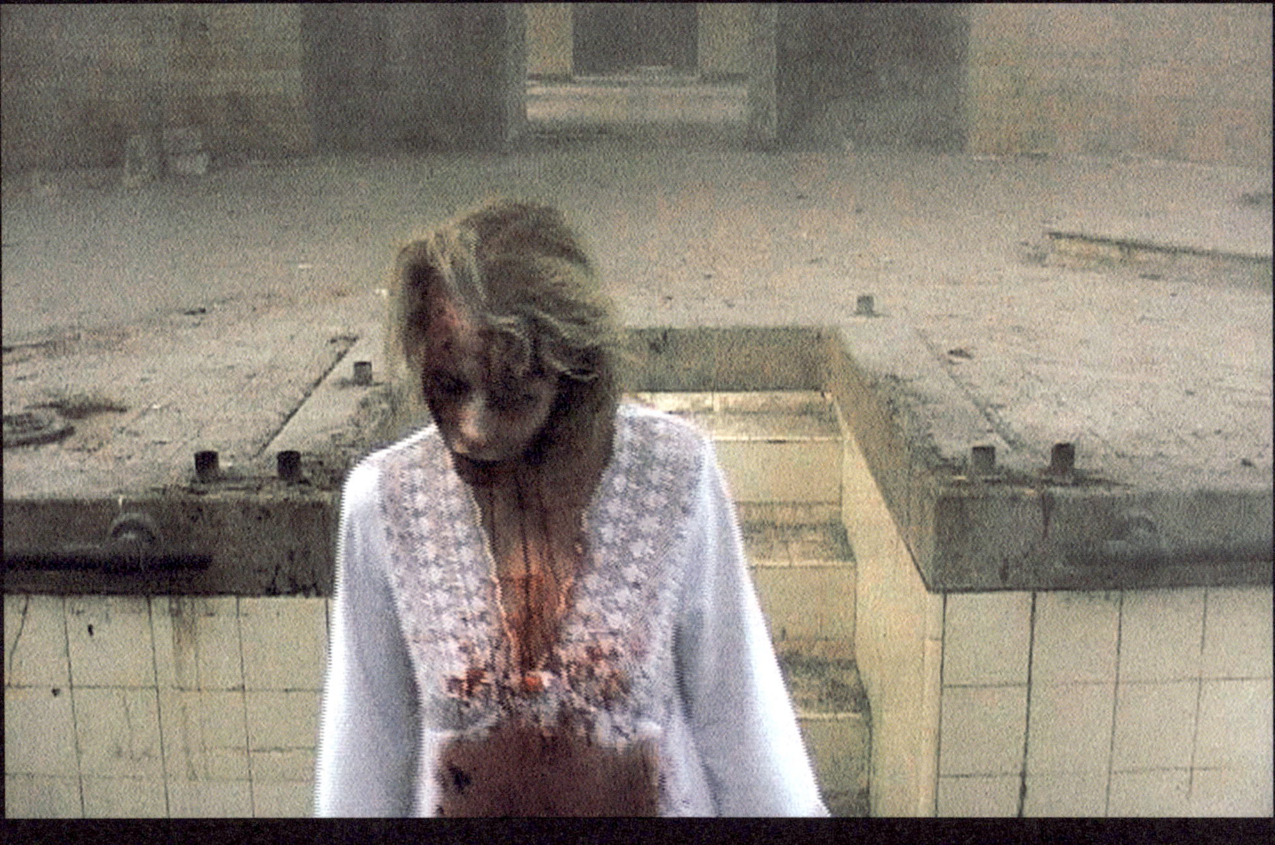

completed in the 1930s. 'It is a work about emptiness, world history, the past, architecture and memory. The film begins with a very realistic approach and then transforms into a strange situation full of drama and illusion. The distant figure works as a metaphoric ghost, one quick hint of a figure, which intensifies the emptiness of the space and, at the same time, changes the viewer's perspective. It is as if showing a person for one second makes the space seem emptier – more phantasmic.' Shots of birds appear throughout the piece – flying in a long corridor, trapped in the prison-like building and watching their own decay. The film ends with the architectural space filling with a supernatural fog – a horror staple.

The idea of a progressively disturbing narrative is something Cera reused in his most horror-infused piece, *The Lost Soul*. It was produced following a period of depression when he was watching a lot of horror films, specifically those of Dario Argento, Jean Rollin and Mario Bava. '*The Lost Soul* is a metaphor for contemporary culture and social collapse. Anyone can turn into a force of evil. It's about the inescapable dark side, exploring the blurred frontiers between mind and body, real and unreal.' The film follows a ghostly woman in a white nightdress who turns into a zombie, blood seemingly pouring out of her stomach. Towards the end the blood becomes intense, gory and disgusting. 'My intent was to capture a feeling familiar to our reality – anyone can be victimized by a terrorist attack. The zombie serves as a metaphor of the outsider, while the ghost symbolizes a lost person devoid of both a past and a future, drifting aimlessly in a decadent space.'

The work was also a tribute to the Italian *giallo*, the French *fantastique* and the European paracinema horror films from the 1970s and early 1980s. 'I greatly admire the cinematography, zoom techniques, lights, set-up, locations, music, the way the drama is constructed and the mixture between murder, the erotic and the thriller. The 1970s were a great period of cinematic freedom when it was possible to realize some of the most crazy, unique and uncanny movies of all time. I believe now is the time for art to appropriate this universe.'

In a more recent work, *A Situation*, Cera comments on terrorism and the culture of fear. The film depicts an office worker who discovers a letter bomb in the post. 'Shocked, he runs out of the office in a state of desperation and panic. The city becomes the landscape where this action, a reflection on subjective terrorism, occurs.' Horror and urban space sit hand in hand. 'I'm interested in exploring the urban context to create fiction – using a city or a specific building as a location for an action or situation. The horror is a reflection of our time. It is dispersed every day throughout the media, turning cities into the ground for terror.'

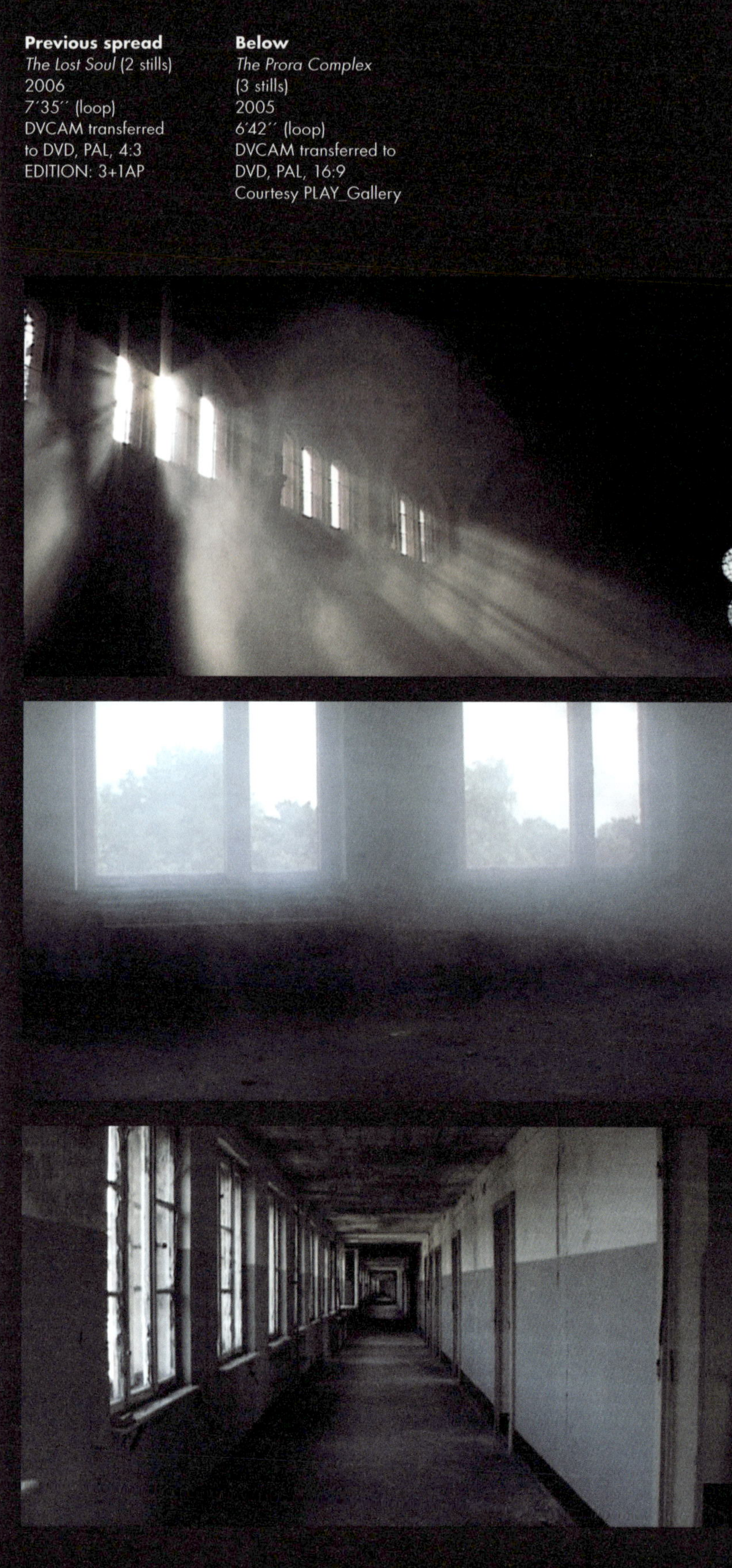

Previous spread
The Lost Soul (2 stills)
2006
7'35'' (loop)
DVCAM transferred
to DVD, PAL, 4:3
EDITION: 3+1AP

Below
The Prora Complex
(3 stills)
2005
6'42'' (loop)
DVCAM transferred to
DVD, PAL, 16:9
Courtesy PLAY_Gallery

Below
Dark Forces (2 stills)
2004
7'23'' (loop)
Colour and B/W
Super-8 transferred to
DVD, PAL, 4:3
Courtesy AH – Galeria
de Arte Contemporânea
António Henriques

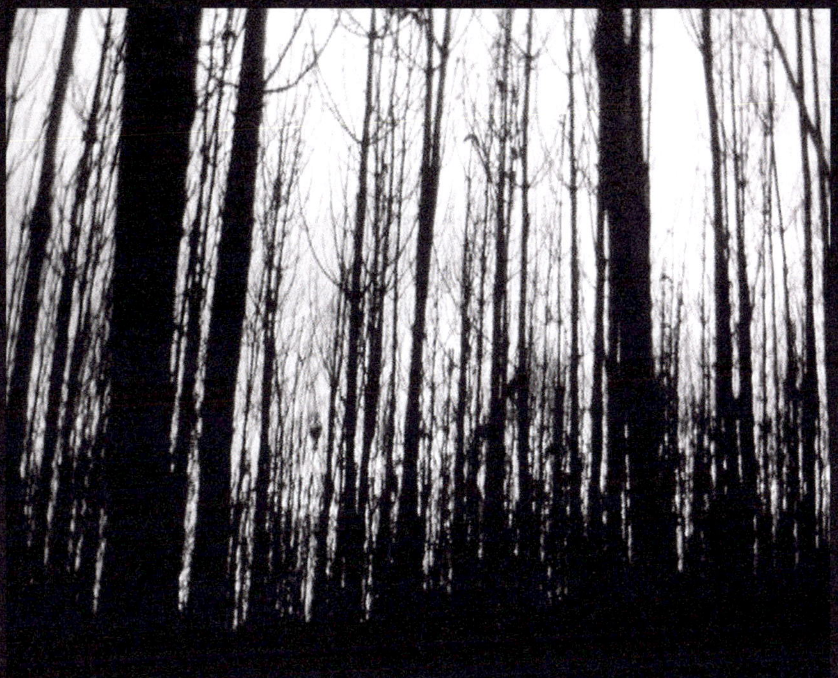

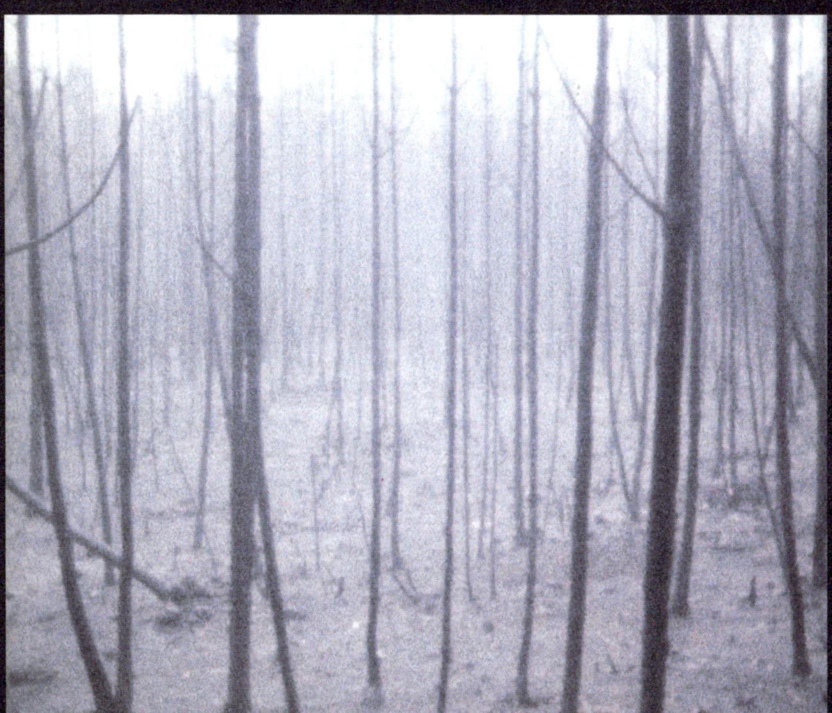

dr lakra

Macabre scrawls and the imagery of horror cover everything in the world of Dr Lakra. Found pin-up images, tinted portraits, old dolls, porcelain objects, kitsch mummified hands, death masks and odd discarded anatomical objects are all surrounded and covered by his tattoo-influenced drawings. He transforms remnants of the past into something strange, interesting and full of action.

Dr Lakra (or El Doctore Lakra in Spanish) came to contemporary art through an unusual path. Influenced by his father, a plastic artist, he began to take an interest in the improvement of other images at school. 'I was always drawing in class – altering the covers of books or making caricatures of teachers in a macabre way. I quit at age sixteen and dedicated most of my time to drawing and painting; I had my first exhibition in 1989. Many of the pieces were collages, some with images from cheap pornographic magazines.' At the time he began working in different workshops, including Gabriel Orozco's, alongside artists like Damián Ortega. Dr Lakra's route was far more left of centre. Involved in the Mexican punk movement, he began to get tattoos from an artist friend, Piraña. 'At this time in Mexico, tattoos were rare and the exclusive of criminals, ex-convicts and punk rockers. The only tattoo machines were homemade ones, using a Walkman motor, a pen and a guitar string with a single needle. Punks used to gather in markets where you could find tattoo stands, trade records or sell whatever you could in alternative markets called *tianguis*.' It was in this unusual environment that Lakra began to collect strange dolls and odd vintage and pin-up magazines, which he used in collage.

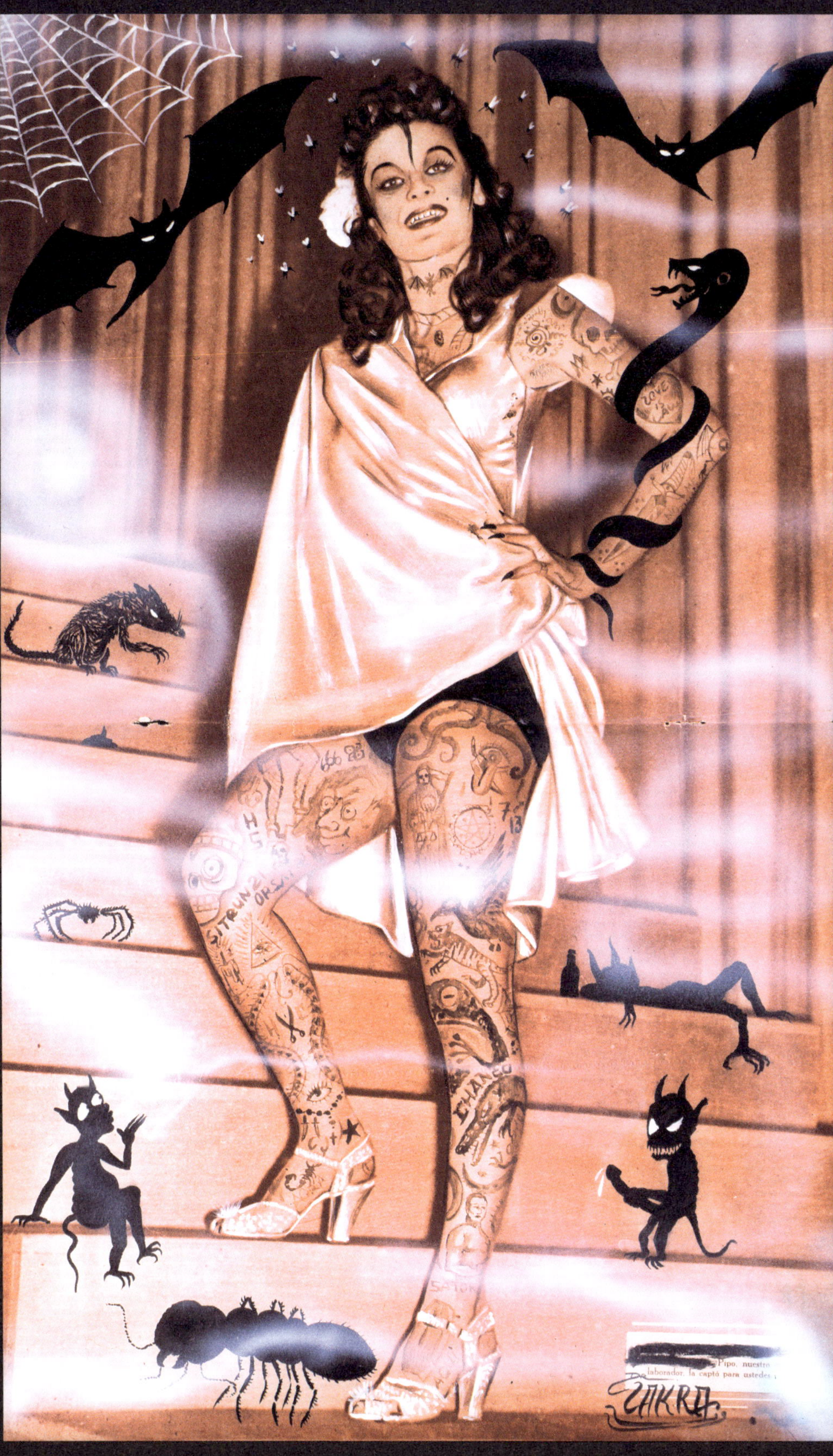
Pipo, nuestro
laborador, la captó para ustedes.
LAKRA

He later moved to California, where he became involved in the tattoo scene and became friends with Ed Hardy, before returning to Oaxaca in Mexico in 1994, where he opened his own tattoo collective and shop, Dermafilia. His imagery strongly reflects a Mexican visual heritage. He is informed by pre-Columbian art, *Lucha Libre* (Mexican wrestling) and the skulls imagery of the *Dia de los Muertos* (Day of the Dead). He is also interested in graffiti and Thai and Philippine tribal tattoos.

His work is the antithesis of the mainstream. Often he 'tattoos' found figures, images and objects. Entire narratives are created around images. Many have a sense of playful horror about them — vampiric fangs or groups of bats, spectral skull imagery. The found imagery is given a layer of power or confrontation. It is filled with a sense of energy.

The pieces play with the history of Mexican pop culture. Straight portraits are transformed into images of vibrant wrestlers surrounded by bats. Old toys and wooden advertising objects become voodoo-like totems. Lakra identifies comic books as his first love, and his work is filled with iconic over-the-top characters brimming with power. Everyday people are remade as superheroes or wrestling icons. There is no sense of marginalization or poverty here. Lakra's work reinvents the clichéd images of Mexico in Western culture.

The artist's work on pin-up images is particularly interesting. He transforms sexualized images of women into something much more controversial. By covering their bodies in tattoos, he makes them appear more formidable, changing their sexuality into something active rather than passive. Sometimes they are made ugly, which highlights how false and deceptive idealized imagery can be. It is always done with humour and a sense of freedom rather than aggression. Throughout his work Lakra walks the line between empowerment and destruction. Like surreal advertisements, these images invite you to roll up and enjoy the pleasurable fear of the freak show and the grotesque.

Untitled (vampira)
2004
Ink on vintage magazine
50 x 31 cm

Untitled (nostalgia)
2004
Ink on vintage magazine
29.3 x 20 cm

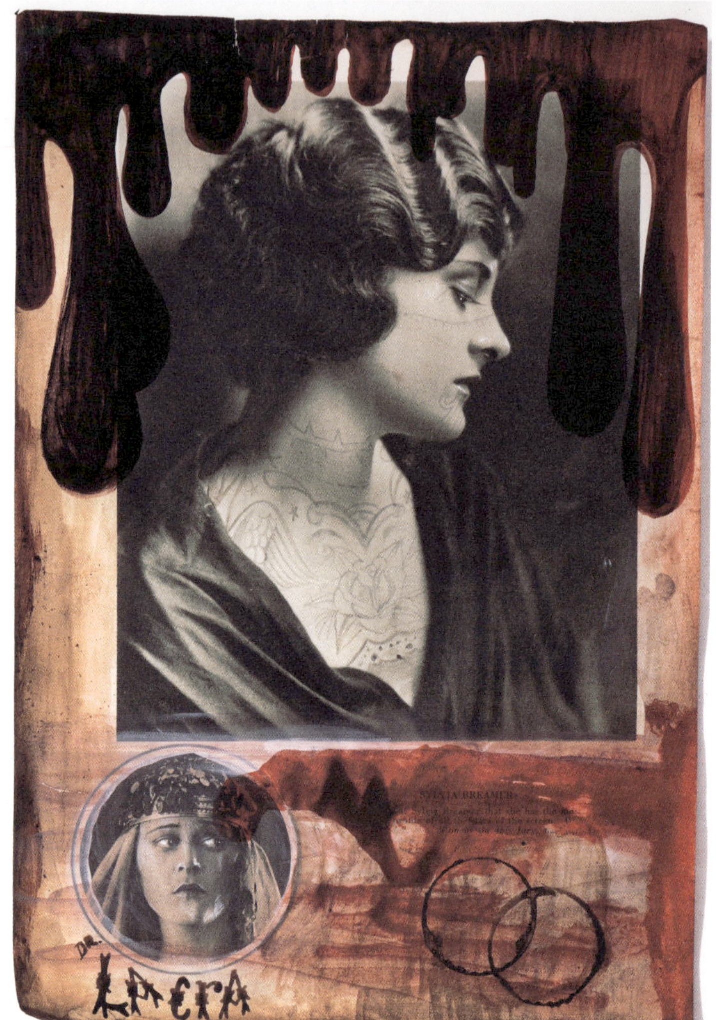

Below
*Untitled (mujer
con gorilla)*
2004
Ink on vintage magazine
21.2 x 23.5 cm

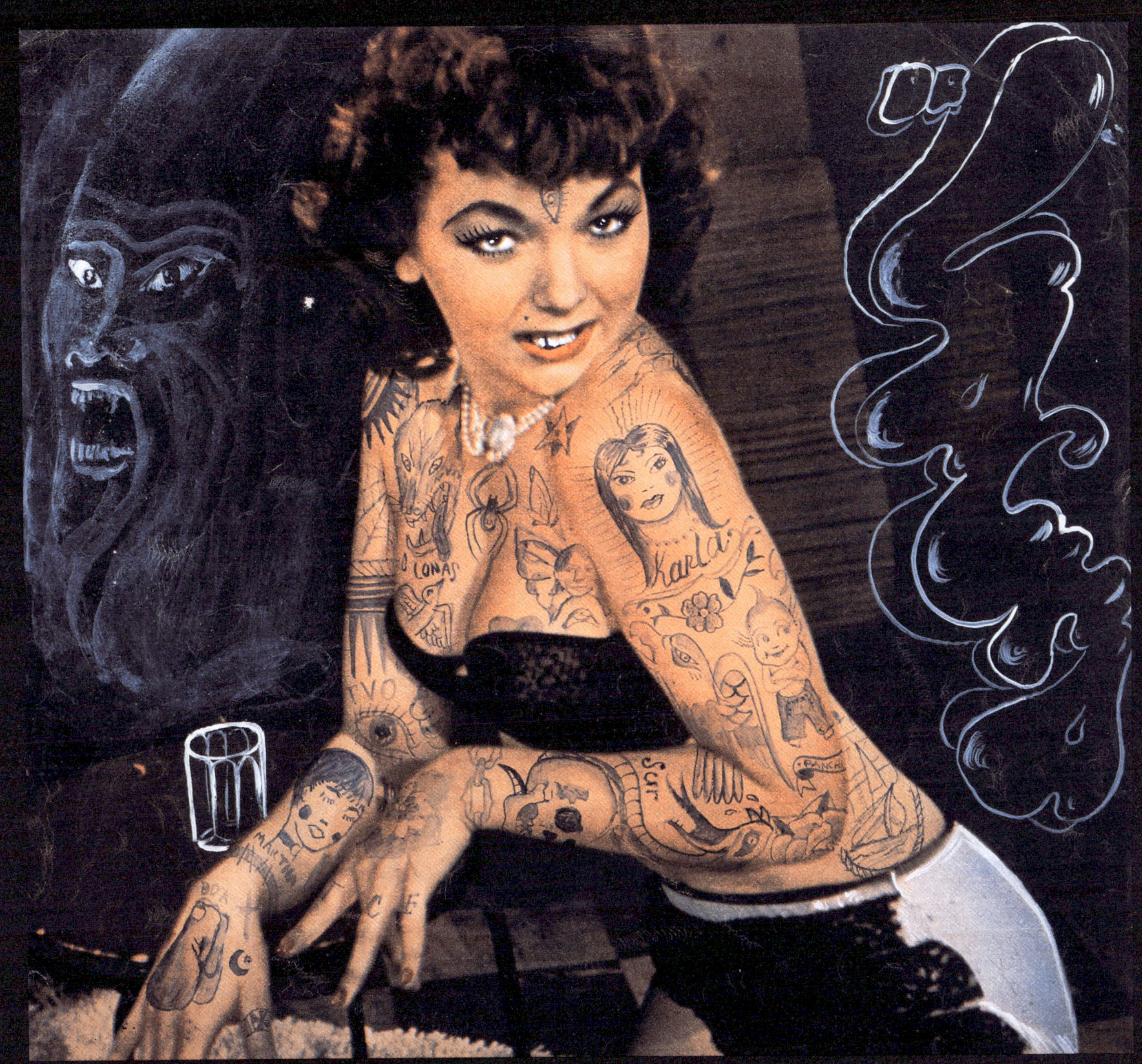

Below
Untitled (La Familia)
2007
Ink on vintage
propaganda
30.4 x 22 cm

Opposite
Untitled (La Familia)
2007
Ink on vintage
magazine
30.4 x 22 cm

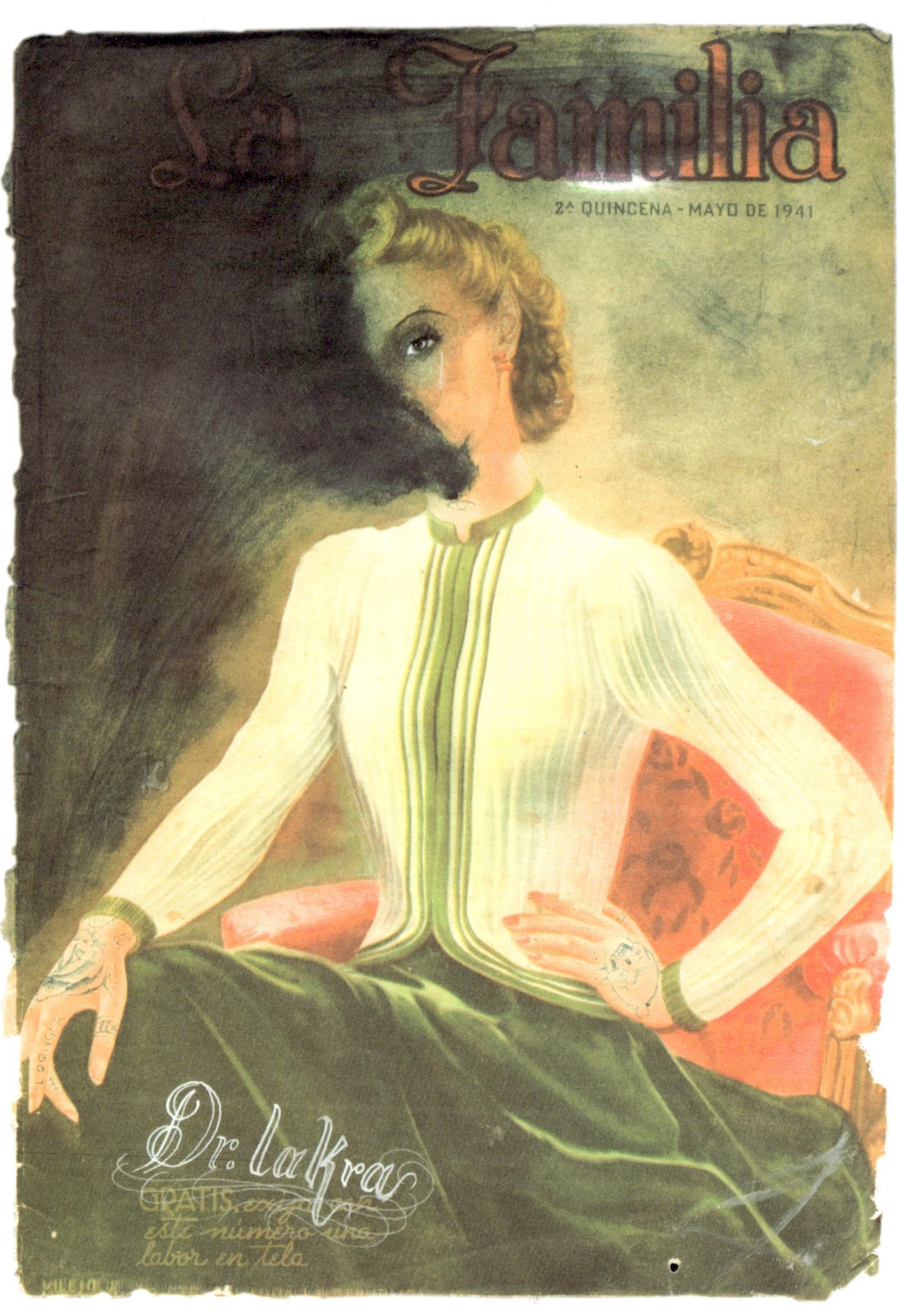

La Familia
2ª QUINCENA - MAYO DE 1941
Dr. Lakra
GRATIS
este número
labor en tela

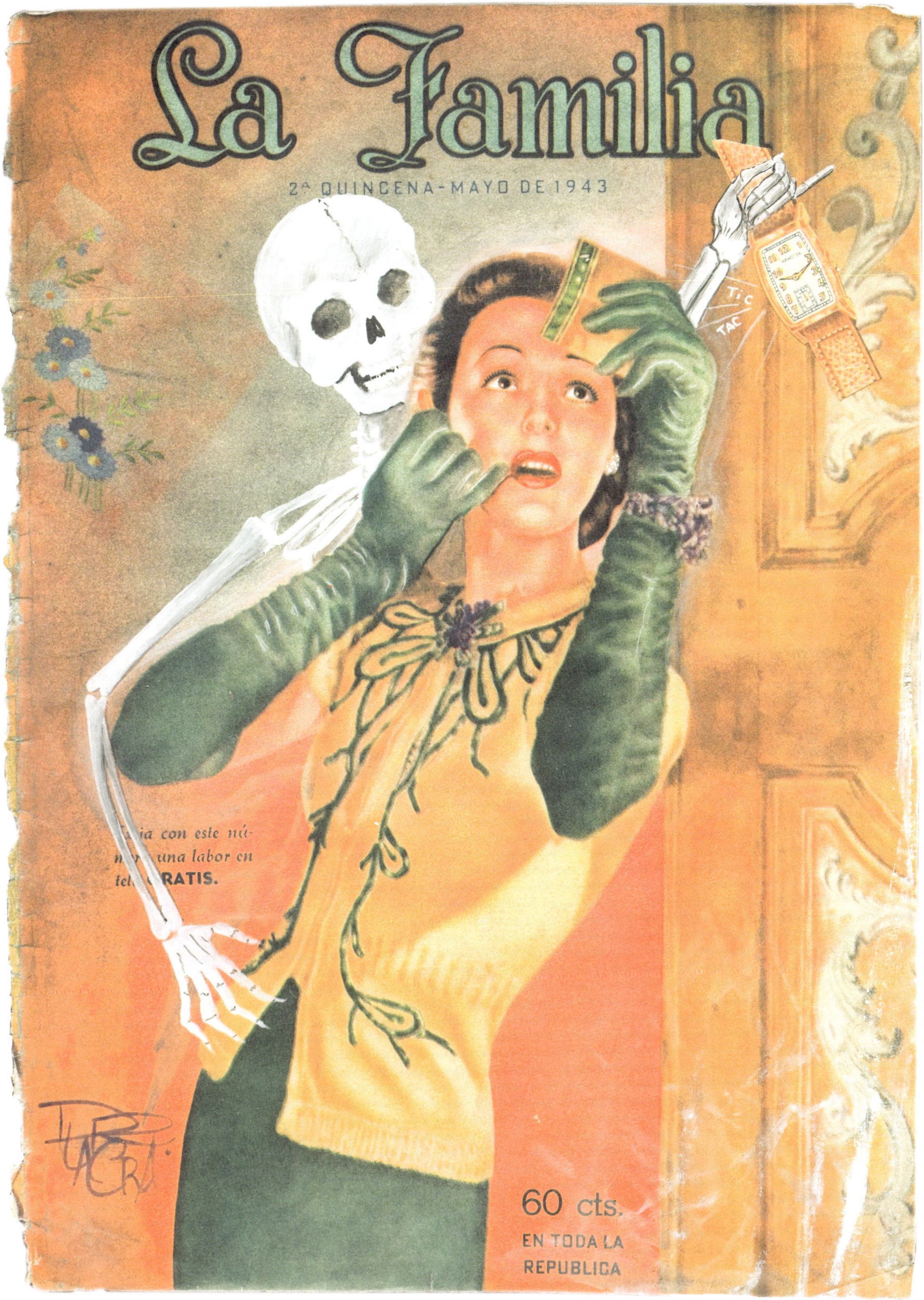

La Familia
2ª QUINCENA-MAYO DE 1943
TIC
TAC
60 cts.
EN TODA LA
REPUBLICA

sue de beer

Sue de Beer has a very personal approach to horror-film imagery. Much of her early work referenced slasher films and a teen take on the gothic. There is a lo-fi aesthetic to her video pieces that echoes the approach and atmosphere of low-budget horror movies. The handmade texture and avoidance of slickness give the work greater impact, adding a touch of realism to its fantasy. 'That isn't intentional, but I don't like digital effects, so I use a lot of "cheats" – special lenses or props – that are truly objects. I guess that would have a link to 1970s film-making.' The camera is a little jumpy in her films. You can sense the mind creating the work behind the scenes.

De Beer often displays her work in sculptural installations. These tactile environments add a whole extra layer to the experience of the film. The atmosphere of film is transformed into something three-dimensional, extended beyond the screen into real space. The sculptures explore ideas around the subject matter and essence of the films they 'contain'. *Black Sun, Willy Rachow* is a two-screen video piece shown inside a sculptural version of a classic haunted house. '*Black Sun* is about a dead body that may or may not exist. It is about "the Thing", longing for the imaginary desire,' she explains. 'I used to break into houses that were abandoned or under construction and do drugs in there when I was a kid. The house is that kind of space for me.' Coloured lights surround the stylized graphic house in *Black Sun*. Her use of tart oranges, blues and pinks veers between Disney and terror to create something acidly disturbing. 'Right now I use a lot of red and green to make evil come

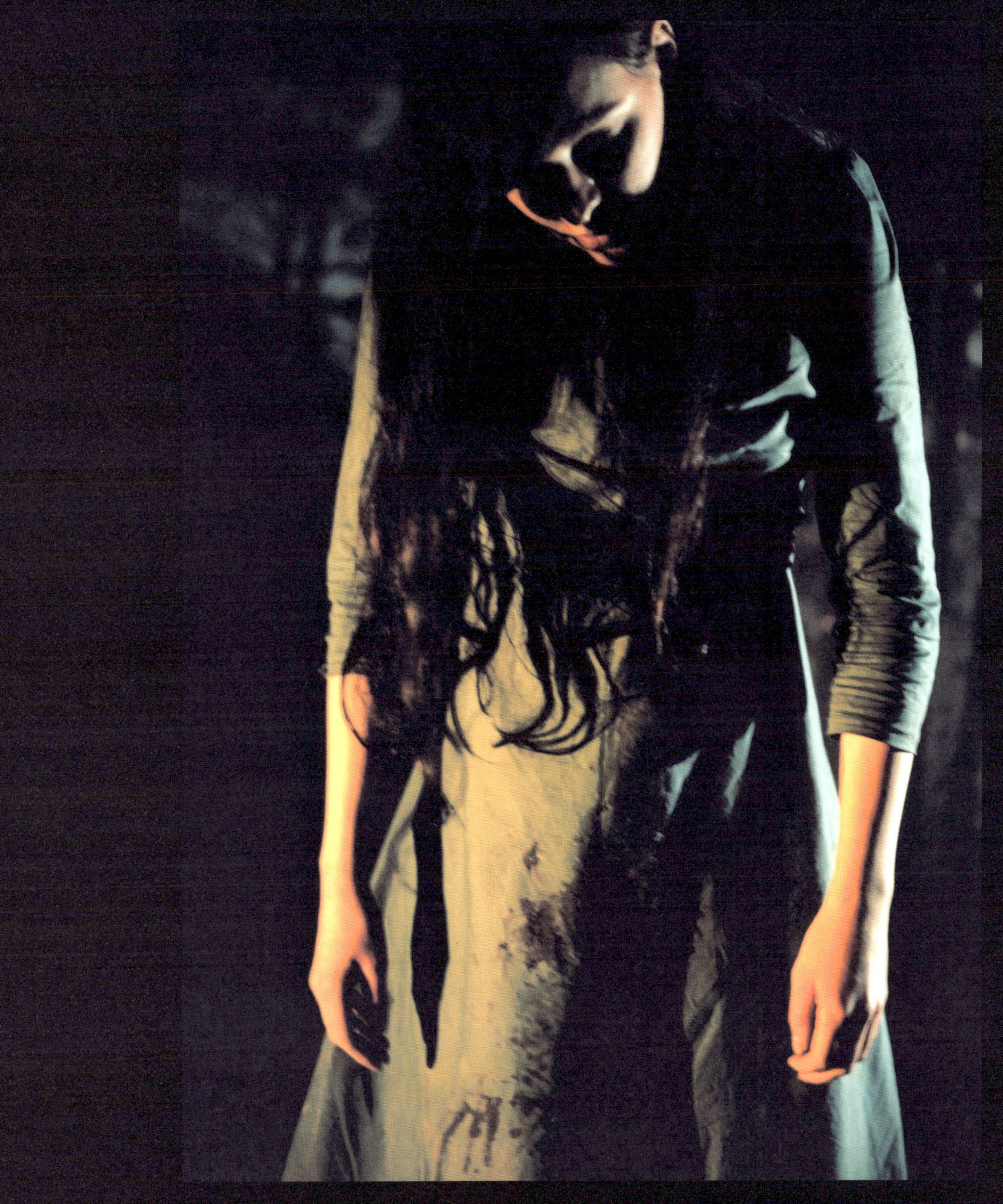

into the world. My cameraman and I call it "Christmas in hell".'

The content of the video element of *Black Sun*, which is shown at the Whitney in New York, is equally infused with horror and heightened emotion. The title of the work was taken from an essay collection by writer and philosopher Julia Kristeva, subtitled *Depression and Melancholia*. It focuses on teenage girls and their desires and frustrations. Walking into the installation to watch the work is like stepping inside the adolescent mind. The piece tries to understand what it is to be feminine. A teenage girl dances in her bedroom, while another is dressed in a sheet like a ghost or kisses a boy in a graveyard. The film flashes forward to images of mature women in everyday life, hinting that the work is about growing up and becoming an individual as well as memory and ideas about the past.

The soundtrack includes a voice-over reading excerpts from books by cult novelist Dennis Cooper. Literature is an open influence on de Beer's work. She links pieces to Cooper, Julia Kristeva, Joris-Karl Huysmans and Nathaniel Hawthorne. 'Dennis was very kind and gave me permission to use his writing. All of the texts I chose were written about George Miles, his ex-lover, whom he wrote five books about. George was dead when he wrote the fifth book in the cycle, *Period*. *Black Sun* is about longing for fictitious love – maybe loving a corpse, maybe loving a shadow.'

The artist's recent work has moved away from an interest in adolescence. Her latest work, *The Quickening*, looks at the seventeenth-century witch trials and this period of hysteric Christianity. 'I was raised in New England, which is a haunted and complex place. Moralism, a kind of sexualized, hysteria-driven violence and ideas of vengeance and retribution – all of these things became seeded into American culture in the 1700s through Puritan evangelism and its relationship to a very present world of spirits, ancestors and crime. Crime can be really animate – it can take the form of an animal or seep into the walls of your house.'

The work has the low-budget props and filming style of her early pieces. She focuses at times on the role of repressed female sexuality, but the male central character is equally important. 'Occult things happen in my film, but they are primarily witnessed by my male character, this inventor figure who makes light machines to pierce the skin of the conscious mind.' *The Quickening*, however, also looks at how the Puritan heritage has affected contemporary America. 'I think there are more layers to this relationship with God and the Devil, with the artist and with the Puritan work ethic, which still structures American thinking – if you remove the red herring of witches and witchcraft.'

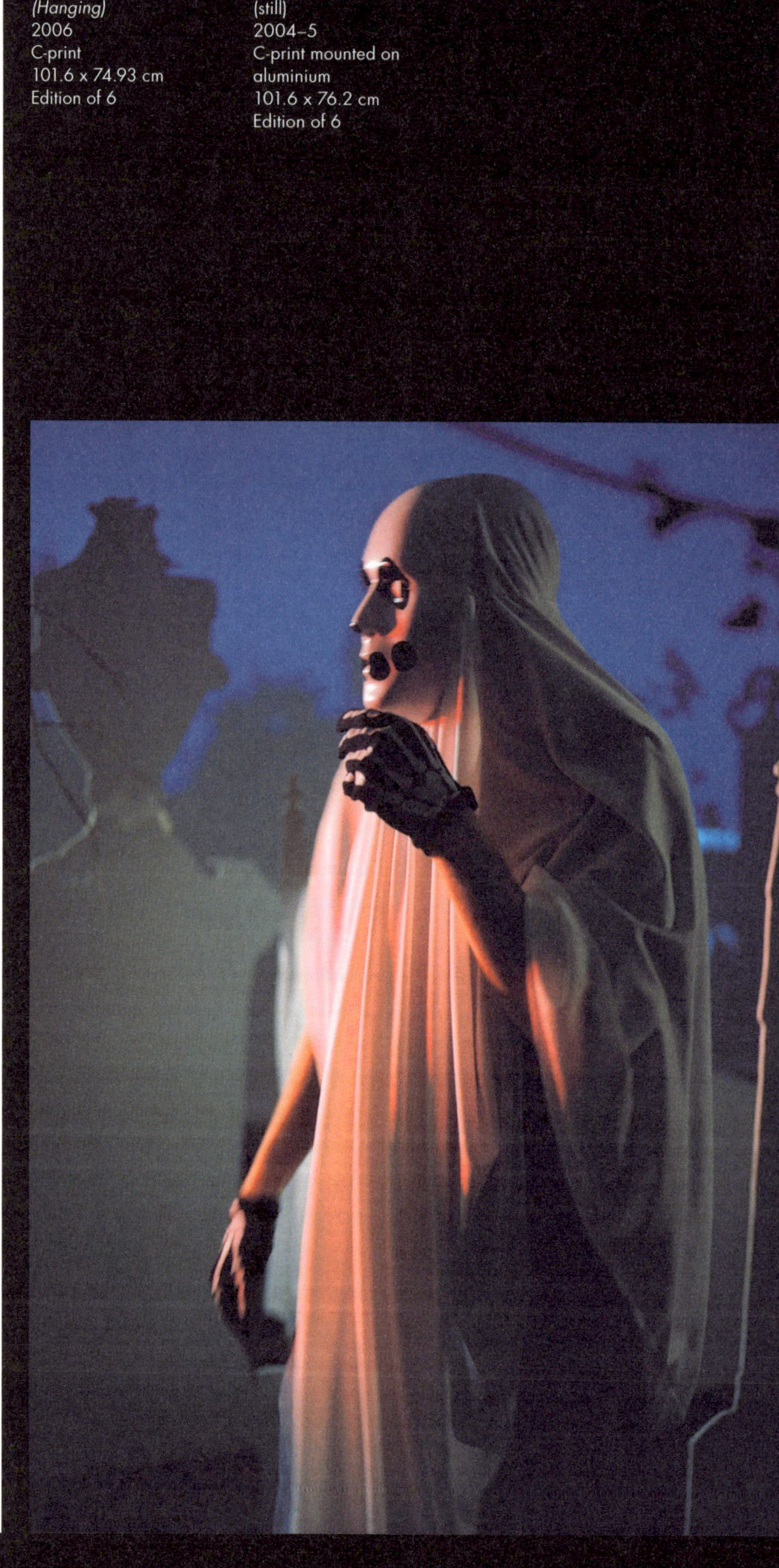

Below
The Quickening (detail)
2006
Video installation:
painted plywood, foofs,
carpet and DVD
Running time: 23 minutes

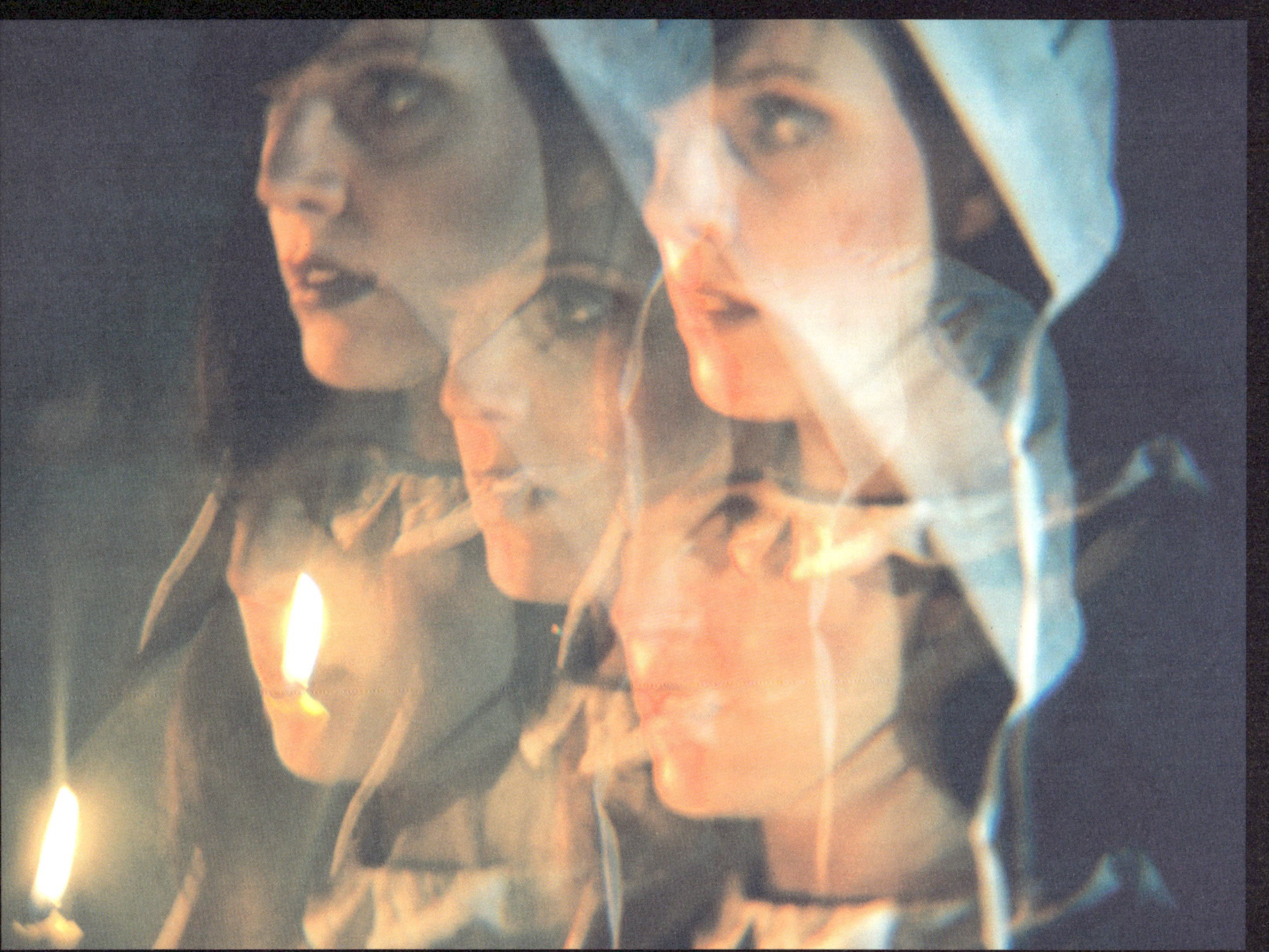

amie dicke

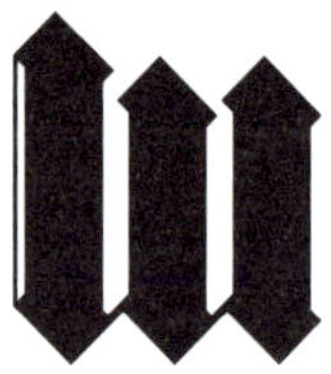

What happens when you dismantle the idealized body? Amie Dicke explores just that in her work. The experience of being a woman is a vital part of Dicke's art. 'It all started with a series of sculptures I made just before I graduated from art school in 2000. I observed other women. I was looking for a personal style or unique attitude or stance and, quite literally, tried to obtain one by studying the positions and shapes of the female body.'

She created pressings of her legs, from crotch to foot, out of marzipan and icing, which quickly (though not intentionally) decayed soon after their creation. 'They are in a state of constant deterioration, through sagging and cracking. The discovery of these deformities provided me with a whole new perspective: uncontainable beauty.' Her work contrasts the 'perfect beauty' of magazines and billboard ads with the inevitability of its decline. 'Perhaps it's the certainty of decay that makes beauty so appealing.'

Dicke first began using and subverting magazine imagery as raw material when living in New York in 2001. 'I found myself surrounded by the world of fashion and glamour. On buildings and metro-stops, glowing lips and shining eyes were tempting me, like they were saying, "All your dreams will come true, just insert personality here". I started to project my loneliness on to the city where the most familiar faces were those of the supermodels on buildings and in magazines.' She started to draw on the faces and bodies of women in magazines, adding flowing lines of black ink and covering the original colours and composition. She

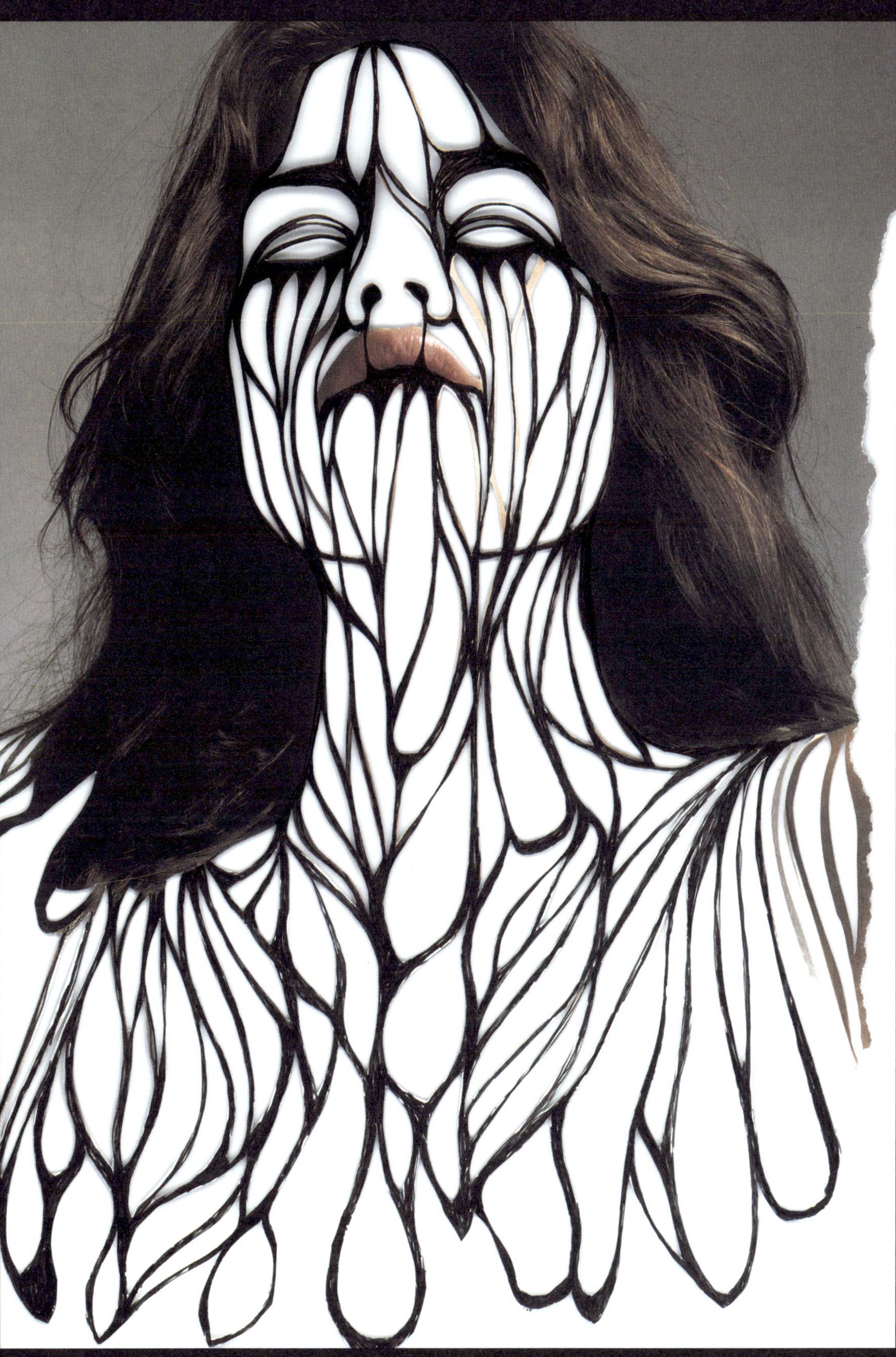

cut away and removed the space between the lines – the fashion, the jewellery, the faces and bodies. 'What remains are fragile figures existing in a gossamer-thin web of contours. I erased the graceful positions and self-confident looks of the models.' Dicke emphasizes that the critique she made on the feminine ideal was directed towards herself, not the fashion or beauty industry. She was more interested in her own response to idealized imagery. 'It's very appealing and at the same time superficial. I prefer the words shallow, skin-deep. Sometimes, you have to explore the surface to be able to go deep. The ambiguity starts with buying the magazine. I like fashion and leafing through the pages of magazines, but at the same time it gives me an empty feeling. It is like the quote by Simone Weil: "Beauty always promises, but never gives."'

The black, spiderous lines of Dicke's work echo a 1970s painted rock, but the connection is totally unintentional. Her aim is not to shock or disturb the viewer, but to reflect her own inner disturbance. Dicke transforms bodies into blood and arteries – forms are reduced to their visceral framework. Instead of rock and rebellion, she is influenced by the drama of sixteenth- and seventeenth-century anatomical drawings, where drawn bodies literally unveil their inner self as their skin is pulled away.

Dicke's work now focuses on sculpture and installation, while still examining the contrast between violence and representations of women. She creates casts of her own body in the position of figures taken from vintage Helmut Newton photographs. In one of her pieces, the eyes and face of a sculptural bust are bound with black plastic tags. Another work features a reclining marble nude contained in a net filled with hair. There's a sense of restrained violence as bodies are bound or controlled.

All is Vanity and Vexation to the Spirit was created during a gallery opening. Here, Dicke performed a semi-religious ritual with incense on an image of a recumbent nude, held within an upturned wardrobe. 'The incense burned through the image, which is lying on dirt in a wardrobe. The burnt places look like the ruins of a bombed city. I like the idea of the unexpected in the works – the fluency, mistake or spill.' Her use of domestic furniture occurs again in *Private Property*, an installation where she uses black duct tape to tie objects to the gallery space. The blackened wardrobes and seats are locked in position, highlighting their isolation. Like her cut-outs, the pieces examine our relationship with the objects and the commercial images around us. Dicke questions whether commodity fetishization begins with the consumer or the consumed.

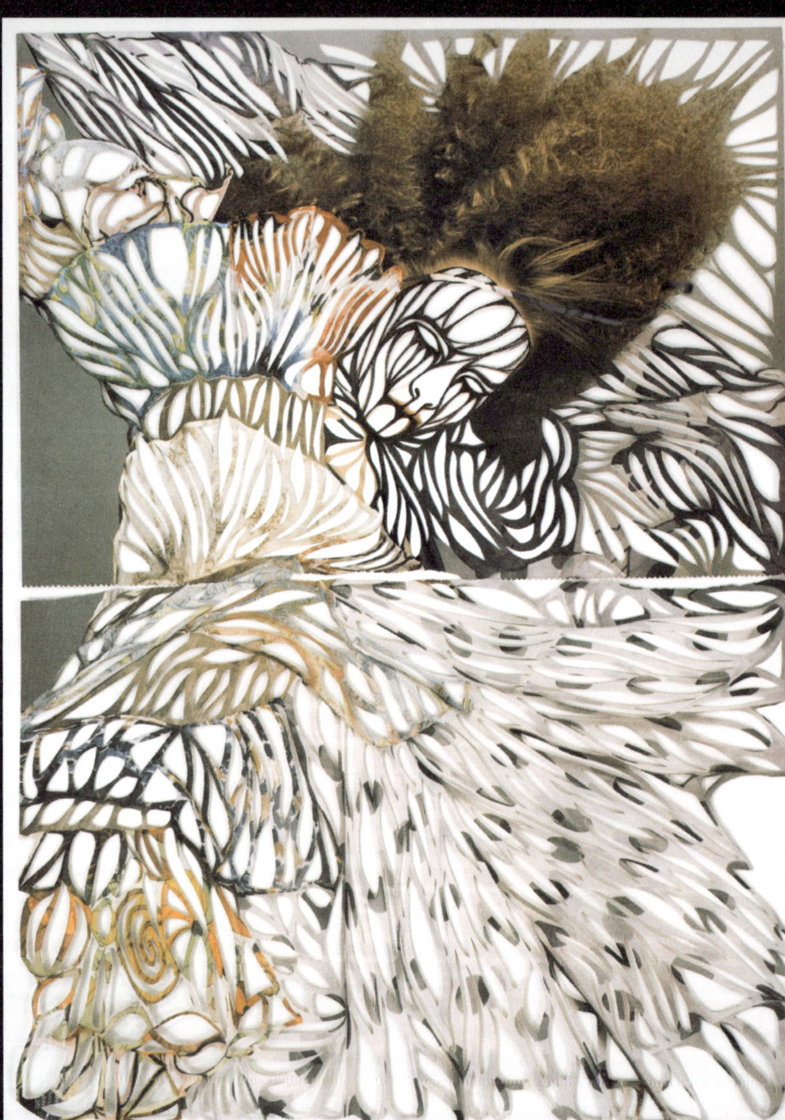

Eye Witness
2007
Mixed-media sculpture:
plaster, plastic zip ties on
pedestal
50 x 60 x 80 cm

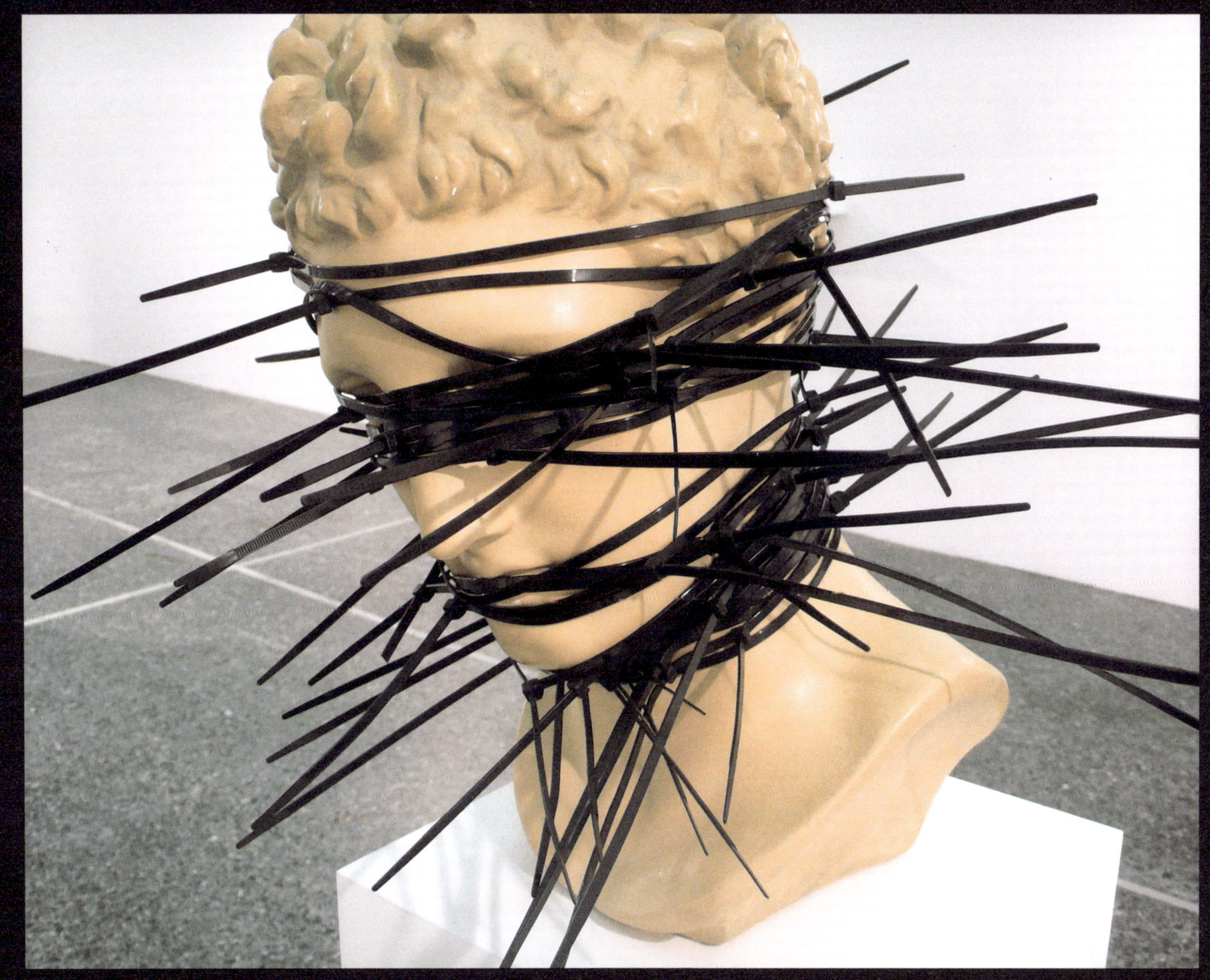

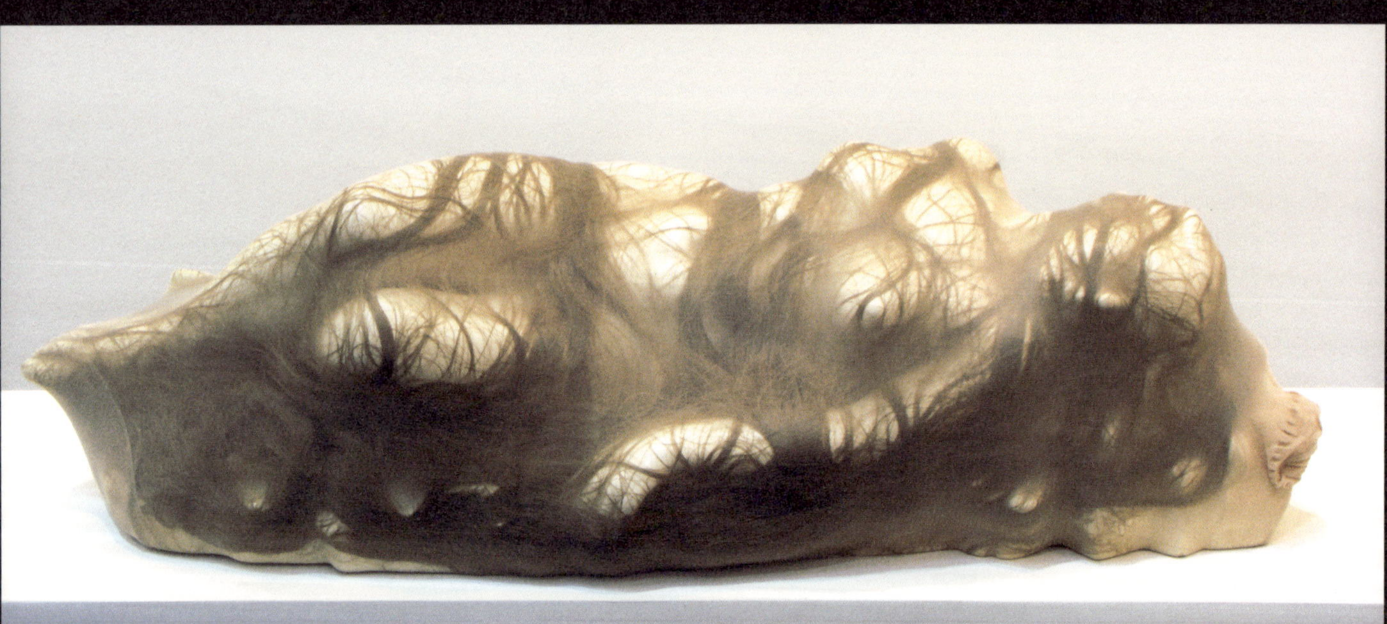

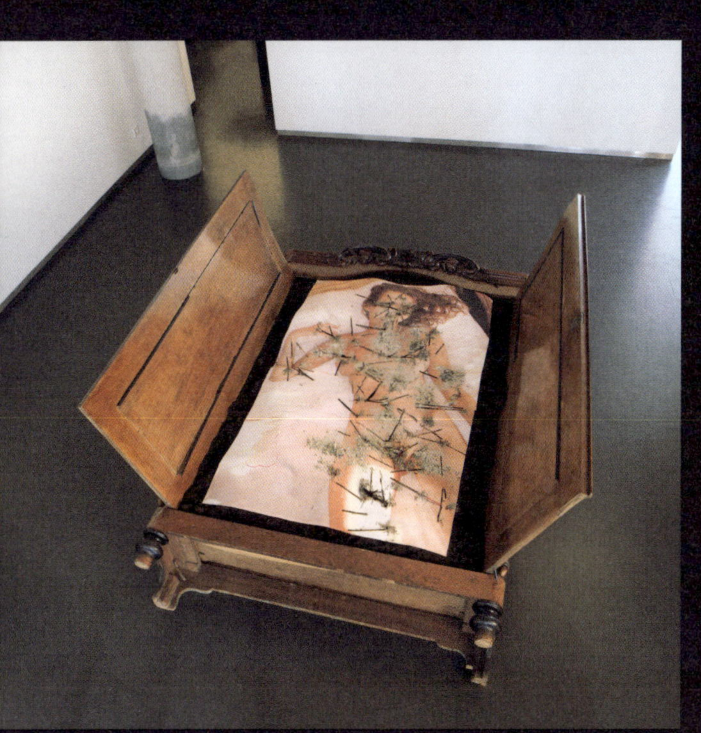

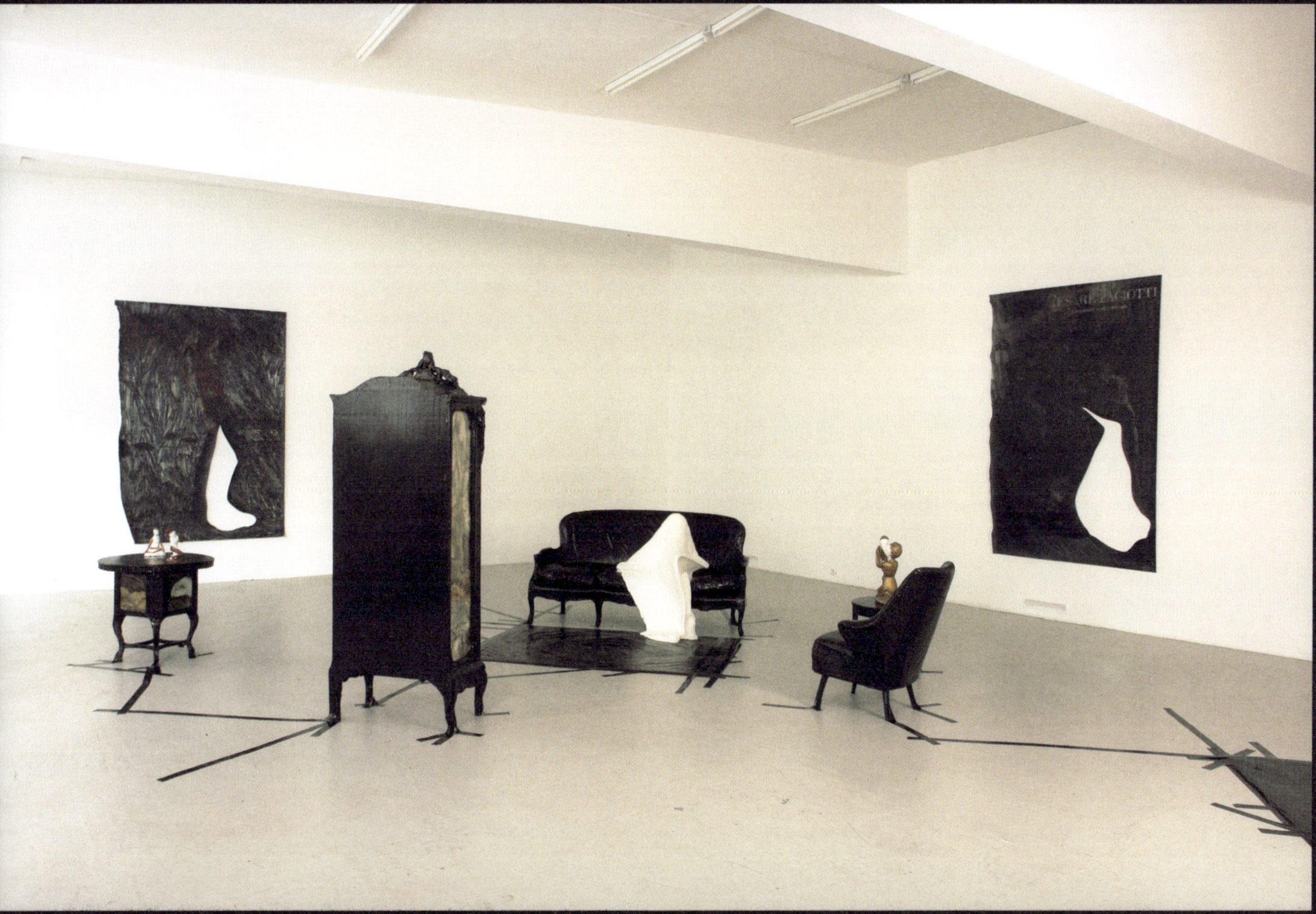

stephen dunne

t all begins with a stain. Stephen Dunne's ink and oil pieces grow out of haphazardly dripped splodges of ink. Images emerge from the shapes and forms of these ink blots, like Rorschach tests. 'I don't have a plan. I just spill ink and make blobs and they suggest images.'

Ink itself adds a specifically important quality to the work. Its fluidity creates a sense of strange atmosphere and warped reality. 'It resonates. Ink has a residual essence.' The sense of horror or darkness in his imagery is also something that comes naturally out of the ink. 'When you show people Rorschach blots, they tend not to see nice things. It taps into the subconscious in a very strange way – it's something that psychologists still use. We don't see happy things. We see horror and misery or weirdness or nightmare.'

For Dunne, the decapitated heads or gory characters in his work reflect the pervasive culture of fear and the 'war on terror'. 'There are political elements to them. There's violence or fear and loathing that stems from a paranoia that's not just internal. It's externalized. It comes from the culture around us.' Dunne does not quote images directly, but his studio is covered in weird and disturbing pictures garnered on the Internet. He allows them to circulate and inform his work indirectly. 'There's a lot of Christian imagery – I grew up in Ireland with Catholicism. The first images of horror you come across are the crucifixion and people coming back from the dead – a zombie allegory.' A past exhibition was entitled *Worship the light, worship the dark*, making explicit the relationship between Christianity and something potentially evil. 'It is important, that balance. The idea of

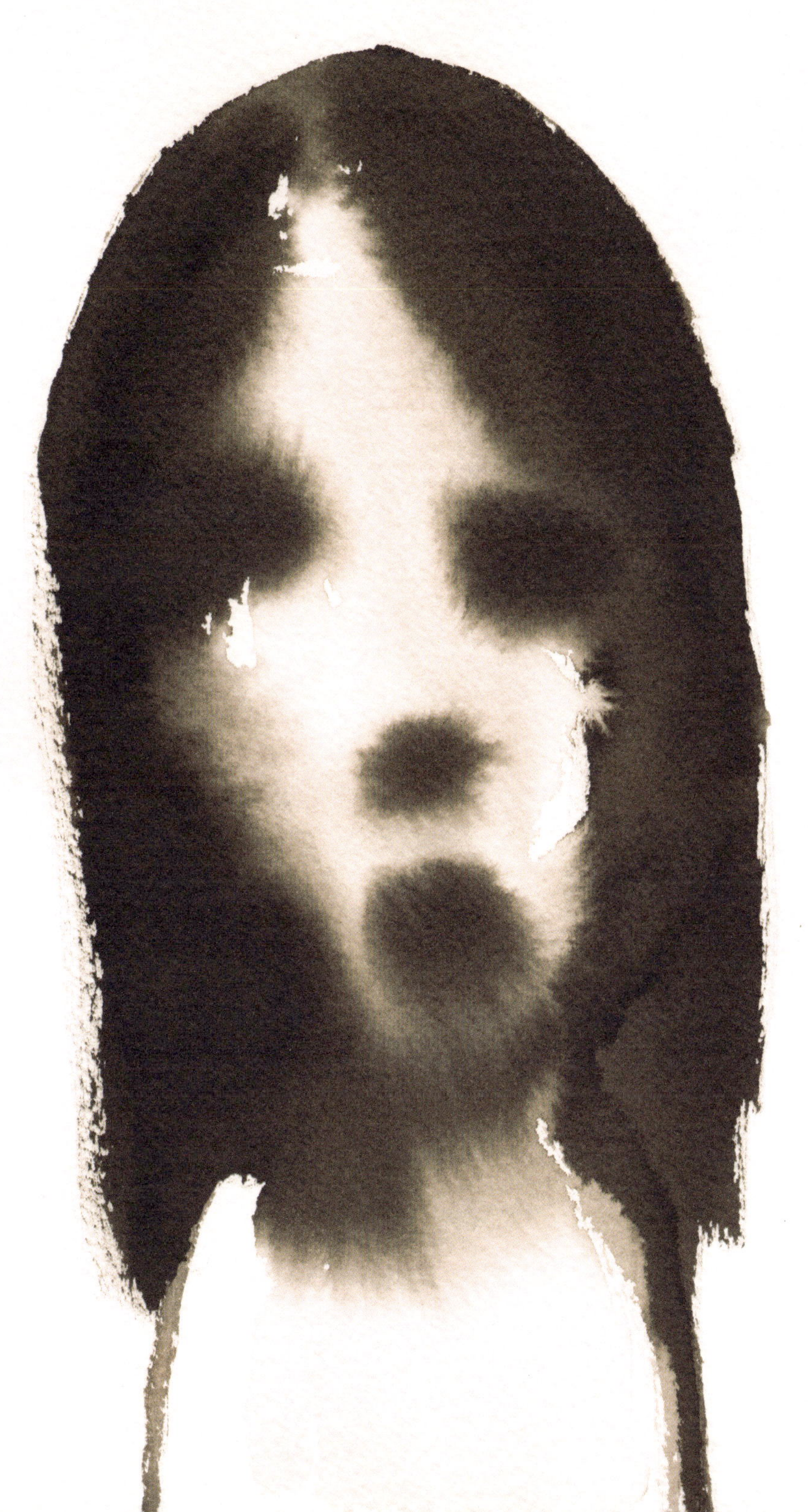

worshipping the Christian light has been perverted into something much more evil. Some more enjoyable stuff happens in the dark – it's a kind of free space to experiment.'

Red-eyed long-haired men appear in a lot of the works. Dunne describes them as an amalgam of Jesus and black metal. Death metal informs the work. 'There's something immensely funny about it. It's about the line between something that's incredibly serious and violent but at the same time slapstick.' That slightly cartoonish balance between horror and humour comes out in the playful, almost childlike style Dunne adopts. 'I think it's important to point out the underlying, inherent stupidity of a grown man painting all day. It's preserving a kind of innocence.' The looseness and wildness of his naive approach fit with the energy and randomness of ink blots. 'I think that the deliberate, virtuoso display doesn't lend itself well to those things – it's not the right way of exploring them. I guess it's more essential or more truthful. It's almost like a developing photograph – trying to capture the energy there and then.'

Dunne's paintings are full of skulls, bleeding ink, rolling eyes and strange men in top hats. 'This was an idea of trying to extrapolate from a very abstract idea of the bogeyman or someone sinister like the childcatcher; trying to personify or visualize an abstract idea of fear. The bogeyman, someone who goes around taking children away, isn't really a fairy tale or a myth. It's a very real fear.' The pieces tread the line between reality and fantasy. A pile of decapitated heads, entitled *Preaching to the Choir*, was inspired equally by zombie movies and the war in Iraq. Dunne was drawn to 'the pure enjoyment of a pile of decapitated heads. At the same time in Iraq there were people being decapitated almost daily. The work was called *Preaching to the Choir* because the American administration was preaching to the choir – only talking to the Christian right. This never-ending circle of violence comes from no one talking to anybody else.'

The ink is largely black, but it is covered with splashes of neon colour to temper the darkness into something more psychedelic. The pieces are filled with eyes, staring out of the page. 'I want the painting to look back at you. There's this sense of looking – they're aware that they're being looked at.' The compositions, often filled to the brim with imagery, loosely reflect horror-film narratives, 'the idea of a collapsed narrative that becomes hallucinatory. It doesn't have a beginning, middle or end – it becomes a loop; a closed loop of violence.'

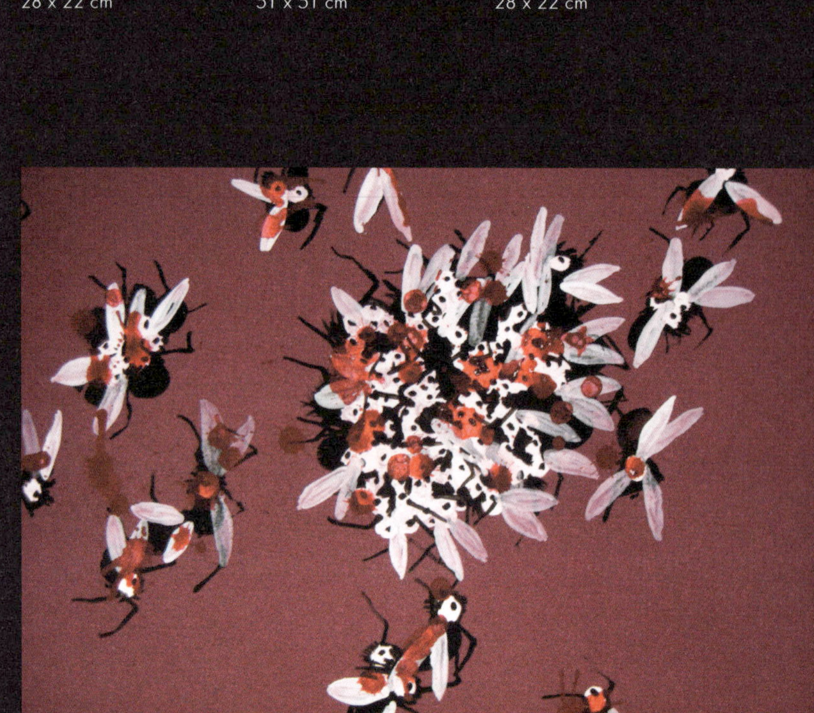

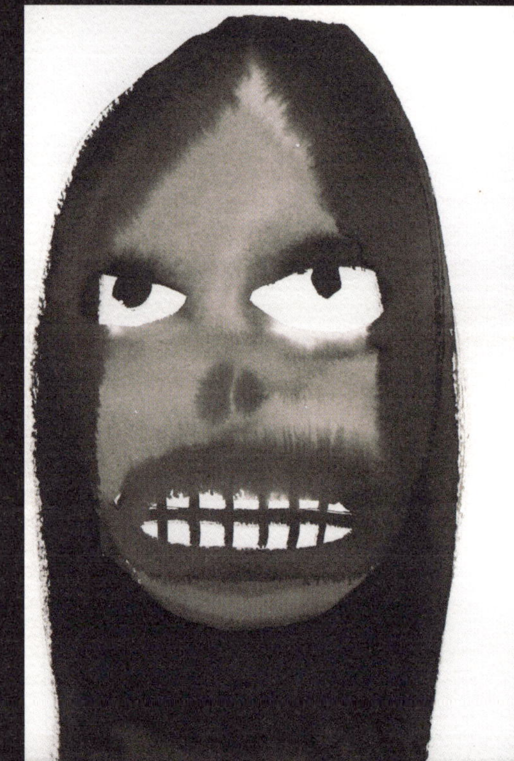

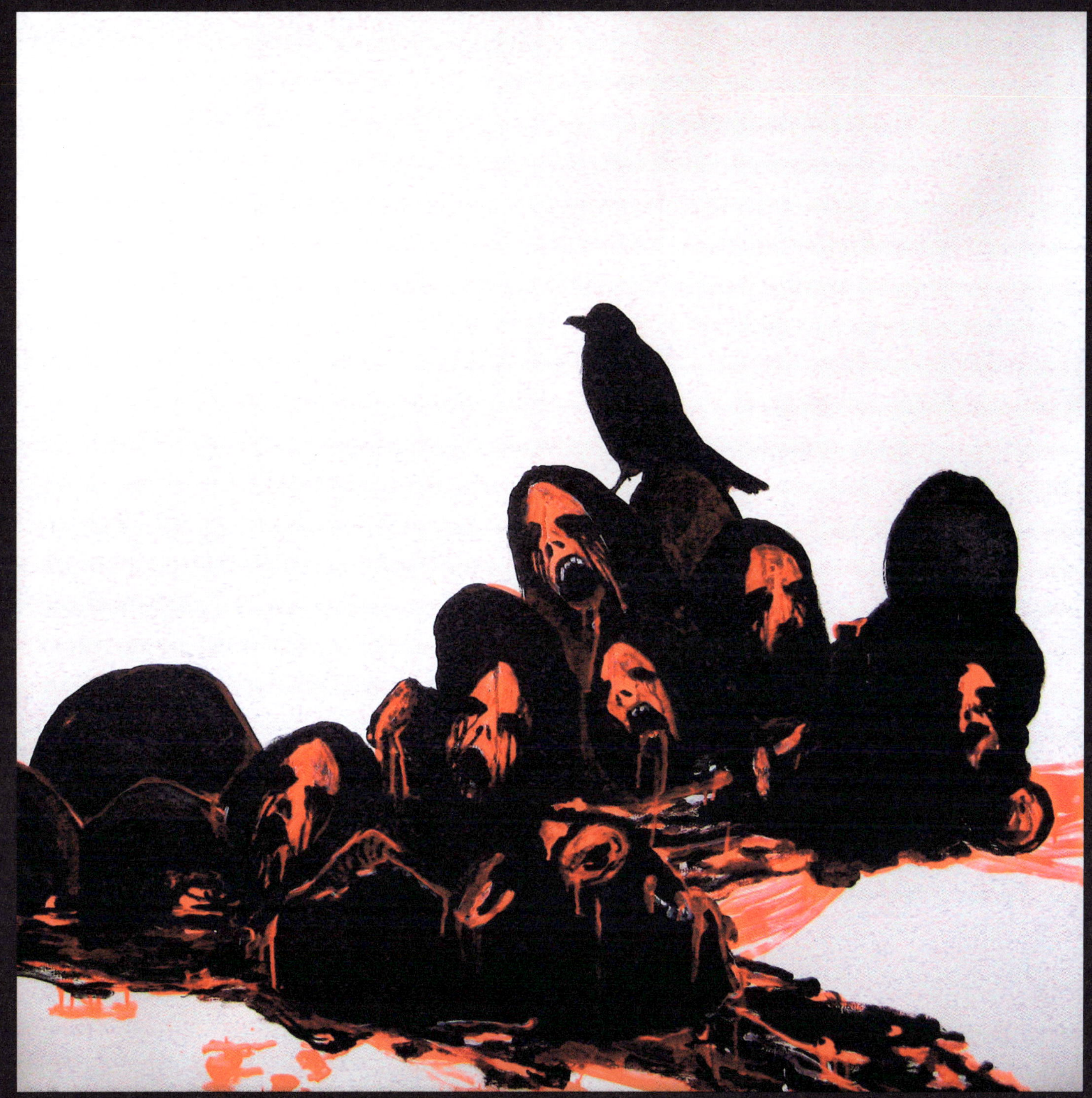

french

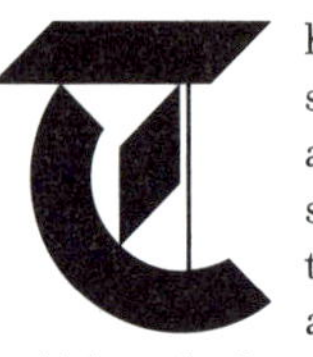There's something very enthusiastic about the way French approaches drawing gore and sinew. Exposed muscles and tendons have a tough texture and meatiness under his pen. Although the work is strange and filled with occult and black-magic references, it is also full of sheer joy.

Drawing was always at the heart of the artist's self-expression. 'I think I started drawing when I was really young. I remember drawing tanks and guns and people getting shot; I was always obsessed with the military. I was probably about four or five.' The British artist's drawings as an adult are intensely visceral. 'I think drawing is the rawest form of art and so undervalued these days. I just love making marks on paper and seeing lines develop and form shapes. You can learn so much from just doing three or four drawings. I probably learn two or three new techniques a week and I think my skills are developing like that. There's something about drawing that is just so much more me than if I was to make videos or weird paintings or anything. I do love painting, but drawing is accessible. I can do it anywhere and all I need is paper and pencils.'

Drawing can often be quite a polite medium, but French's work is quite the opposite. His pieces are openly violent and bloody. A rotting soldier stands on a pyramid of skulls. Eyeballs hang on the end of sinew as they fall out of a decaying face. Metal is an obvious influence on his approach and subject matter. He grew up listening to Iron Maiden, Saxon, Slayer, Napalm Death, Obituary and Bolt Thrower. 'Obviously metal has been a massive part of my life. It really

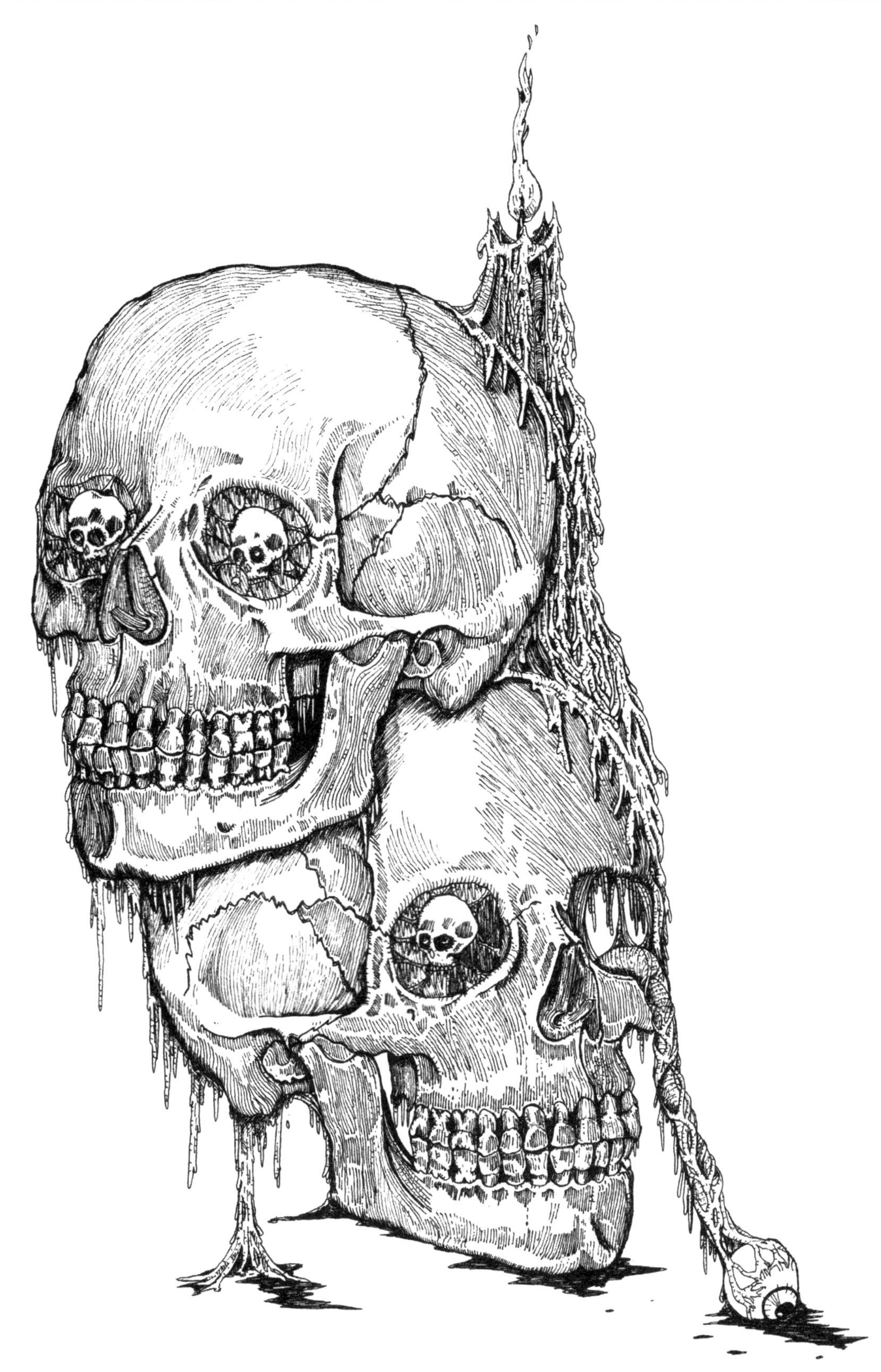

influences everything that I do. It comes into my work all the time. I think your work always shows a part of your personality – mine is in love with metal.' The music genre's visual heritage also plays into his horror-filled subject matter, particularly underground artists creating album cover art and band T-shirts.

French creates large black and white pieces, often with figures floating in white space. 'Using black and white means that I can concentrate on the detail and line work. I really feel that with some work colour would detract from the actual drawing. Also the simplicity of it is amazing.' His pieces range from piles of discarded skulls to ritualistic images drawn from black magic iconography. In particular, he is drawn towards muscle and sinew. 'I got this anatomy book from a car-boot sale and I liked the way it was all drawn. I wanted to learn how to draw in that anatomical style, so I started to draw body parts and bought more books and developed that way of drawing. I also think that's a pretty nasty, metallish way of drawing. There's a lot of drawing and work like that on old Carcass albums and other grind death metal bands. Learning how to draw like that has helped my draftsmanship overall.'

Deer and antlers are other recurring images in his work. The heads of deer are depicted wearing gas masks. A strange demonic religious icon character has an antler surrounded by a halo. The antlers sometimes resemble increasingly complex branches of trees. French often creates images where objects overflow. There are too many roots under a tree, too many bones on a pile or too much hair on a figure. There is a sense of nature in excess.

French does commercial illustration work alongside his art pieces. Its subject matter is all reasonably dark, though his personal work can be more gore-obsessed. Often his commercial subjects are even stranger than his bloody and violent drawings. 'I had to draw a skeleton eating a hamburger; Ronald McDonald being put through a mincer and coming out a clown; a wolfman kissing a girl. I have just been asked to draw the nativity scene, with Mary giving birth to a goat; that's pretty weird, but I'm really into that one. I always draw from images and photos, so I'll need a bunch of nativity scenes – pictures of goats and of women giving birth – to draw from.'

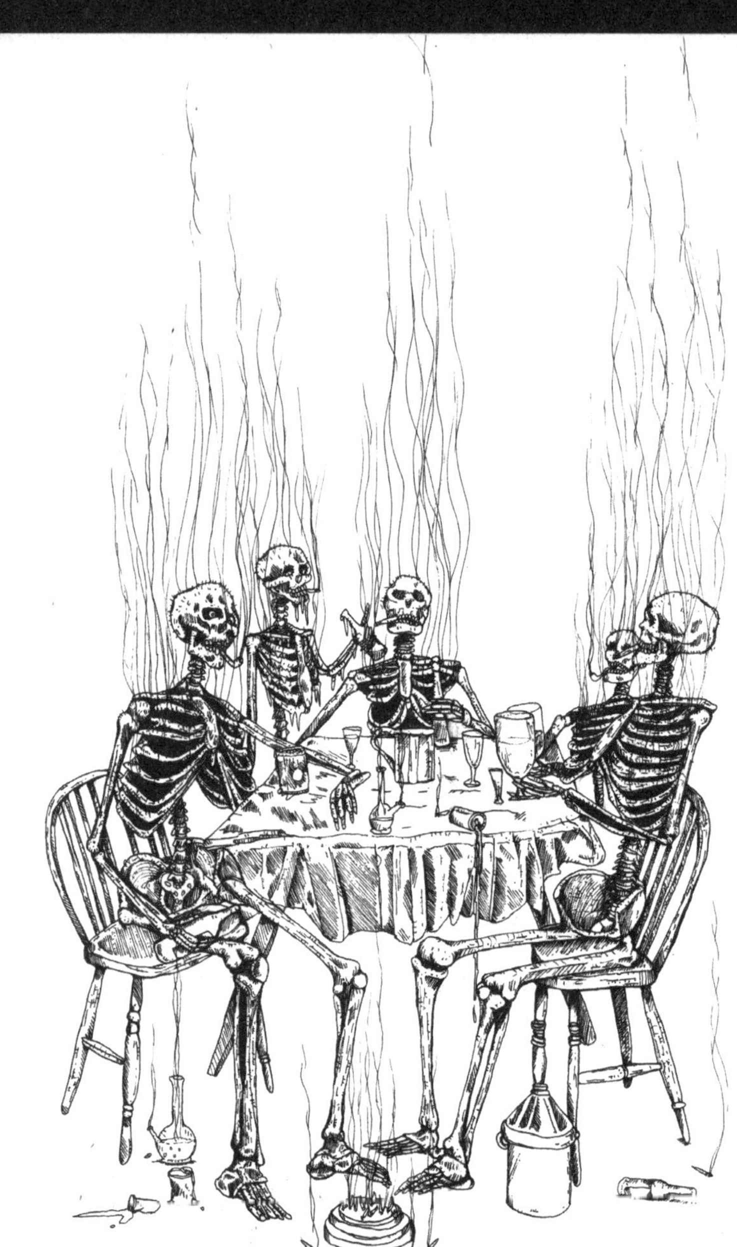

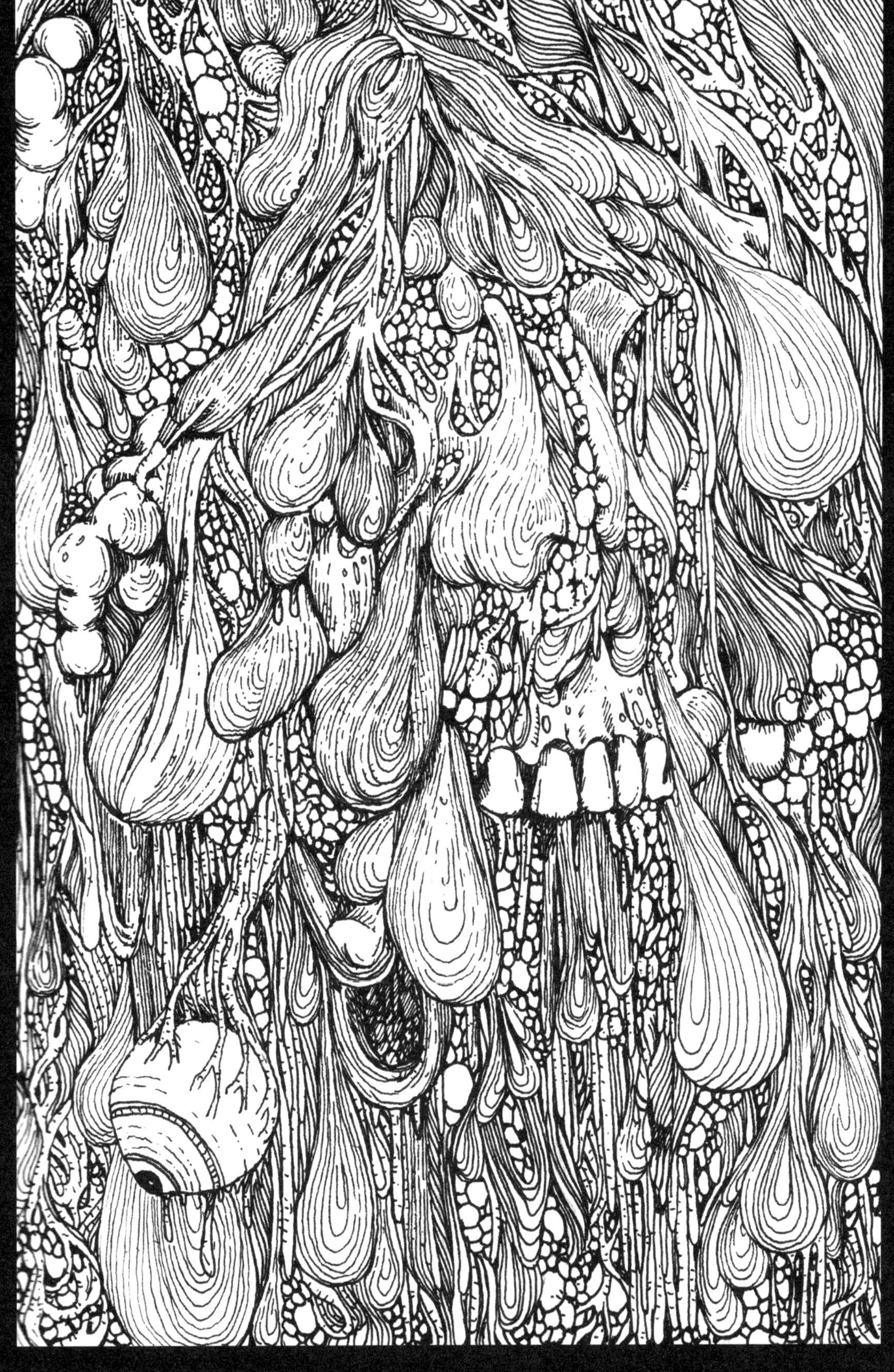

gabriela fridriksdottir

abriela Fridriksdottir sees her native Iceland as an unusual influence on her work. 'I came up with a theory that maybe one's mind could be compared to the ground one derives from. The Icelandic approach towards art is young and immature. If it has function, it is beautiful.' Fridriksdottir's work, however, veers in a completely different direction. She creates a world of poetry and chaos.

She studied sculpture, but Fridriksdottir is best known for her drawings. 'Drawing has always been such a natural part of my life. To begin with I never thought of it as a piece of art or something you would want to frame. I never looked at it as a part of my art-making; it was merely a tool that I used to start up my mind entering a new project. When I began making a piece of sculpture, or part of an installation or a painting, I would throw the drawings on the floor of my atelier and not think about them anymore.' From 2002, she realized that drawings were a central form of expression. They were the source of her entire creative practice.

Fridriksdottir often creates warped monster characters. There's something tender about these strange, fluid mutants. 'Imperfection is maybe what I love the most. When a thing is not perfect, when it has a crack or flaw, that affects you. When a drawing or sculpture merges between the abstract and figurative, and between the animal and human, there opens up a certain space that is full of possibilities. That is my favourite space.' Her creatures represent a feeling or mood, but nothing as obvious as happy or sad. 'I am not interested in the basic bad and good,

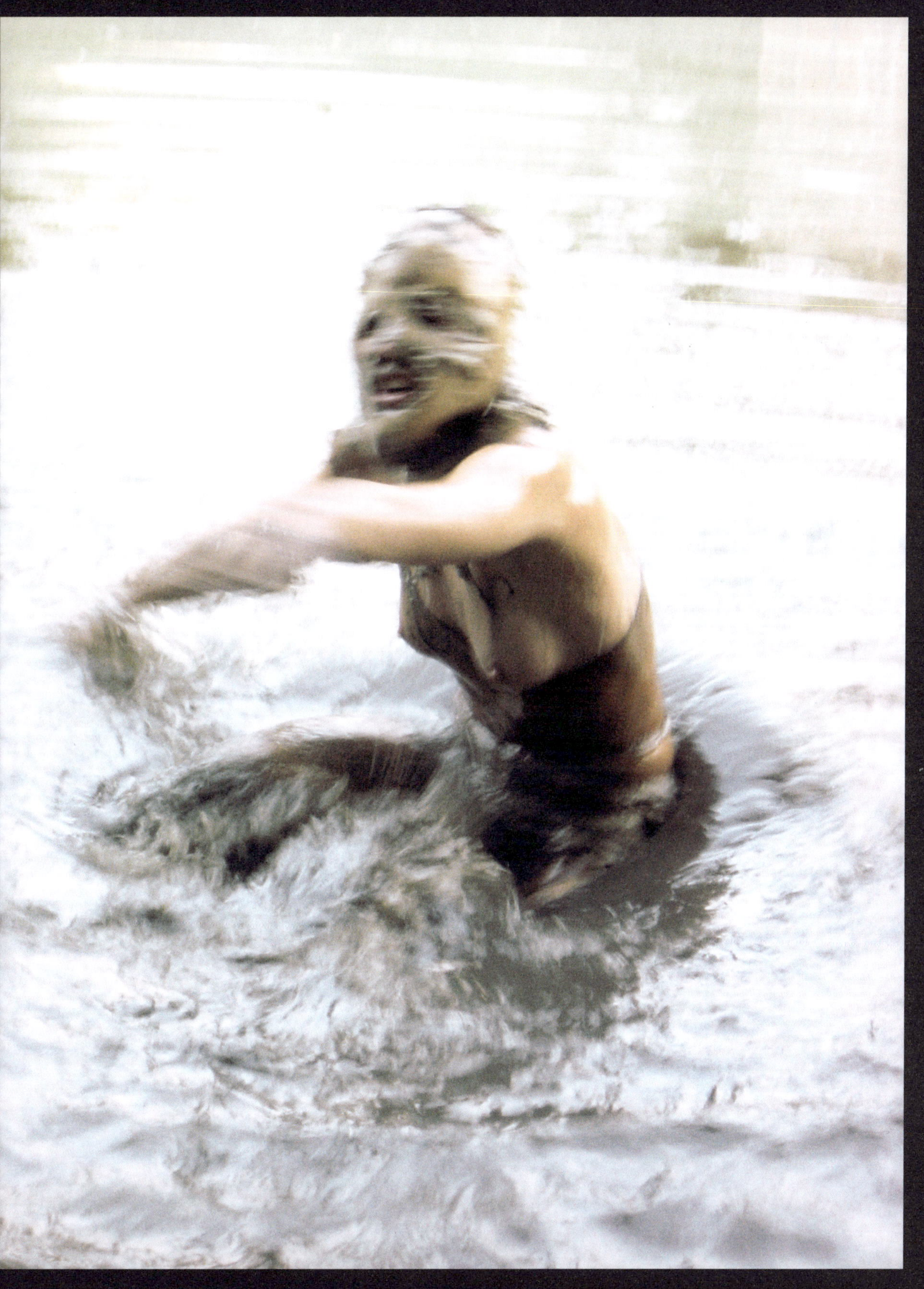

happy or sad, horror and sweetness contrast. I like things that are really hard to match.'

Fridriksdottir's work becomes more violent and visceral in her performances. She uses bread dough, creating experimental masks thick with bodily textures. 'As a child we used to make clay out of bread dough. We called it "troll-dough". You could always go and make a lump and make all kinds of figures and forms. It was not the visual, aesthetic effect that it had that made me use it again. It was more the memory of how it felt touching it.'

She began using the dough when developing an alter ego called Morris. This bohemian poet was intentionally ambiguous. 'The character needed a face that wasn't fixed – an unbaked face. The dough was a perfect mask.' Dough is always changing as it ferments. It is a substance permanently in metamorphosis. The material inspired Fridriksdottir to use video in her practice, in order to capture the dough's changing nuances and expressions.

Often the dough is used as a mask or disguise. 'By covering your face with a lump of dough, it changes you into something that is so dramatic, that it is unbelievable.' Her performance pieces explore that sense of dramatic transformation. 'I like materials that are strong, expressive and tell a story – like dough, mud or hay. I choose them for their ability to present a certain feeling, mood or soul.' She works with materials that produce a gut reaction in the viewer.

Fridriksdottir explores the emotional restlessness of melancholy in her sculpture and drawings. She is particularly interested in the four humours – the concepts that were the basis for medieval medicine and psychology. She created a video of an operation made on the melancholic body, where the surgeon was seeking the black bile produced in the liver of a melancholic. The film, *Melankolia*, is a metaphorical narrative of her fascination. It shows the artist soaked in black goo, rising up to a heavenly place of ideas.

Music and sound are other important aspects of her work. 'In the videos there is no dialogue. Instead, I try to find language in different musical instruments.' Wet mud is the sound of a bass clarinet. The cello is the voice for the branches of a tree or the nervous system. In all of the artist's weird and wonderful work there is a very personal language of visual poetry.

Previous spread
Katharsis (still)
2004
Video
Duration: 7:49 / ed.
3+1AP
Courtesy the artist, i8, Reykjavik and Spielhaus Morrison Galerie, Berlin

Below
Operazione Poetika, Selfportrait
2002
Print
17 x 11 cm, 1AP
Courtesy the artist

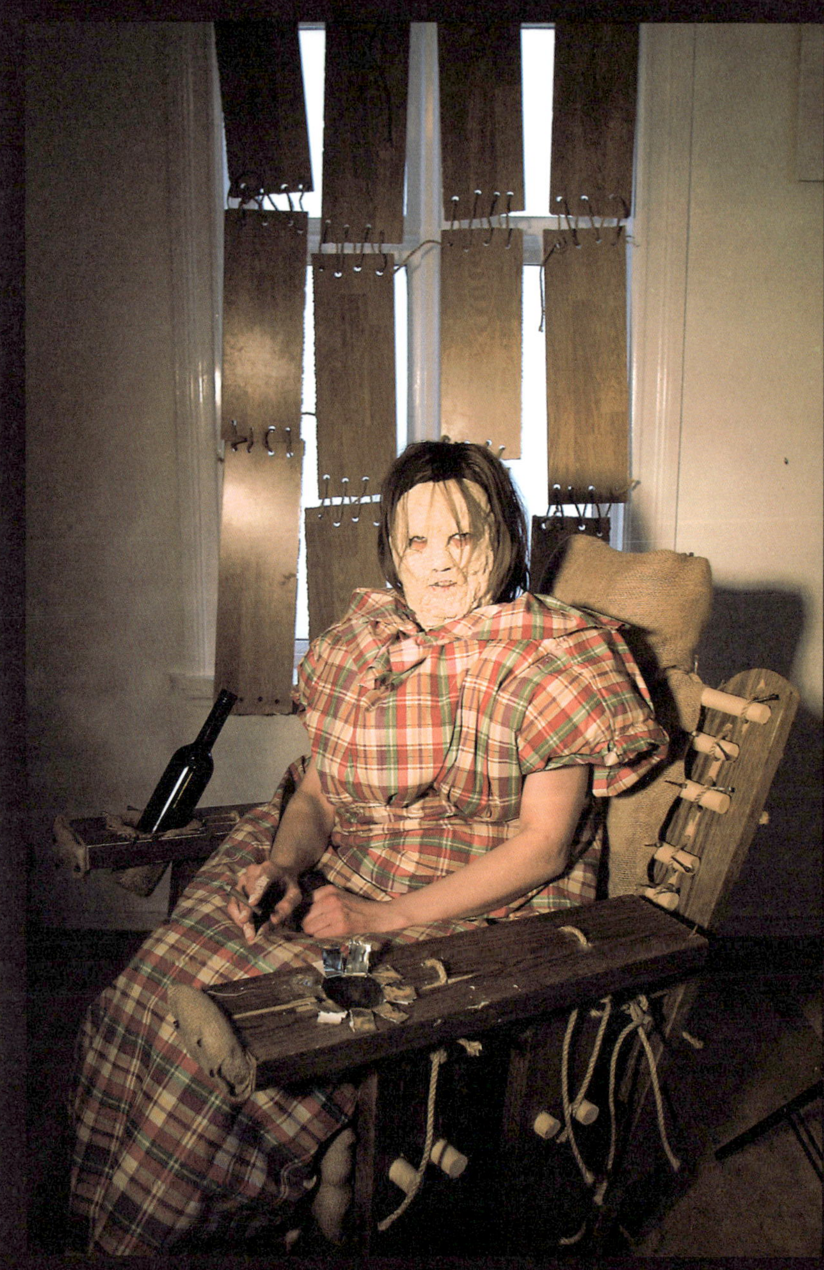

Below
Tetralogia, North (still)
2005
Video
Duration: 9:30 / ed.
6+1AP
Courtesy the artist, i8,
Reykjavik and Spielhaus
Morrison Galerie, Berlin.
Ed. 2/6; Collection
Migros Museum für
Gegenwartskunst, Zürich

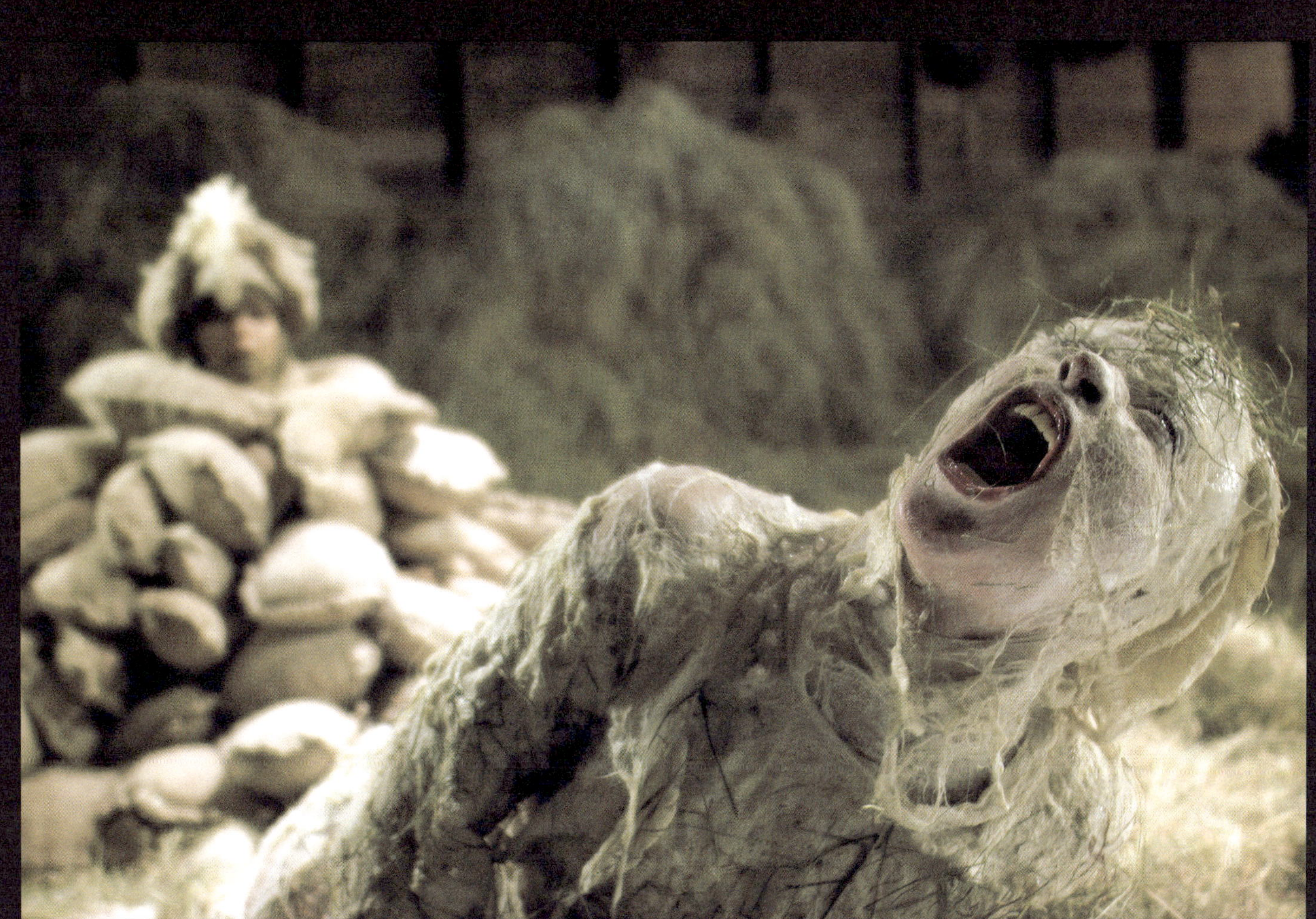

Below
Operazione Poetika,
Selfportrait
2002
Print
17 x 11 cm, 1AP
Courtesy the artist

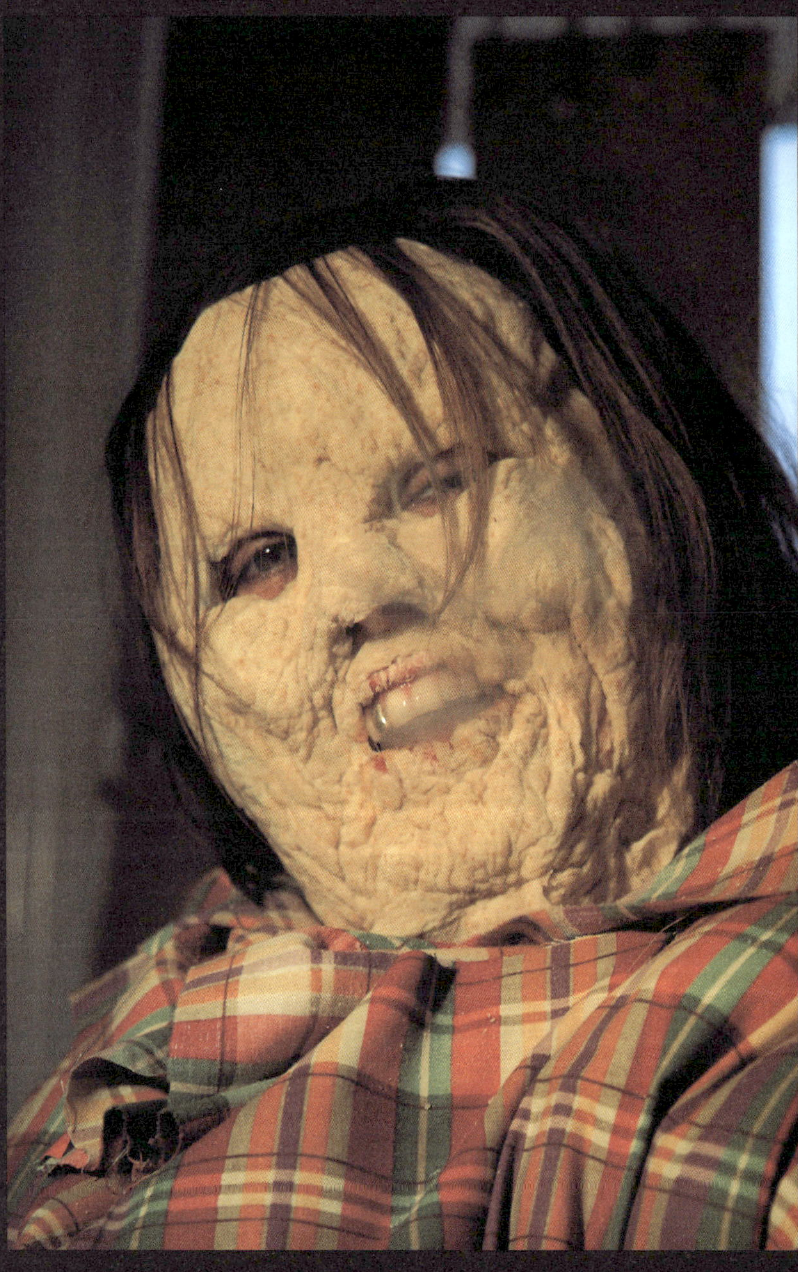

Below
No. 1, Inside the Core
2006
Print
89 x 89 cm / ed. 7+1AP
Courtesy the artist, i8,
Reykjavik and Spielhaus
Morrison Galerie, Berlin

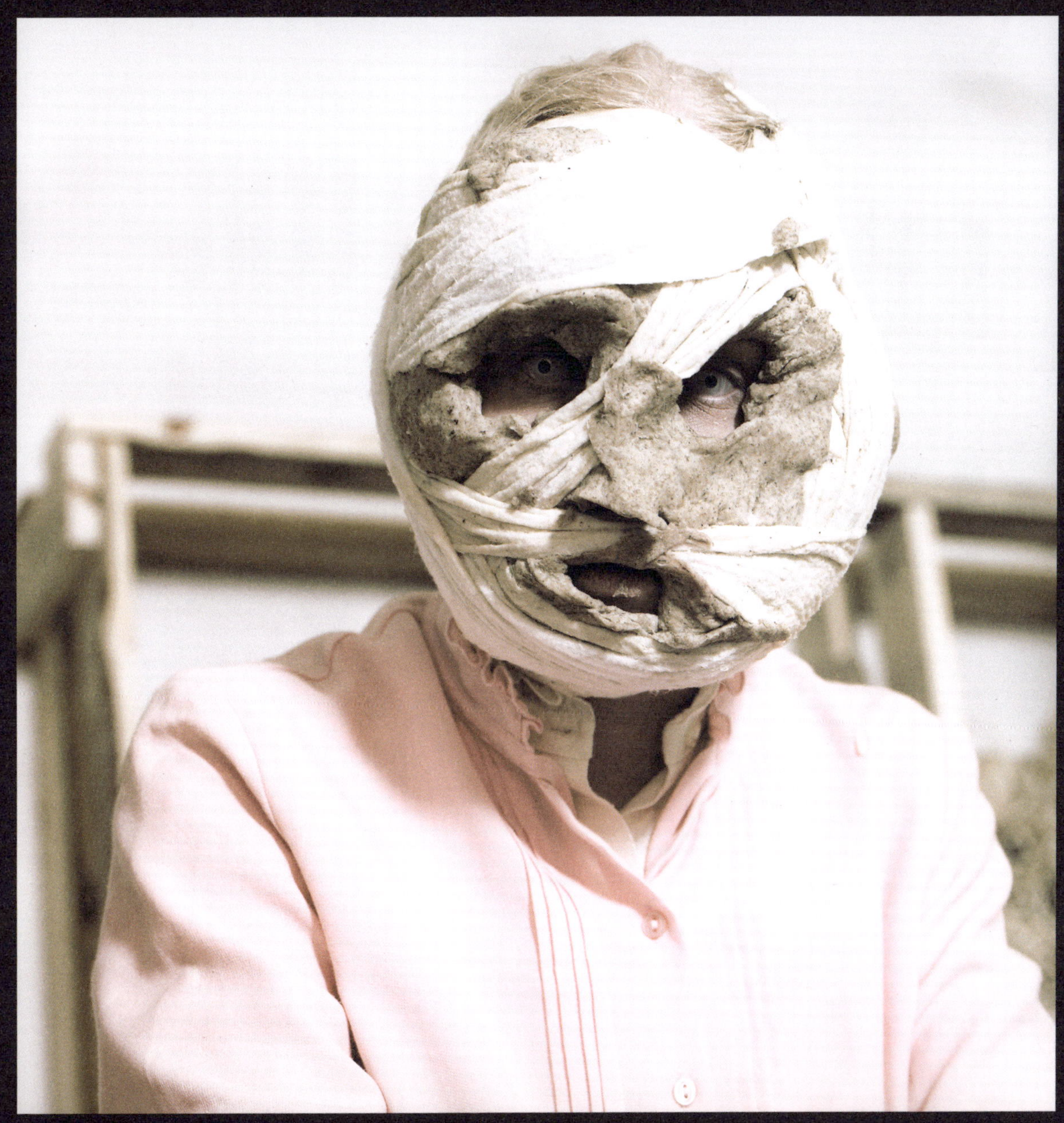

matt greene

There's a fluid darkness to Matt Greene's paintings. His ethereal pieces are filled with mushrooms, overtly sexual female bodies and heavy-metal imagery, but nothing is harsh or violent. Instead, his works feel like visionary hallucinations. Magic and irrational spaces are recurring themes. This disturbing, dreamlike atmosphere is intentional. It plays into a fascination with prophetic dreams and shamanism. 'I want to look back to early cultures' ideas about the importance of dream-spaces in decision-making. I want to show a world in which many modes of thinking can coexist simultaneously.'

There is a sense of ambiguity in Greene's work. The choice of painting as his central medium relates strongly to this feeling of uncertainty. 'It's a pretty basic art form that will always represent the struggle between the mind and the physical world. Our pictorial conventions are so deeply ingrained that they mirror the experience of reality as a screen,' Greene explains. 'I like that painting can be read as almost purely physical or purely intellectual, but it's never able to be completely one or the other. Ambiguities require longer and slower interpretations; I like the slowness of painting. It reveals the flaws of fantasy.'

Metal-band imagery infuses a lot of his pieces, but music itself is not the central attraction. Instead, these allusions reflect an interest in the drag aspect of heavy metal and its alleged relationship with witchcraft. 'I'm really interested in things that don't fit into categories.' That lack of fitting in, or clarity of identity, is also about gender and androgyny. 'I was interested in how so many early cultures not only

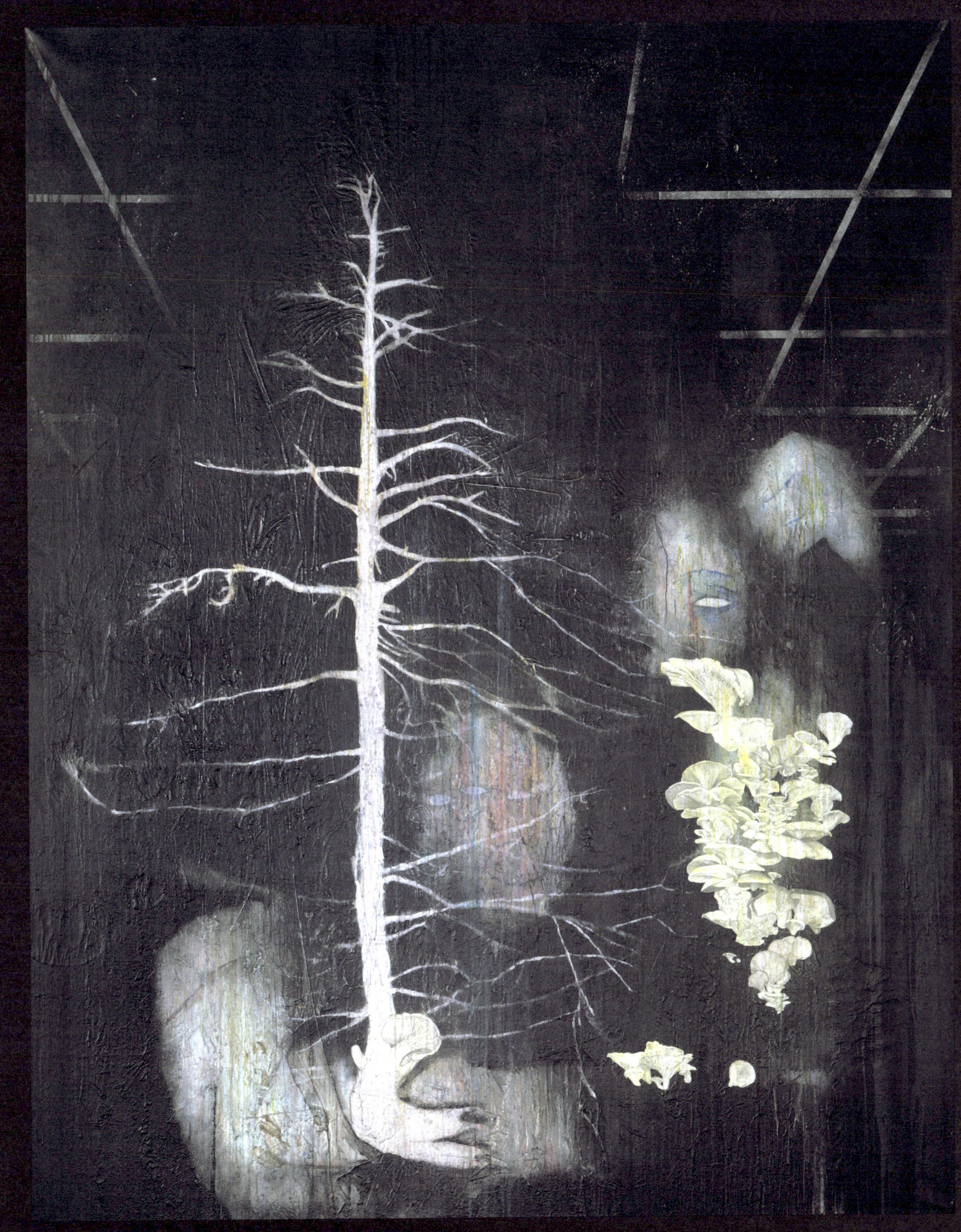

Matt Greene / 055

tolerated people who were between genders, but they frequently saw them as holding special magic powers. This theme recurs in alchemy with the idealization of the hermaphrodite. The early Alice Cooper records were especially interesting to me as descendants of this lineage. I wondered to what extent a pop star could be thought of as being shamanistic.' This is more about accessing an archaic or 'primitive' aspect of human culture than something New Age.

Another aspect of the shamanistic nature of creativity is the visual references to mushrooms, although these are not intentionally about their psychedelic effect. For Greene, the mushroom motif is about seeing the world through new eyes. 'I started learning to identify the mushrooms I was seeing on hikes in local mountains. Once I knew something was in the landscape, I would be able to see it all over the place. What had once been invisible to me was now recognizable, because my thinking about it had changed. I wanted to make art like this, to create something that looks chaotic, but is actually an accumulation of very ordered events.' Neither plant nor animal, mushrooms, like the androgynous cultural figures that interest him, live in a state between. 'It also crosses my mind that it gives the organism immense orgasmic pleasure to produce mushrooms. Interspecies empathy.'

Sex is something that is at the heart of much of Greene's less black pieces. There are paintings of women in black tights and white French maid outfits wielding swords, or in corsets mid-battle. Here, characters openly quote positions taken from pornography. These pieces have titles like *The Orifice* or *The Pollinators*. There's an interesting crossover between aggression and the erotic, but the women here do not appear passive. In fact, they force their bodies into the viewer's gaze.

Much of Greene's work is filled with black paint, washes of colour emerging out of a misty darkness or an unknown or negative space. Alongside his paintings he also creates drawings, which, like Hans Bellmer's, are full of layers and a multiplicity of angles. Here bodies, skulls, sex and death all literally overlap. 'It's Baudelaire's concept of bile and the ideal – the perfection of the idealized fantasy paired with the absolute non-existence of such a thing in the physical world. In this equation death is related to castration – the denial of access to pleasure. Drawing is a direct battle between the ideal and the material, one that is more or less doomed to failure.'

The artist has said his work is borne out of frustration, but it is an intangible frustration about expression and communication. 'My endless source of frustration is the disparity between what can be imagined and what can be done; the desire for things that do not exist; the inability of language to describe an idea.'

Previous spread
For the eyes of our fathers
2005
Acrylic, collage and
graphite on paper
305 x 244 cm

Below (top)
*That We Do Not
Appear to Fly is of Little
Consequence*
2006
Acrylic, ink and collage
on canvas
244 x 305 cm
Courtesy Peres Projects,
Los Angeles/Berlin

Below (bottom)
*O))) (indicating enormous
sound pressure)*
2004
Acrylic, collage and
graphite on canvas
294.6 x 365.7 cm
Courtesy Peres Projects,
Los Angeles/Berlin

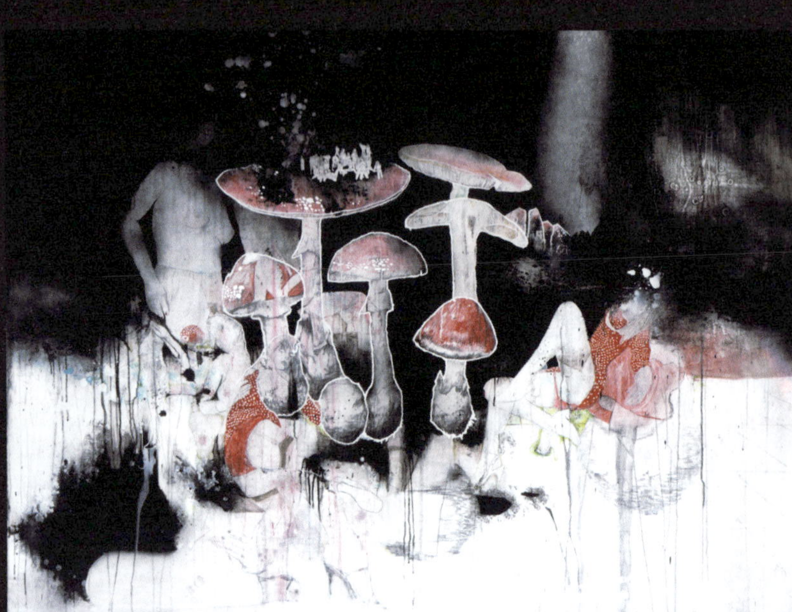

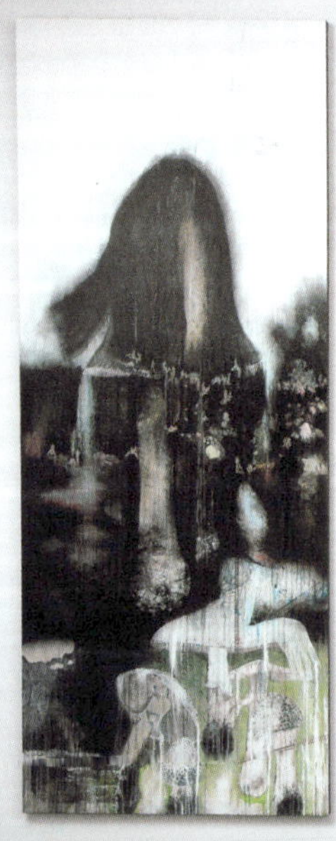
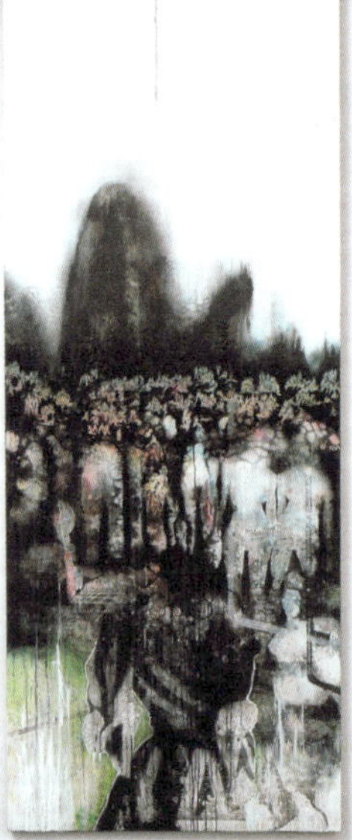
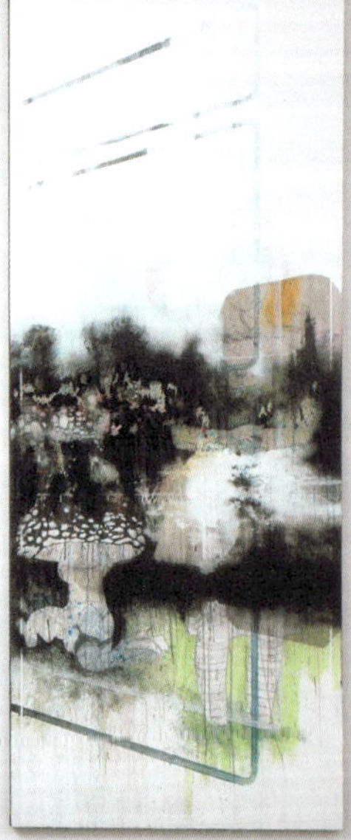

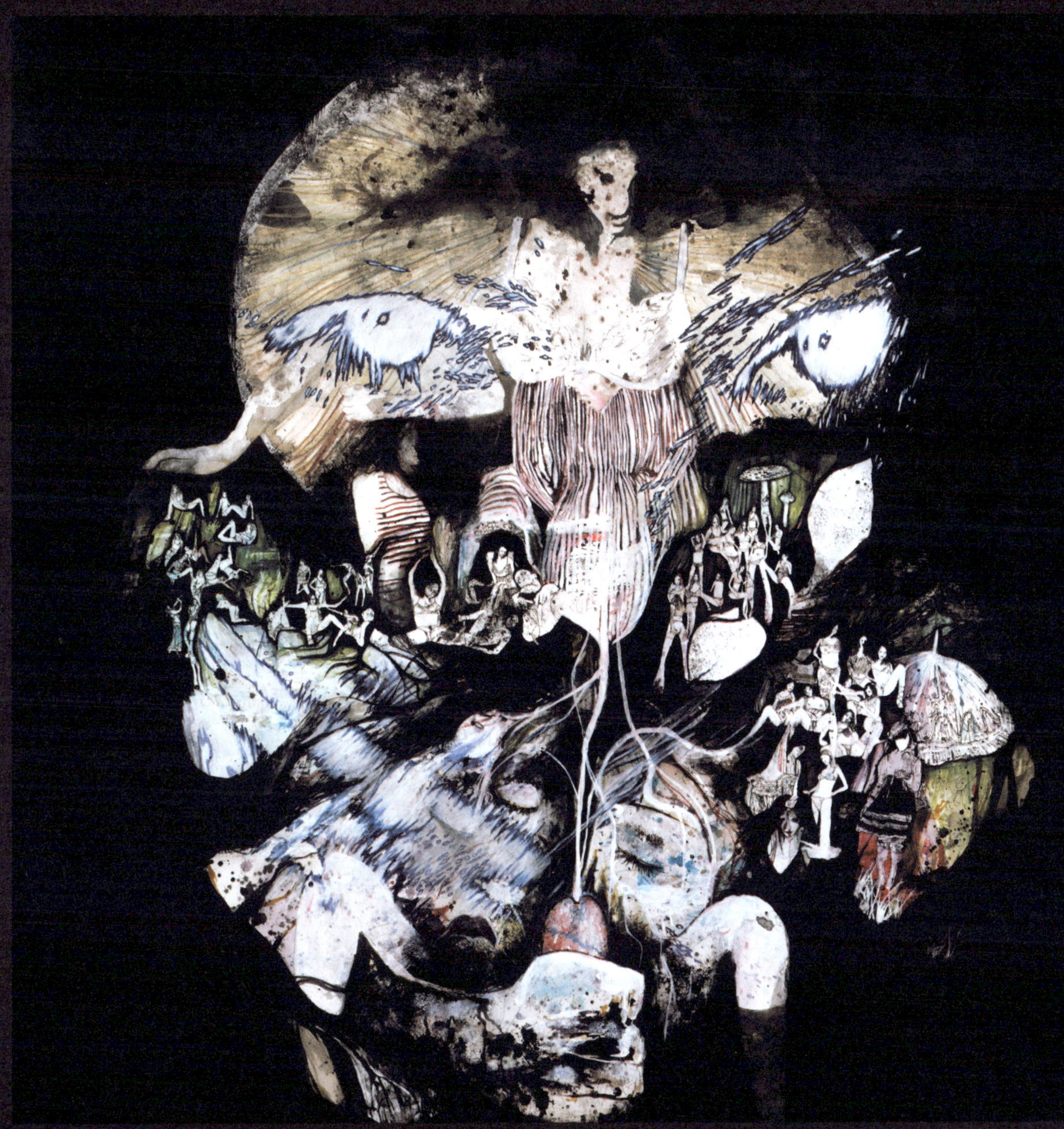

Below
Mater Tenerbrarum
2004
Acrylic and ink on paper
120 x 120 cm
Courtesy Peres Projects,
Los Angeles/Berlin

james hopkins

Vision can be deceiving. James Hopkins's sculptures look like normal, everyday objects stacked on shelves. They also resemble grimacing skulls. It is an unusual approach. The trompe l'oeil effect Hopkins creates is something more traditionally used in painting rather than installation, but it works brilliantly. 'I am particularly interested in scenarios that deceive the eye, because they allow us to question the discrepancies between the real and the illusory. Our senses can be misleading in certain situations. What the eyes see, the brain can mistakenly believe.'

Here truth and reality become blurred. Hopkins's visual tricks play with what we take for granted. 'The real is momentarily suspended in a state of disbelief. I like the experience you have at the moment when your perceptual apparatus is thrown into disarray, and your notion of the real is ephemerally unhinged. It's a disconcerting experience.'

Hopkins first began making sculpture seriously after seeing an engraving by Albrecht Dürer from 1527. He became fascinated with the old master's use of perspective from a single, isolated viewpoint in the work. 'For me that seemed an interesting aspect of sculpture – that we can only see what is directly presented to the eye within a constrained field of vision. Our perception of the process of vision is never complete.' We can only see one aspect of something, never an object in its entirety. In his series of skull shelves, Hopkins plays with this same approach to perspective. When the viewer looks at the object straight on or from different angles the piece is either revelatory or unclear. 'The effect is similar to a partial loss of vision.

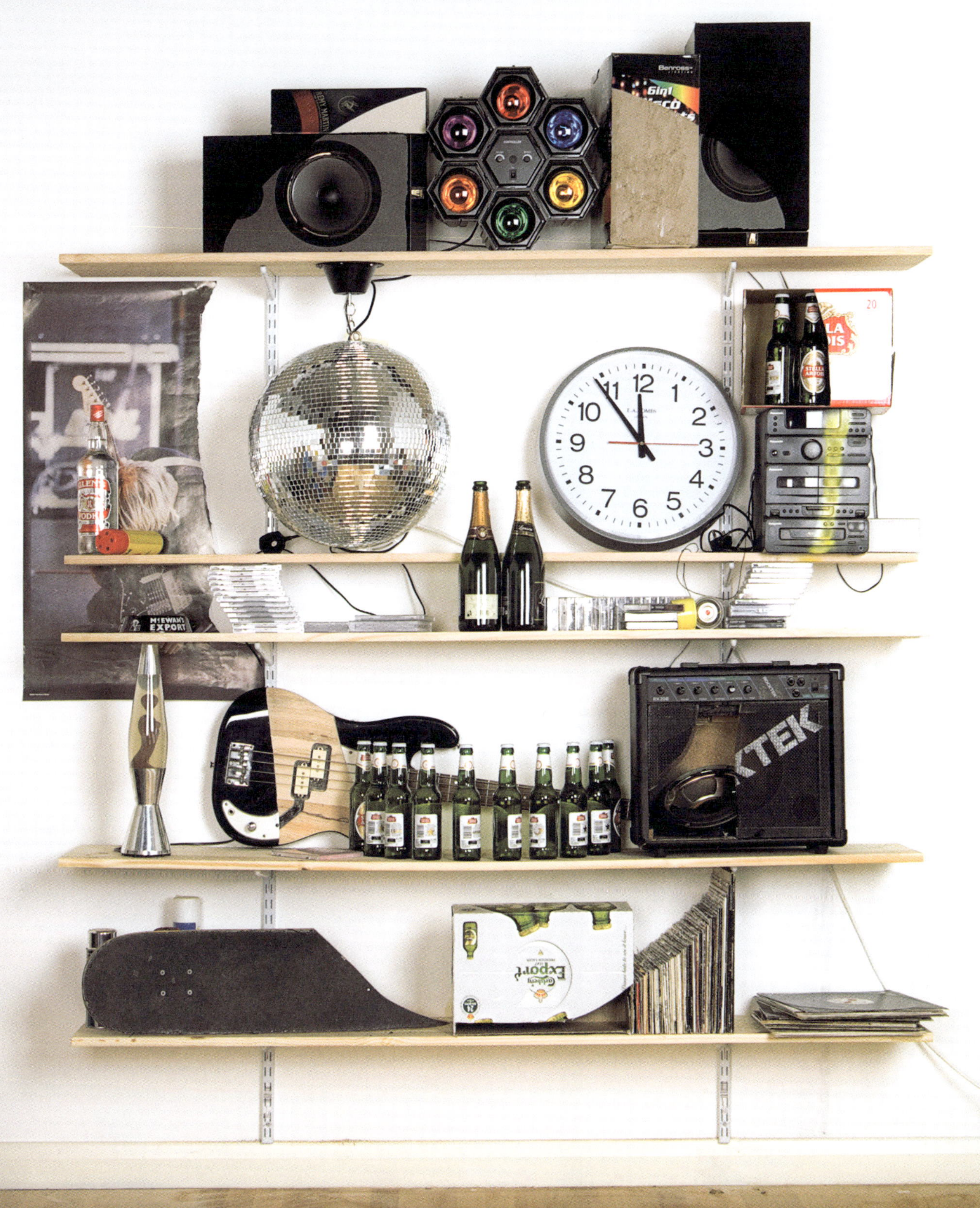

The mind chooses to see what is first presented or most familiar in favour of the secondary image of the skull.'

The artist is drawn to the imagery of death and the skull's place as an iconic symbol of demise. 'Everyone understands what skulls look like, so when making an illusion, this familiarity is a huge help. My skull portraits are not always instantly recognizable, so I often rely on visual clues to lead the eye in the correct direction in order to decipher the camouflaged aspect of the imagery.'

There is a serious allusion to the meaninglessness of consumerism in Hopkins's work. Many of the pieces' titles, such as *Prosperity and Decay* or *Le Visage de Vanitas*, reveal that association. 'I got interested in the connections between death and consumerism from looking at the seventeenth-century Dutch movement of vanitas painting. I really liked the objects they depicted, what the objects were saying metaphorically and how these items would be juxtaposed with a skull. This genre of still-life painting is a celebration of life. I wanted to convey that in my own work, but in a more contemporary manner. In other words, when we die we lose all our indulgences and possessions. So the work is saying: enjoy life while you can.'

The artist chooses to transform everyday items into art — from stationery to hi-fi systems. The pieces show how we give meaning to the objects around us. Like many contemporary sculptors, Hopkins subverts an object's original purpose in order to comment on its values and function. The objects he uses are often almost invisible items you would expect to see on a shelf — but their emotional or symbolic meanings are as important as their shapes or original functions. This metaphorical or symbolic approach is classic seventeenth-century vanitas. 'I use books or computers to convey a sense of knowledge. Bottles of alcohol and instruments to refer to indulgence. Mirrors and other consumable items to suggest vanity. I cut into, peel back and remove the surface of these objects to reveal the image of the skull, acting as a *memento mori*, a reminder of the fact that one day we will lose life and all our earthly possessions.'

There is a lightness here, despite the 'live today as you die tomorrow' message. There is delight and humour in creating and looking at the illusionary effects. 'Humour is one of the ways people deal with death. I use illusion as a means of hiding the image of death, and find it fun to play with the viewer's perception. My work often has intrinsic wit. I have noticed that viewers often laugh, in a similar way to the punchline of a joke.' Death never looked so entertaining.

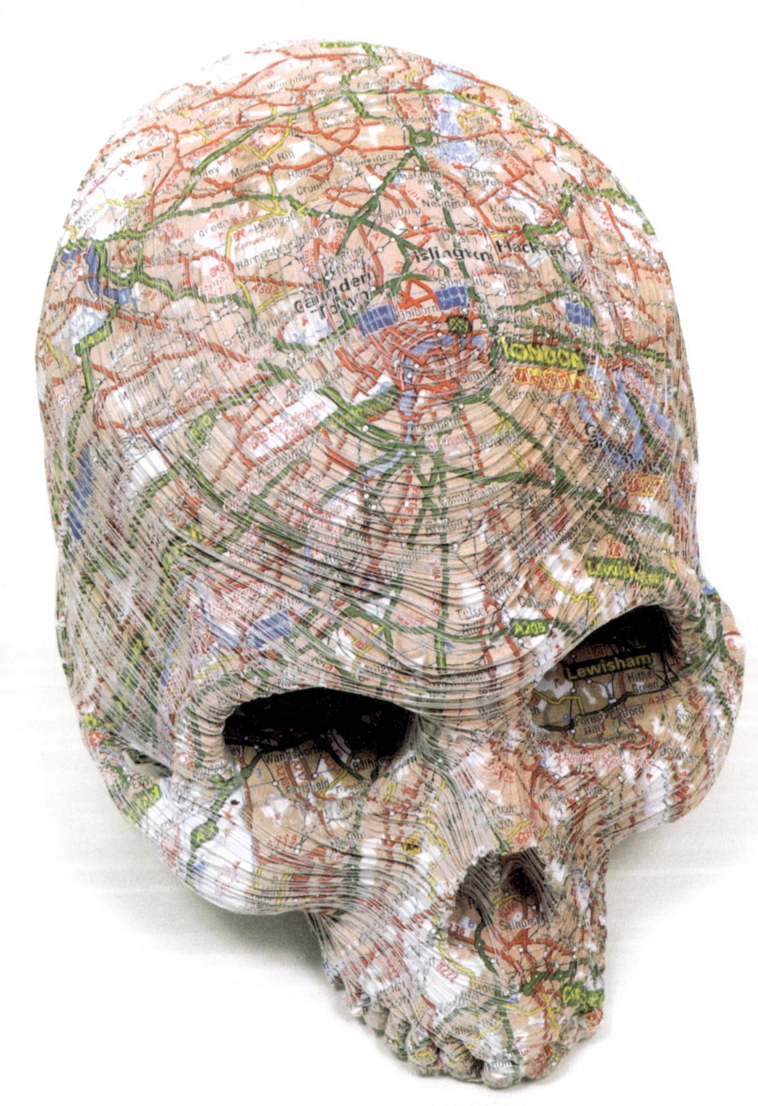

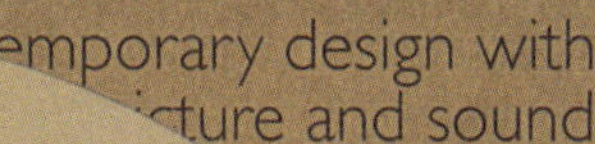
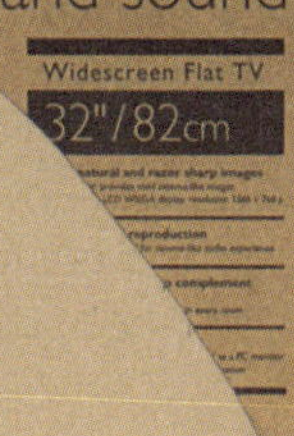
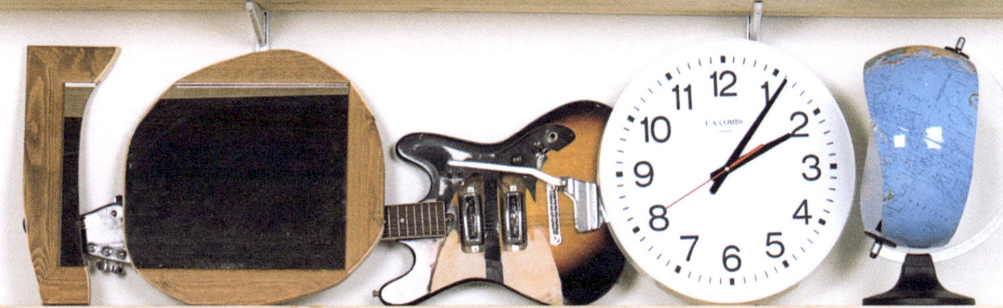
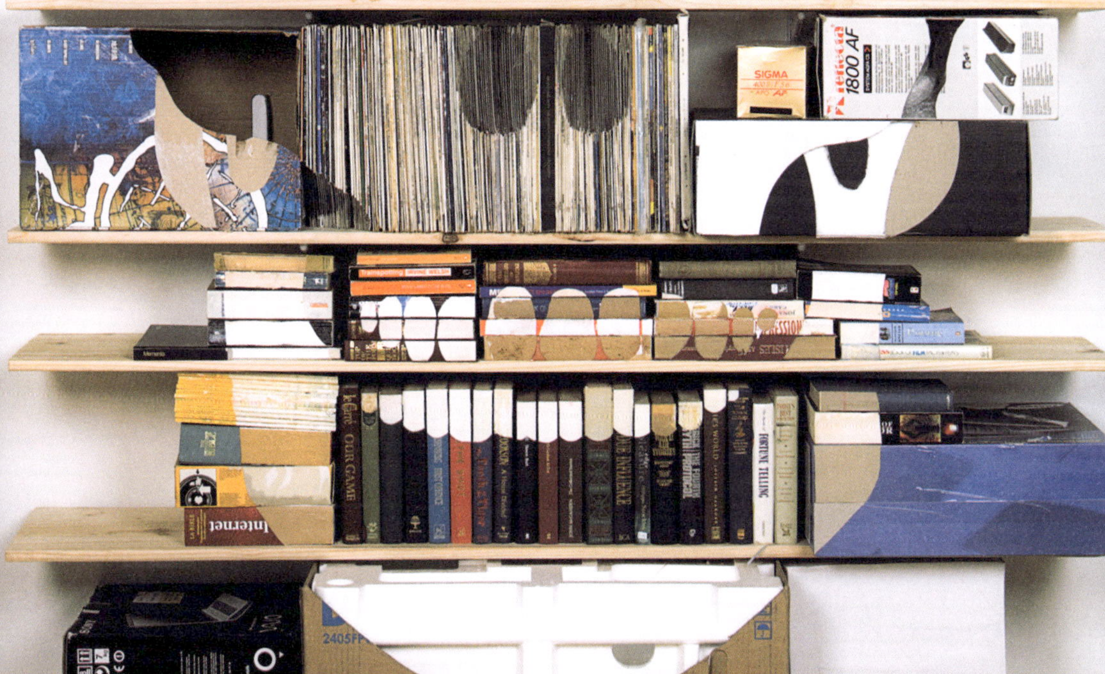

PHILIPS
contemporary design with
picture and sound
Widescreen Flat TV
32"/82cm
enregistreur de DVD
SIGMA
1800 AF
SONY
VAIO
Internet
OUR GAME
FORTUNE TELLING
2405FT

des hughes

es Hughes's approach to sculpture is inventive and hard to define. No medium is too prosaic to be transformed into a sculptural object. 'I'm beginning to realize the significance of being brought up a Catholic, alongside my parents' obsession with eccentric DIY. I remember furniture extended to grotesque proportions, unusual-shaped holes in the walls and various tree trunks indoors.' His work brims with humour, but it is not in the hyper-real hysteric way of some of the other artists who are drawn to similar subjects. 'I never really set out with humour in mind, but it might be the connection to certain types of horror films and the clean graphic or cartoon nature of certain gestures, like chopping something off. The limitations of using unsuitable materials often give the objects a pathetic, tragic feel.'

The disembodied hand is a recurring theme through Hughes's multimedia pieces. 'I think there is a connection with fragments of classical sculpture, saintly relics or even the practice of producing bronze casts of the hands of renowned sculptors, as if it might offer some insight into their genius.' His hands, made of wax or sausages, intentionally reference the horror staple of the reanimated chopped-off hand, such as *The Adams' Family* character 'Thing'. For Hughes this 'object' still has a powerful resonance. 'It is a device that is disturbing and comic, that has the ability to express itself, move and still to be a threat; castrated yet defiant. In terms of sculpture, the narrative of the chopped-off stump is a convenient way to finish. It results in a compact and precise form that only includes the bits that interest me.' His sculptures have included gloved hands made from sausages and skeletal fingers made from dog biscuits.

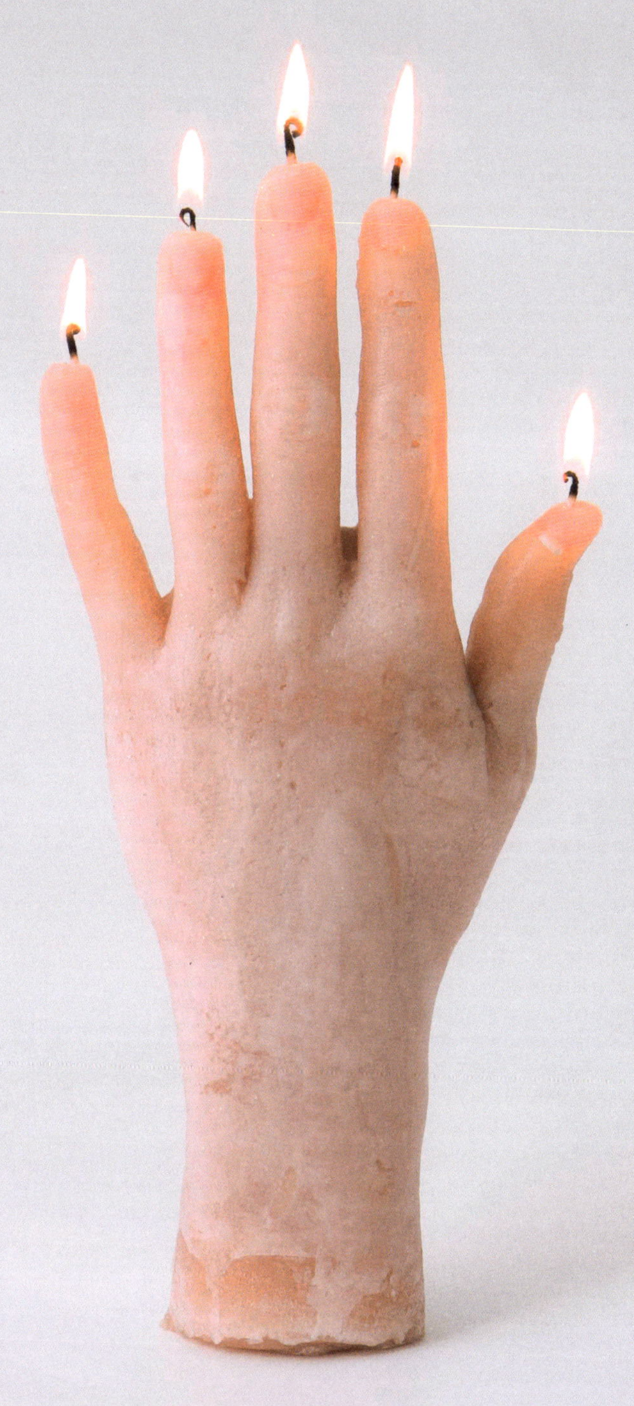

Some of his most resonant pieces play with the idea of the Hand of Glory, a pagan spell or charm, originally created out of the fists of hanged burglars during the Middle Ages. 'It was essentially a candlestick that was thought to open doors and ensure that victims were deeply asleep.' Hughes created a gas-powered version to address ideas around sustaining a particular moment or image. 'As an object, it seemed to have the power of a significant curiosity or a relic. I was interested in the belief systems that need to be in place to sustain magic, or in fact any religion, through their use of sacred objects, and the obvious parallels with works of art.'

The burning flame coming out of the artist's own cast fingers adds a living, unearthly edge to the work. One sculpture replicates the hands in different positions – like a small, burning army of gestures. 'I am interested in the effect of the "live" elements (the fire and rusting) on casting and how it might be possible to create a theatrical effect with obvious and modest means.' The Butane gas used to fuel the sculptures seems to cause drowsiness and sickness if you are in the room with it for any length of time – adding a brilliant visceral edge to an already physical piece.

It is not just hands that are cut off in Hughes's work. Other pieces include chopped-off ears, 'pierced' to the wall with multiple polished nails and screws. Many of his objects mimic the texture of real bodies – limbs and skin appear sticky and tactile. 'I am as interested in the potential of materials as I am in inventing or recreating images. The material and the object are inseparable. It might be that a chance encounter with a particular pile of raw sausages might suggest a hand of distorted fingers. It is a bonus when the stickiness, the seeping and the smell come for free. I'm often reminded of the gruesome accounts of serial killers' creative disregard for their "material".'

There is something uncanny about the physicality and repetition in Hughes's work. The innate discomfort of seeing something that looks both human and inhuman simultaneously. His use of everyday and domestic materials increases this sensation. 'Everything that I make seems to be either assembled from, or attempts to mimic, or is cast into material that is everyday, domestic or at least suspiciously familiar. There always seems to be one characteristic that invites distortion to grotesque extremes. I think the work exists in the tension between the material and what it has become.'

Previous spread
Hand of Glory
2007
Wax and string
28 x 15 x 6 cm
Courtesy Ancient &
Modern, London
Photography Gerard
Hughes

Below
Sculpture for Dogs
2006
Jesmonite, sandstone,
powder and steel wire
27 x 17 x 11 cm
Courtesy Ancient &
Modern, London

Opposite
I in the Triangle
2007
Cast resin, copper,
natural gas bottles and
found materials
140 x 85 x 48 cm
Courtesy Ancient &
Modern, London
Photography Andy Keate

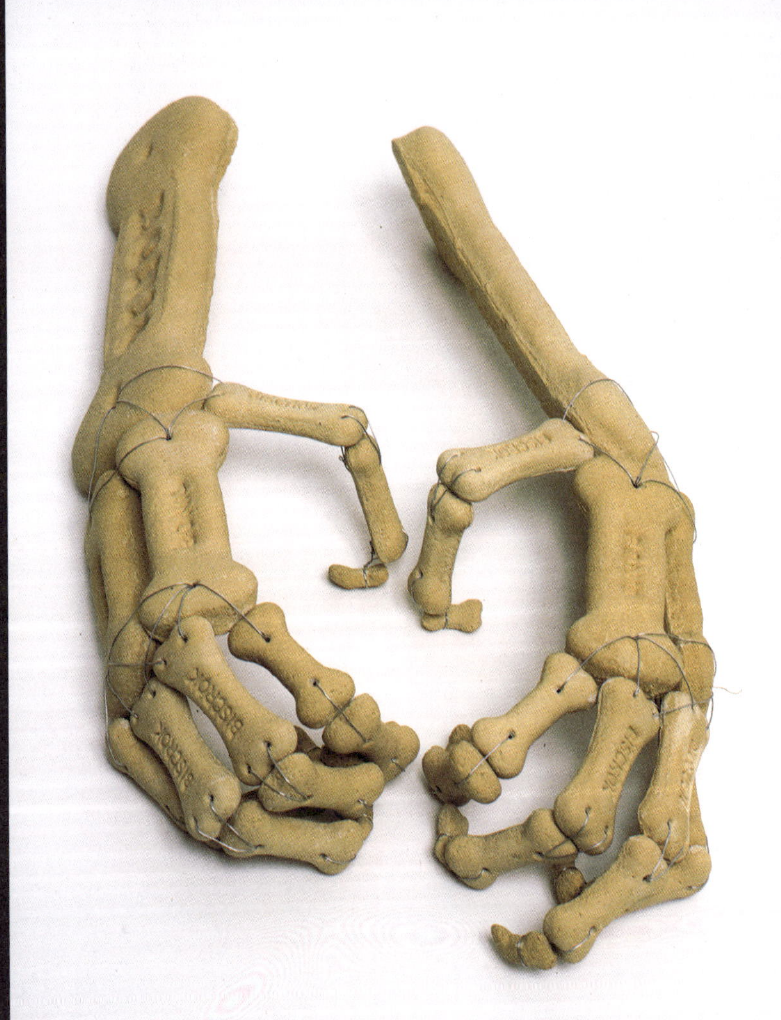

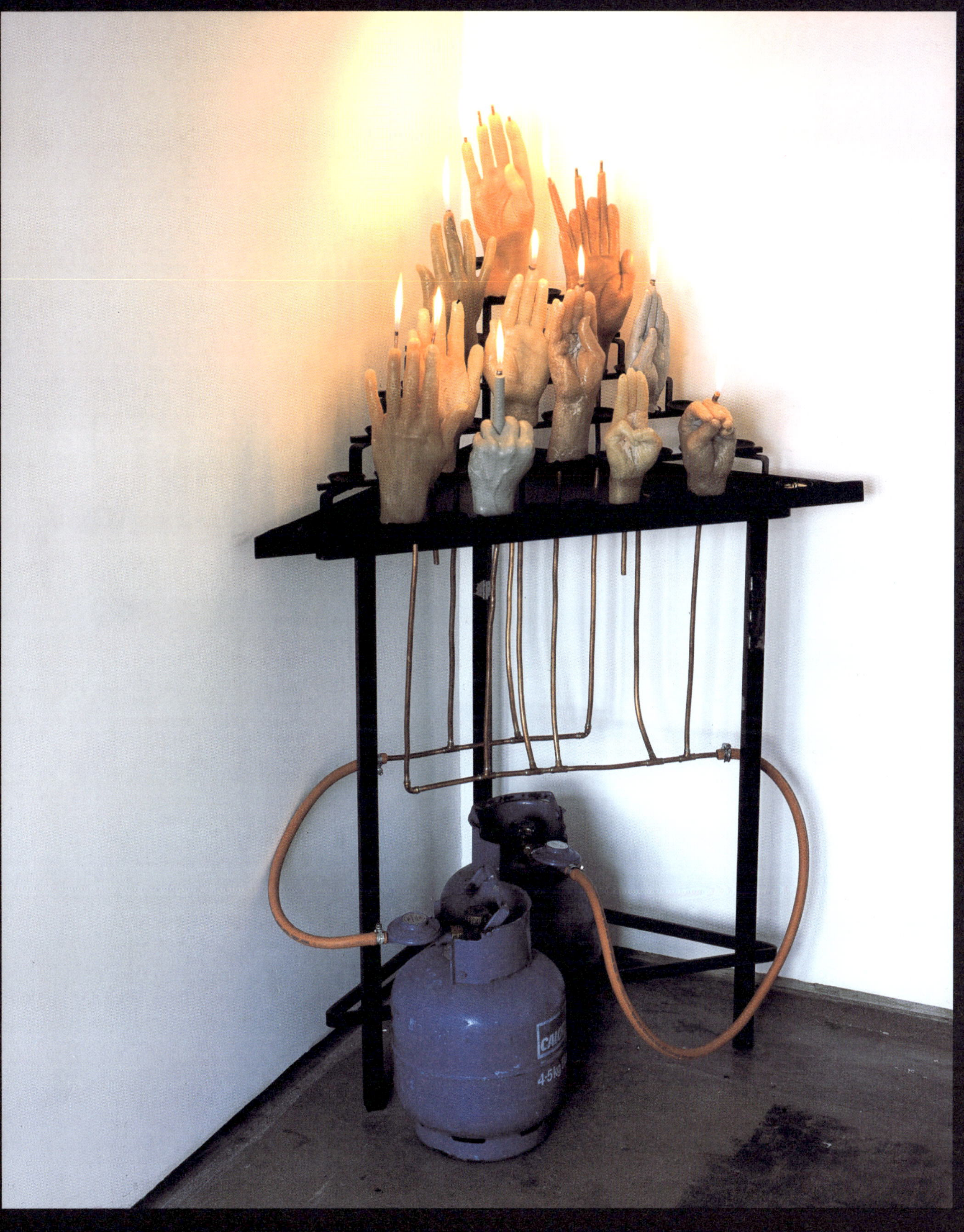

christian jankowski

orror films are in Christian Jankowski's blood. When the German artist's parents were dating, they created an eight-millimetre horror movie in their spare time. Jankowski was attracted to many aspects of this genre in his art: 'the visual impact, the huge fan community, the attraction of monsters and the obsession of people working in this field. I like the surreality. Everything is possible. Even when we know that all we see is fiction, it affects us in a very physical way. It plays very directly with our senses.'

Jankowski explored the many nuances of horror in a series of work in 2006, following on from earlier works that had examined other genres in popular culture. The horror pieces were originally inspired by a talk at Massachusetts Institute of Technology (MIT) by media studies professor Henry Jenkins. Jenkins showed stills from horror productions – a grotesque face sticking out of an ass, a screaming bleeding body – alongside theoretical quotes on the meaning of these violent images from popular culture. 'This was the first time I experienced the feedback these horror productions get from academics.'

Working with New York City–based art institution Eyebeam, Jankowski began to create his own interpretation of a low-budget horror film. *Angels of Revenge* was created during a horror convention in Chicago in 2006. 'It all just started with the very abstract idea of working inside an existing horror film production.' He came across the horror convention on the Internet and hired a conference room next door. 'The structure of these horror films is often

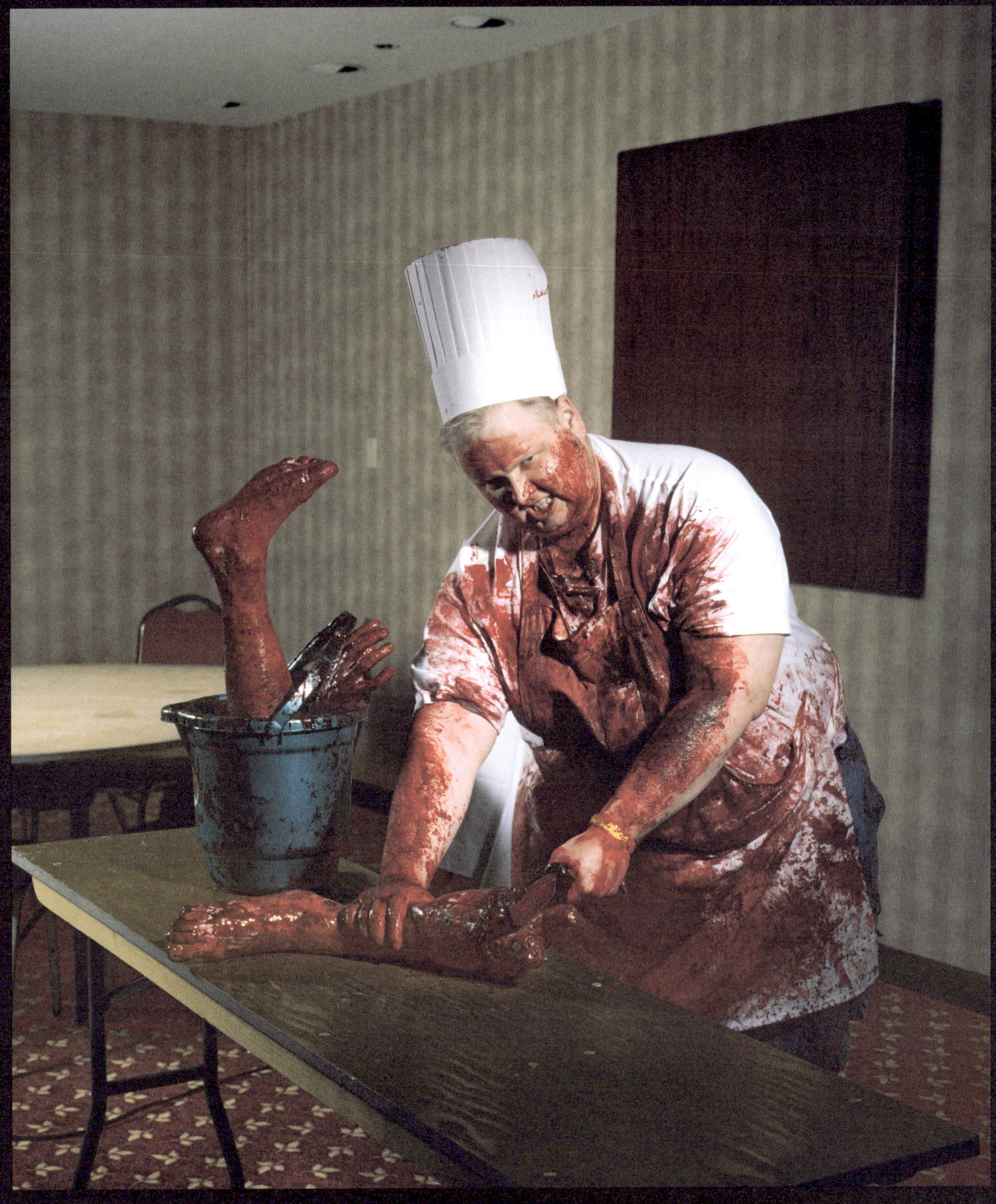

a revenge story — that a ghost or someone is coming back looking for justice.' He became fascinated by the formula of revenge.

The artist asked horror fans two questions: 'How were you most wronged in your life, and what is your revenge fantasy against the person responsible?' 'Punishment is also a creative act. That's how I explained it: that they should come up with a punishment that best suited what had happened to them.' The result was a claustrophobic video and series of photographic diptychs, where costumed participants shared their very personal, hand-scrawled revenge stories alongside images of themselves dressed as horror characters. Their choice of character was personal. Before they arrived at the convention they were unaware of Jankowski's project. Their fictional alter egos were an expression of their own inner desires and fantasies.

These photographic pieces are incredibly scary, even within a gallery context. The characters include an insane butcher covered in blood and wielding an axe, a blue-faced child demon, a werewolf and a masked serial killer. It is the intimacy of their handwritten fantasies that make them so disturbing to look at. Often stained with fake blood, these evil daydreams are frequently incredibly violent, describing mutilation and torture. It was an interesting insight into the minds of horror fans and contemporary America.

Another horror project that Jankowski created during the same period was *Lycan Theorized* — a werewolf movie filled with philosophical quotes about the nature of horror. It starred high-profile academics and cultural historians. The result was a brilliant combination of academic theory and unintentional comedy. 'I wanted to do a film about the crisis of the whole genre. Many theorists claim the end of the American horror film — there are only the remakes of already existing ones. I wanted to map out the existing theory and sew it together in a kind of Frankenstein style. And do it all in an existing commercial horror production — to see what is left from the potential it once had — to stimulate discussion and meaning.'

Alongside this fusion of highbrow and low pulp culture, Jankowski exhibited the prosthetic faces and bloody limbs made for the film. These simulacra of blood and gore were presented like museum artefacts or the debris of an autopsy. 'I asked the theorists I interviewed to give me their body parts, which the actors in the film scenes would drop and lose in a similar way to the theory. I was interested in showing a physical experience of the people who normally have a distant, analytical look at the genre.' He created a world where theory became immersed in action.

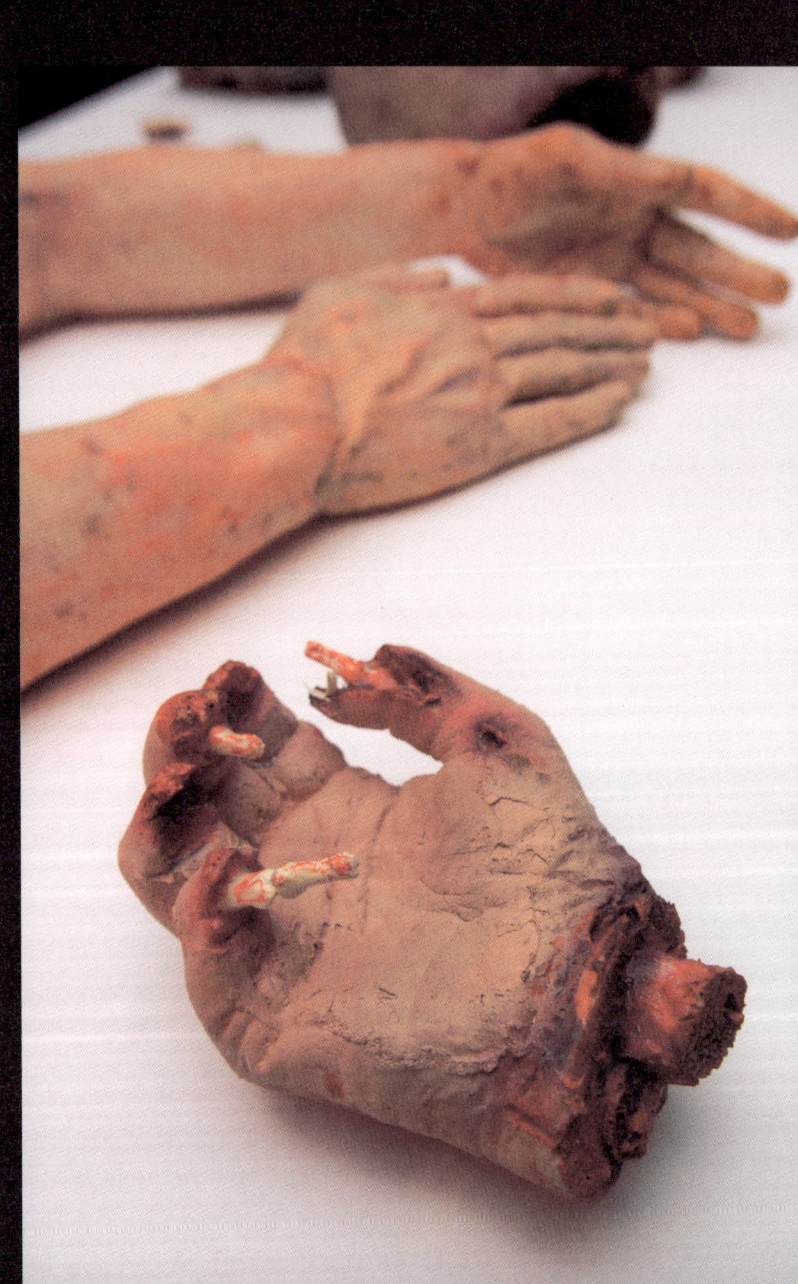

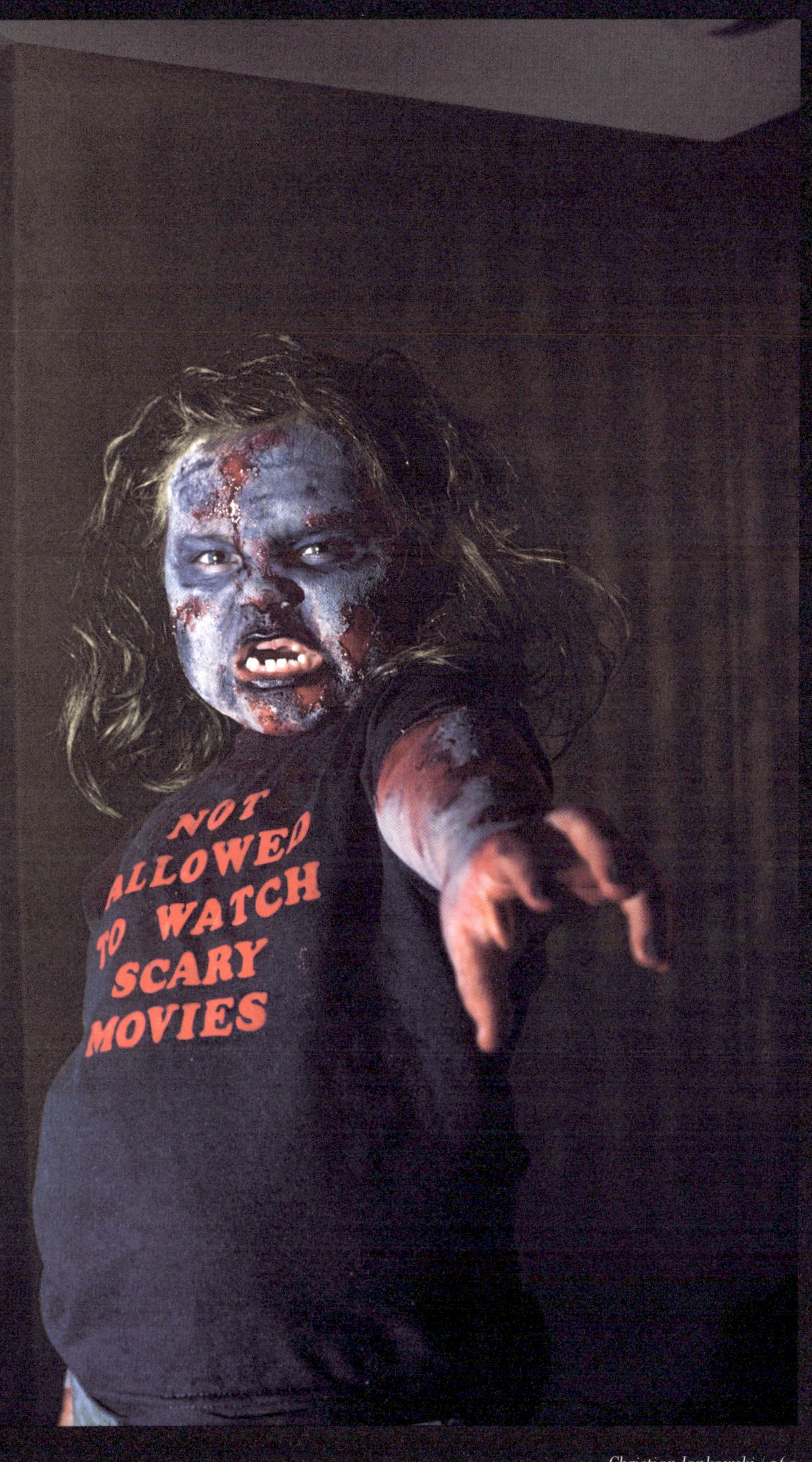

NOT
ALLOWED
TO WATCH
SCARY
MOVIES

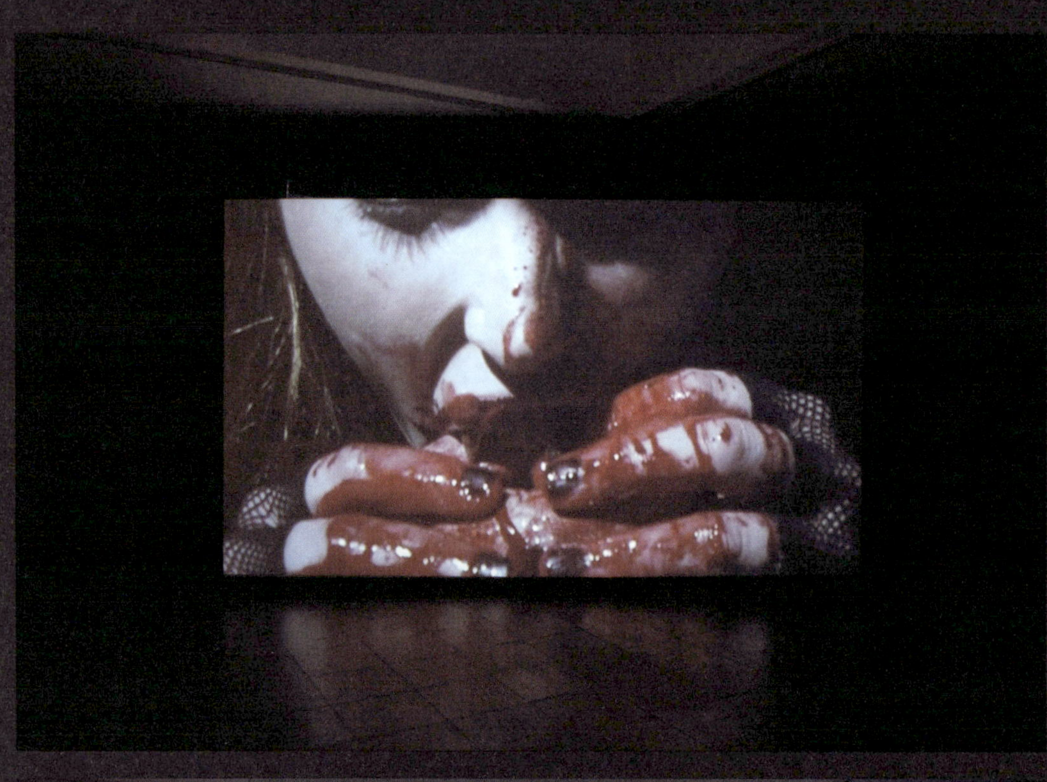

Left and below
Lycan Theorized (2 stills)
2006
Film and mixed media
Courtesy the artist and
Lisson Gallery, London

Opposite
Angels of Revenge
(Jason 1)
2006
Print
100 x 75 cm

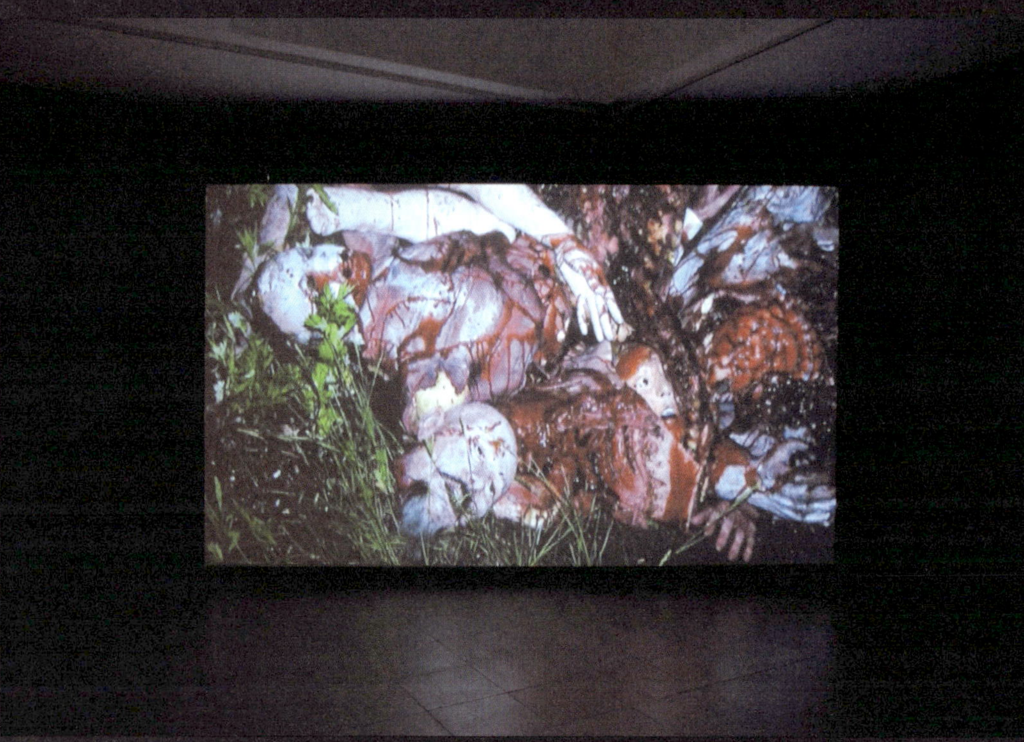

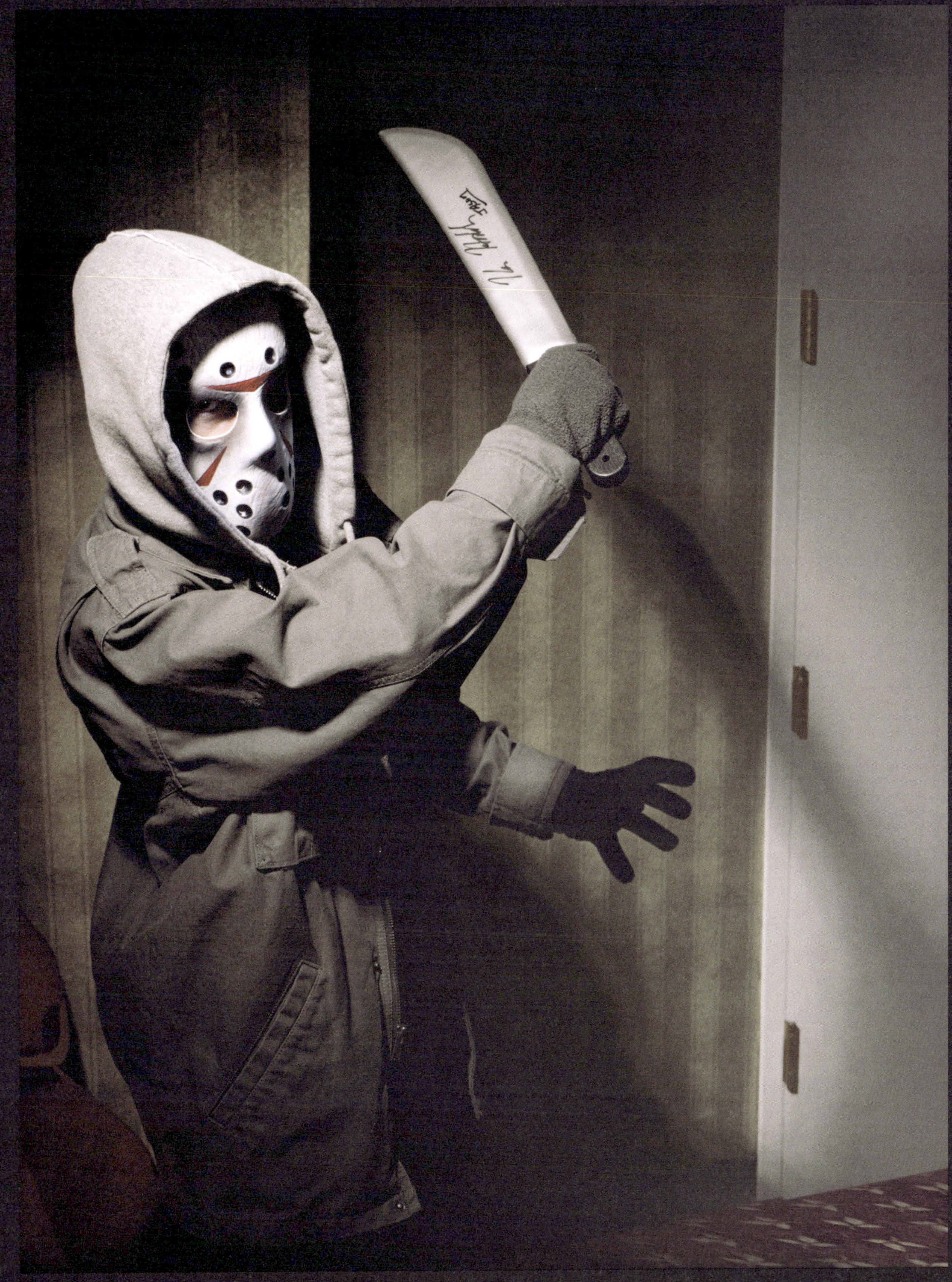

Ken Kagami

here is nothing like the horror and violence in a child's mind, when the boundaries of pain and cruelty are still being formed. Ken Kagami's sculptures, made from plastic toys and vibrant drawings, are openly childlike. 'Recently, I realized that the inside of my brain has not changed much since I was a child.'

There is something innately playful about Kagami's art. He originally began working in fashion but the connection is not obvious in his pieces. His imagery is delightfully violent: toy children fall over and bleed; monsters slash their own bodies; dolls fry dismembered hands. Somehow the gore is hilarious and light-hearted. 'In my childhood, I often used to watch horror movies on TV alone, keeping the room dark. I remember that my mother was really worried about me. I do not know if such experiences had an influence on me. I am fascinated by violent imagery. It is not real violence but the absolute fake violence of horror movies. I have no interest in real violent actions at all.' Here, aggression is slapstick, uncontrollable and comedic. Kagami sees a similarity between humour and hostility – human nature draws us towards both in an almost instinctive way.

The colours in Kagami's work are strong, with Crayola crayon intensity. These are primary-school brights – brick red, sunshine yellow, royal blue. His drawings are made largely with felt pens and coloured pencils on paper. The simple lines are highlighted with areas of black, red, yellow and green. Often Kagami adapts cartoon imagery – transforming iconic characters from Disney or Charlie Brown into horrific, sexualized hybrids. 'The characters that I use

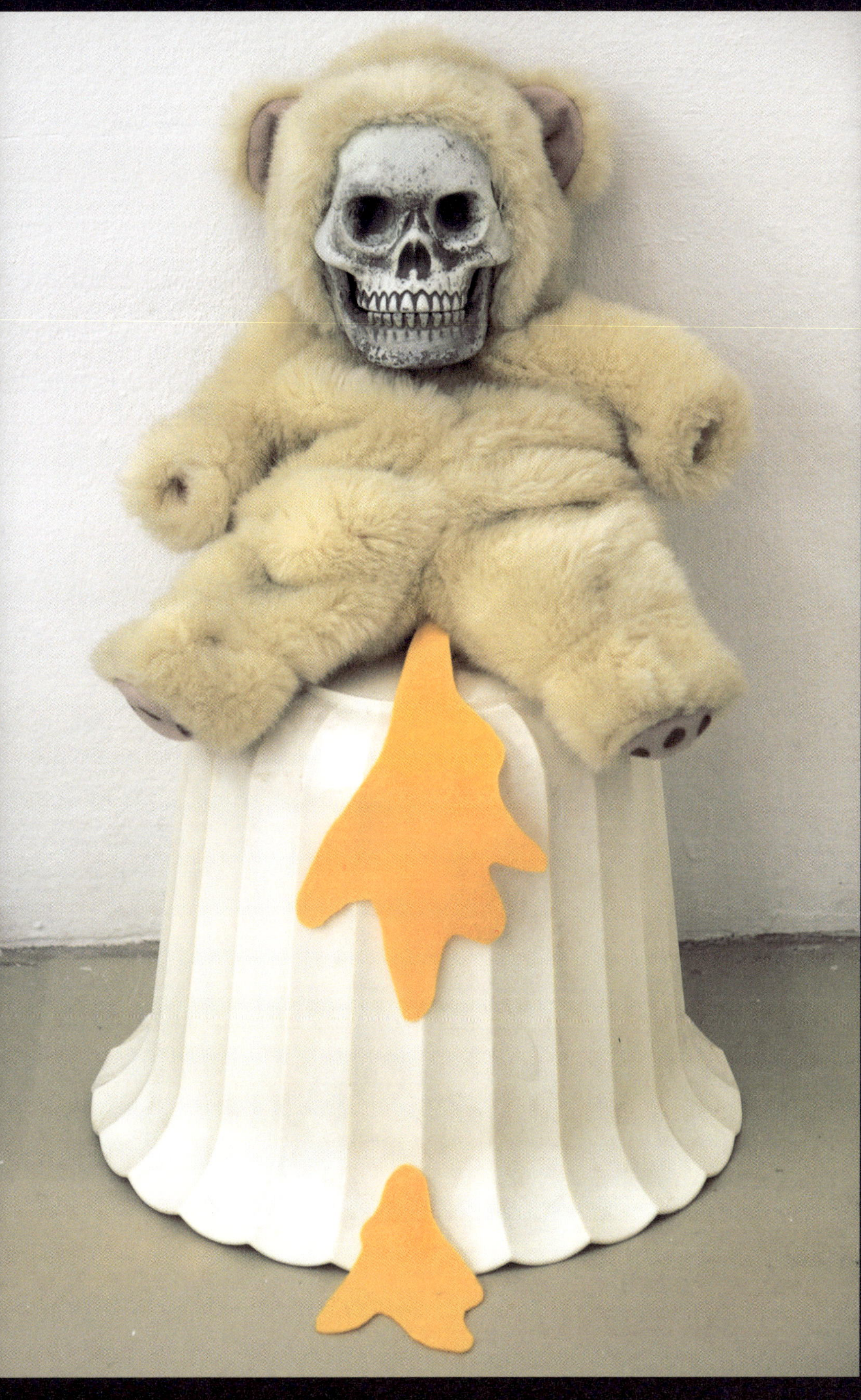

are very popular, which makes it easy for people to get into the works.' Kagami quotes emblematic creatures then mutates them, adding blood and humour. '*Sexy Brown* is a man with a big bust and a sexy pose – bleeding through his mouth. He might be a real Charlie Brown.' The characters strut and pose for the viewer like distorted porn stars for an imaginary camera. These bloody models cut off their own limbs while smiling inanely for the audience. Kagami also experiments with performance, striving to retain his focus on humour. He often uses props that move in response to sound. The aim is to explore what people cannot laugh at in reality, to bring the humour out of tragedy and fear.

Mutants and monsters are a recurring motif in Kagami's work. Many of his sculptures quote a kind of kitsch pop horror filled with bloody mouths, hosts, skulls and bats. 'My works might have been influenced by American horror movies from the 1970s and 1980s. The important point is that everyone has a particular image of these motifs, such as disturbing, scary or creepy.'

His sculptures appropriate toys and tacky horror props. The pieces are made from objects that most people discard or ignore. Naked dolls with skull heads sit around a giant bagel. Plastic dismembered feet rest their bloody forms in fluffy bunny slippers. 'The stuff I find on the street, or second-hand toys, are very stimulating for me. The used baby blankets are dirty, with a lot of stains, which is an important source of my ideas. My parents did not buy me many toys in my childhood and that could be a reason why I use toys.'

There is a tension in Kagami's art – some of his most disturbing pieces are his most playful. 'Just being disturbing is so boring for me. Whatever is playful and makes me laugh is very important. I am always inspired by daily life. I am fascinated by something between modesty and vulgarity – there is a fine line between them.' His work is intentionally naughty and dirty, exposing cultural taboos. The pieces are sexual and childish at the same time, filled with smells, excretory substances, food and animals. Toys piss themselves. Drawings have giant banana-like erections. A penis is drawn with two skulls for testicles.

Kagami aims to create work that prods at the universal subconscious. Understanding the visual references makes communicating the emotion behind the work graceful. If it makes you a little uncomfortable, then you know it's working.

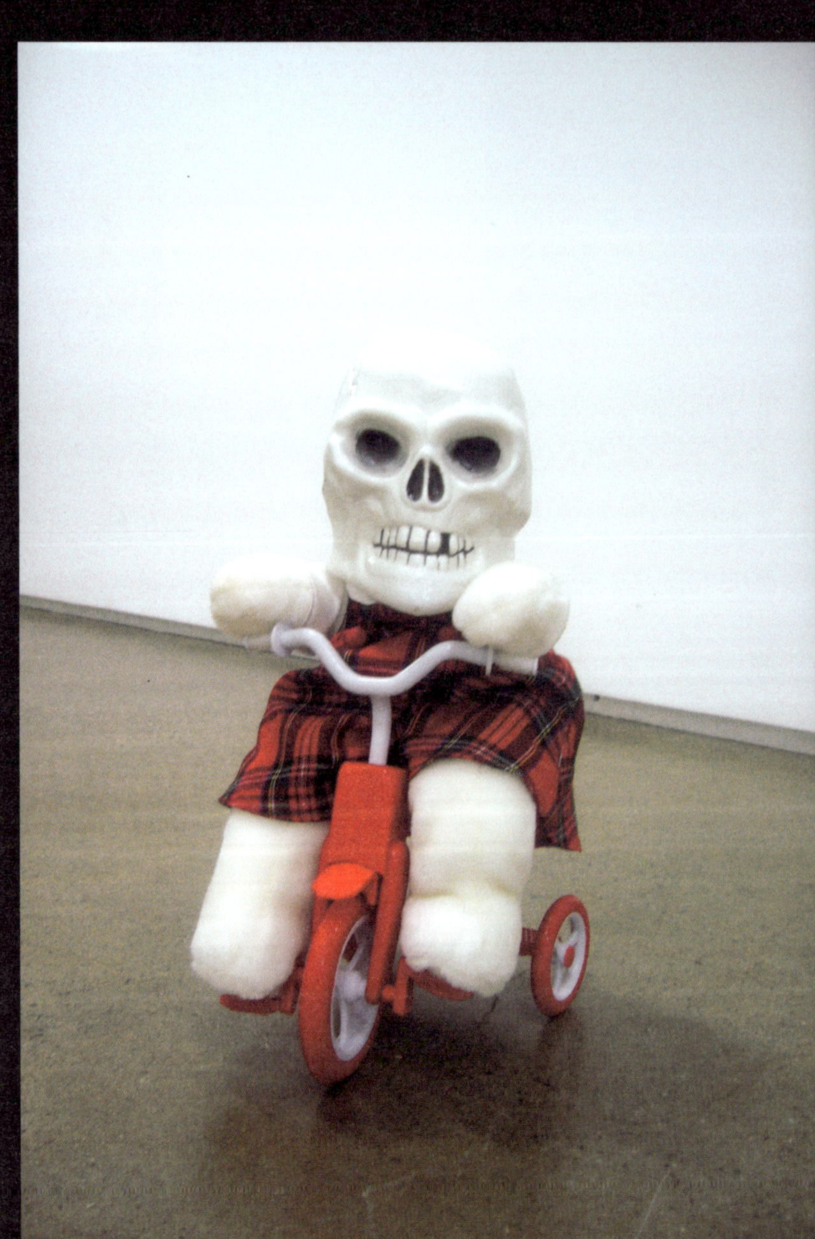

Right
Kitchen
2005
Mixed media
86 x 44 cm
Courtesy the artist and
gallery.sora., Tokyo

Below
Shopping
2006
Plastic and mixed media
48 x 53 x 23 cm
Courtesy the artist,
gallery.sora., Tokyo
and Galerie Krinzinger,
Vienna

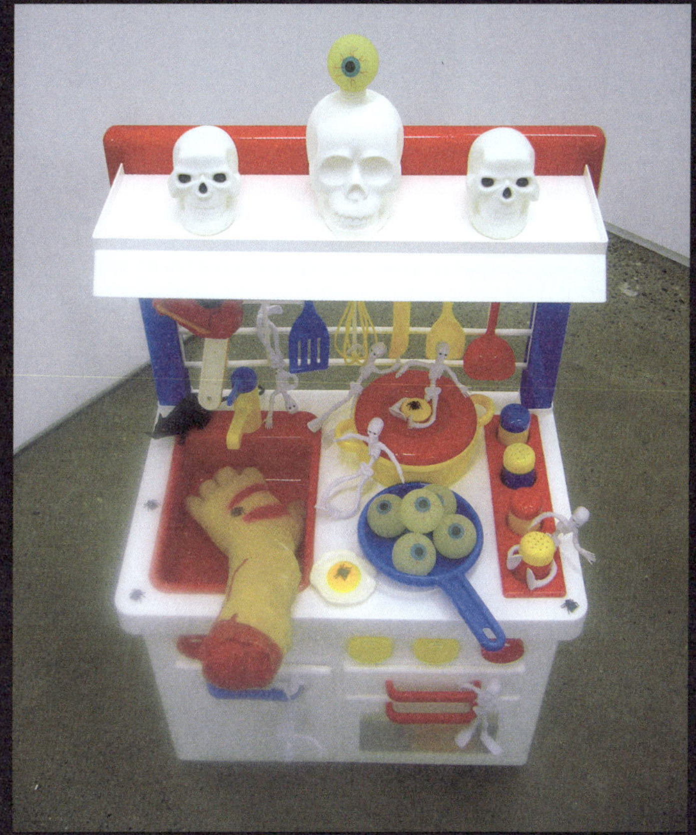

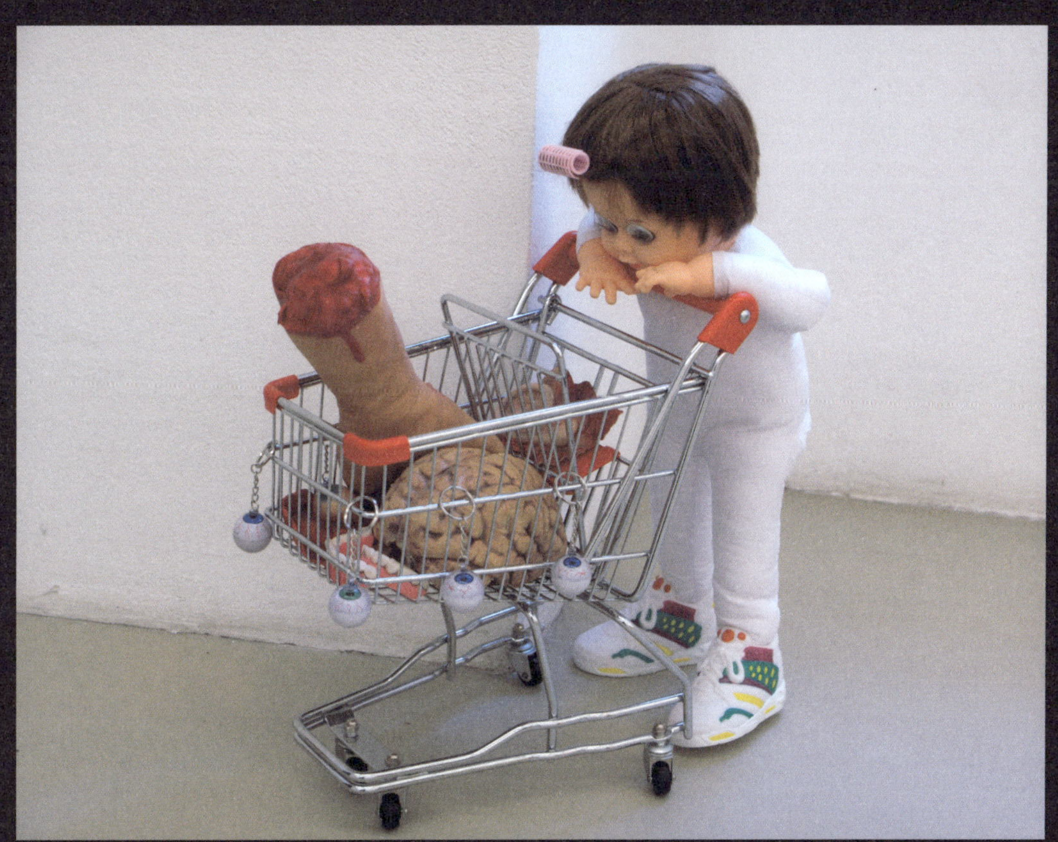

Below
Angie
2006
Textile and plastic
60 x 20 x 10 cm
Courtesy the artist,
gallery.sora., Tokyo
and Galerie Krinzinger,
Vienna

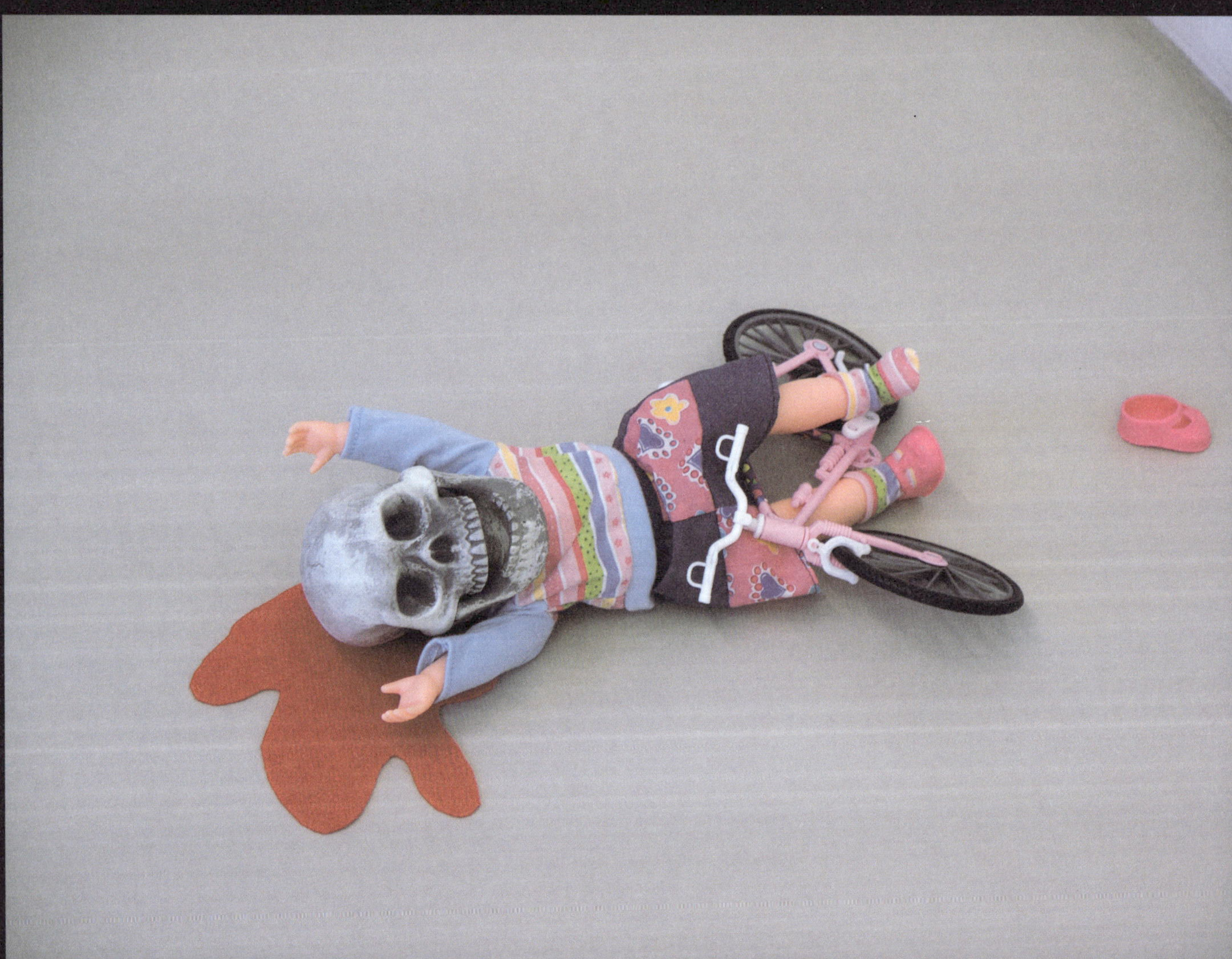

Below
Ballon (detail)
2006
Textile, plastic and
stuffed animal
Courtesy the artist,
gallery.sora., Tokyo
and Galerie Krinzinger,
Vienna

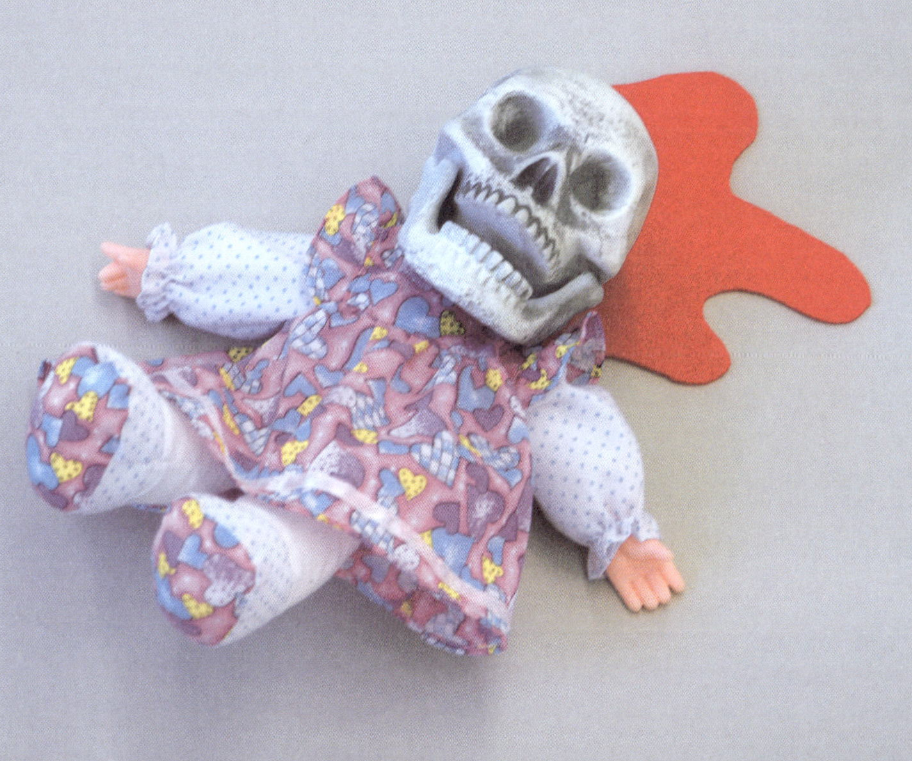

izima Kaoru

here's no point in avoiding the inevitable – and there's nothing more inevitable than death. Japanese photographer Izima Kaoru creates images that try to show that death is not to be feared. 'Be it sickness or accident, death happens to everybody. How does one become able to accept that? This is the question I reflect in my work.' He focuses on the fantasy of death – or rather fantasy deaths. He depicts actresses and models in their idealized moment of death.

Kaoru was working as a fashion photographer in Japan when he began his *Landscapes with a Corpse* project. 'I was attracted to the idea of creating a very powerful and provocative setting for fashion shoots.' But the work had wider implications about death and consumerism. 'I wanted to illustrate the fact that fashion is part of our everyday life. I wanted to raise an awareness that death is always there. It's a part of life. Why, then, can't it be appropriate for a fashion shoot?'

Editors ignored the idea, so Kaoru founded his own fashion magazine to publish the project. At first the photographs were constructed as a straight fashion story, but as the project continued Kaoru's personal views on death and its place in society came to the fore. 'The series has became more conceptual. What interests me now is the way in which one looks at one's own death. What would the scenery with death look like, especially to the person who is looking back at his or her own death?'

The work concentrates on women in particular. Kaoru explains that the focus on female deaths is a result of the fashion audience largely being women. When he produces a series, he

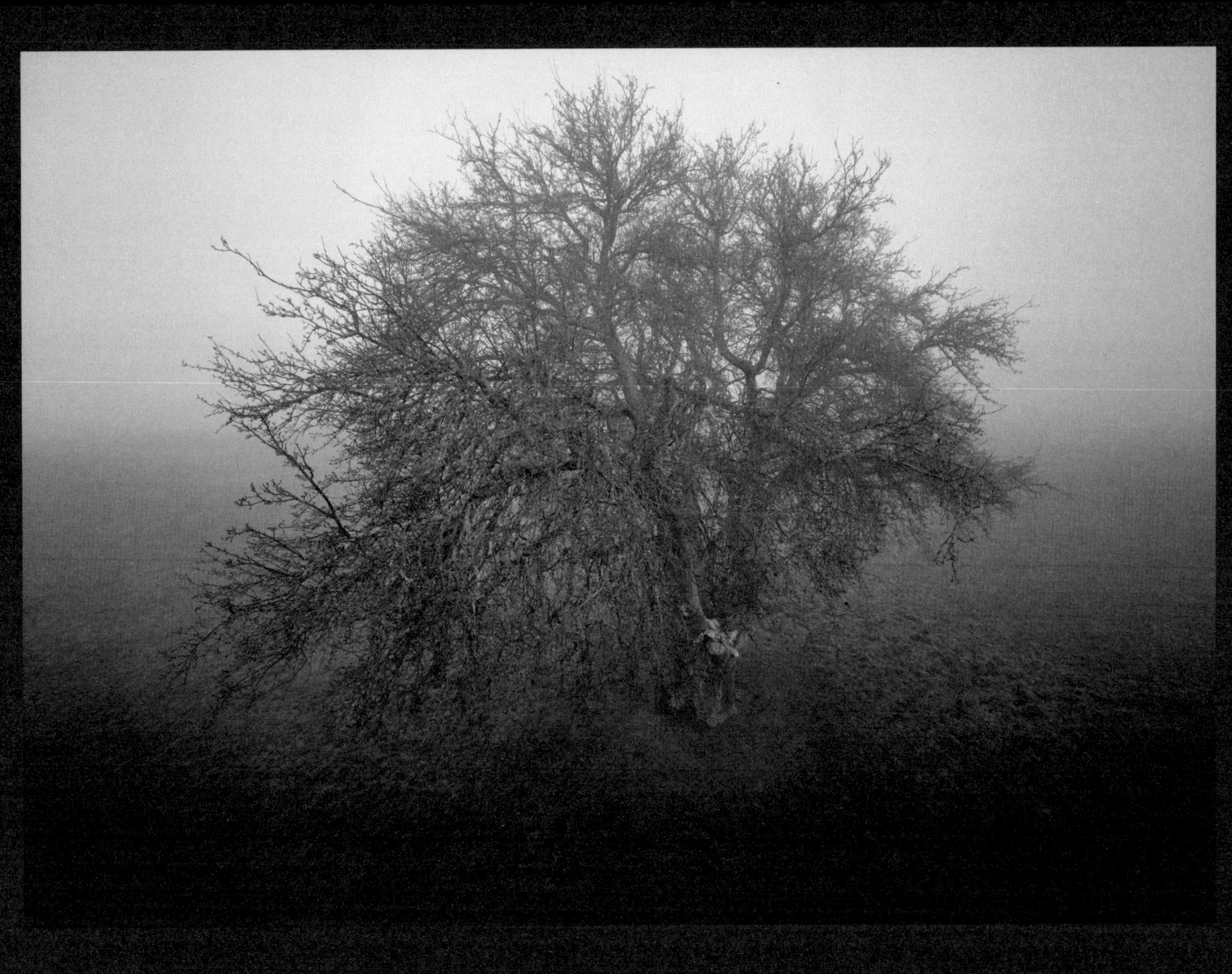

asks his models to share their death fantasies with him. He looks at how and where they would like to die, and wearing what. 'Women's answers are generally more imaginative and interesting than men's.' The work is in fact empowering rather than exploitative; women are expressing their own alluring death fantasies, rather than being 'killed' by the photographer. It is more of a collaborative process. The photographs always credit the famous fashion designer whose clothes the protagonists are wearing when they die. The work is a bit like a glamorous game of 'Cluedo': Miss Scarlett, killed by strangulation, in a field, wearing Hermès.

The work also makes an interesting comment on the deathly nature of photography itself – that it conceptually captures and kills its subject. There's a very interesting contrast between Kaoru's highly beautiful, stylized images and the horror of death. He appears to depict these deaths in the same way as a cinematic camera closes in on a figure – first from afar, then zooming into the death in detail. 'The multiple angles do not come from cinematic techniques but from copying inquest photographs. Each series has a setting, which should be viewed from close up to far away. It's composed as if the soul of the person who has died leaves its body to go higher up into another world.' Looking back on life is part of what interests the artist – how we see ourselves at the end. There are spiritual connotations to his approach. 'My intention is to visualize the views of a soul as it looks back at the body on its way to another world. I mean to reflect a sense of acceptance that I hope the dead have. These thoughts make me take beautifully stylized images and I think, by taking them, the fear of death softens.'

There is something positive about Kaoru's approach, despite the obviously macabre nature of its content. His aim is to make death a positive part of life, something accepted rather than feared. 'Developing this series over the years, I have begun to think about death more than ever. I ask myself: "What is an ideal death for human beings?"; "How would I like to die?" Today most people die in hospital. This has distanced us from death. It takes place somewhere outside normal life. Working on the *Landscapes with a Corpse* for so long, I now believe that human beings, including myself, should take death back to the day-to-day experience of life, rather than keeping it at a distance.'

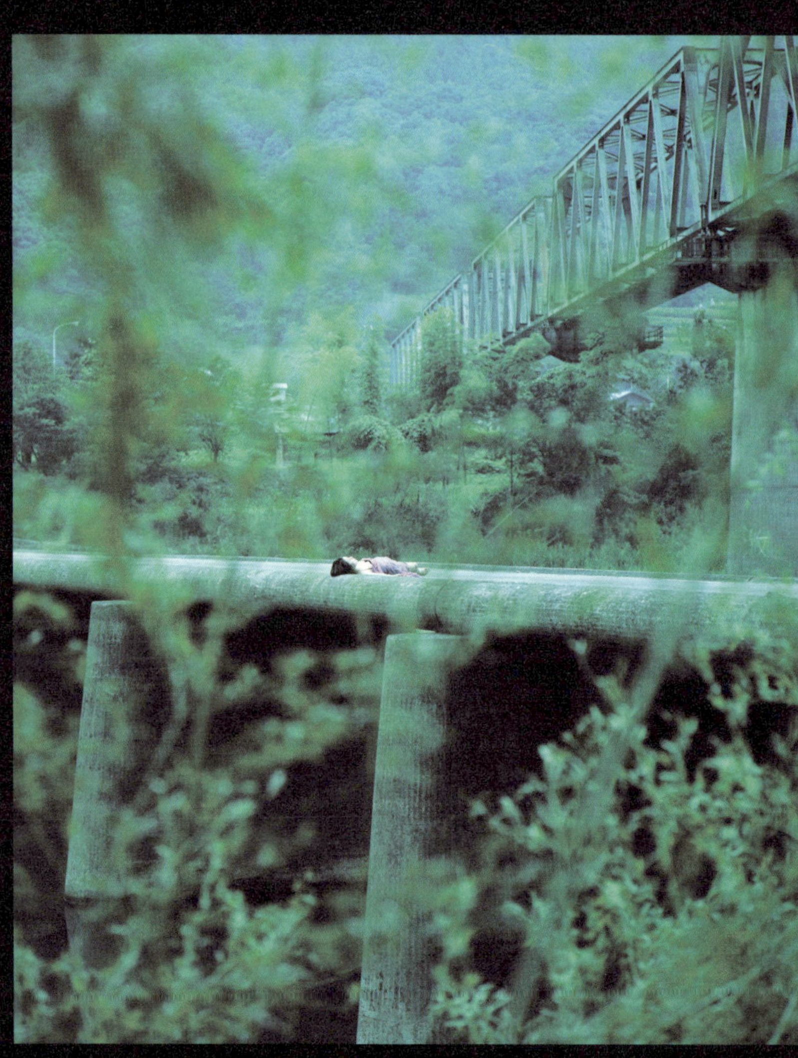

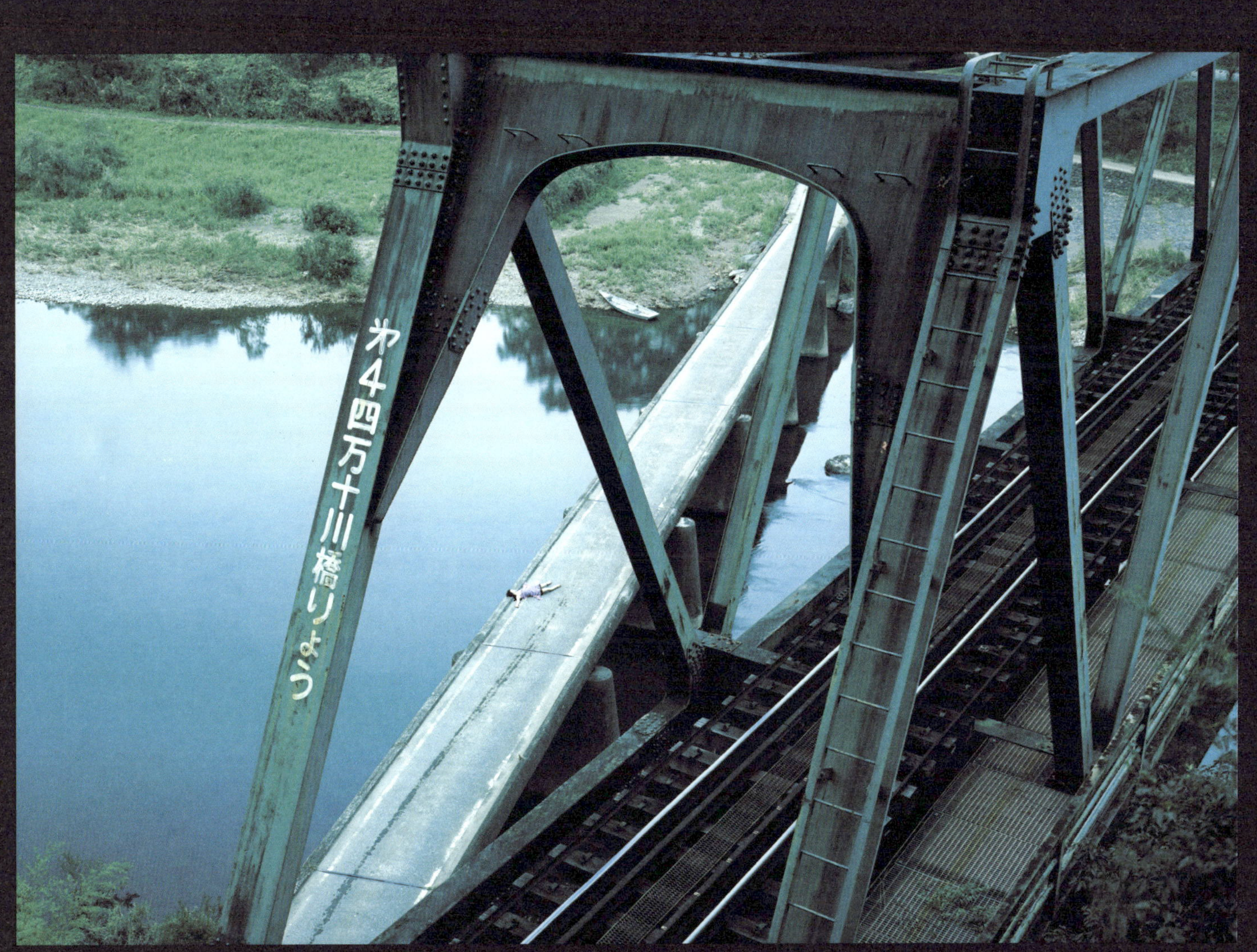

第４四万十川橋りょう

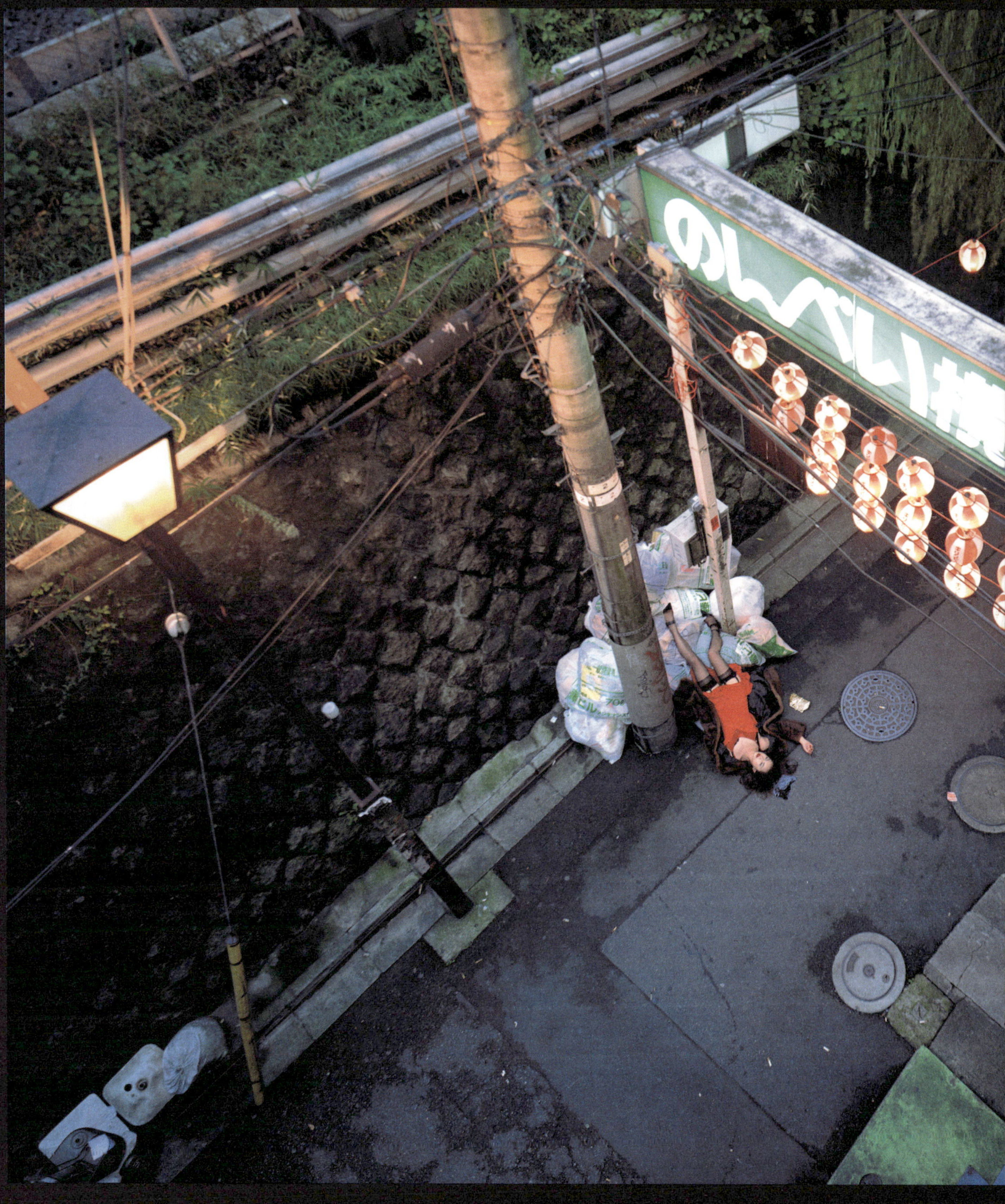
のんべい横丁

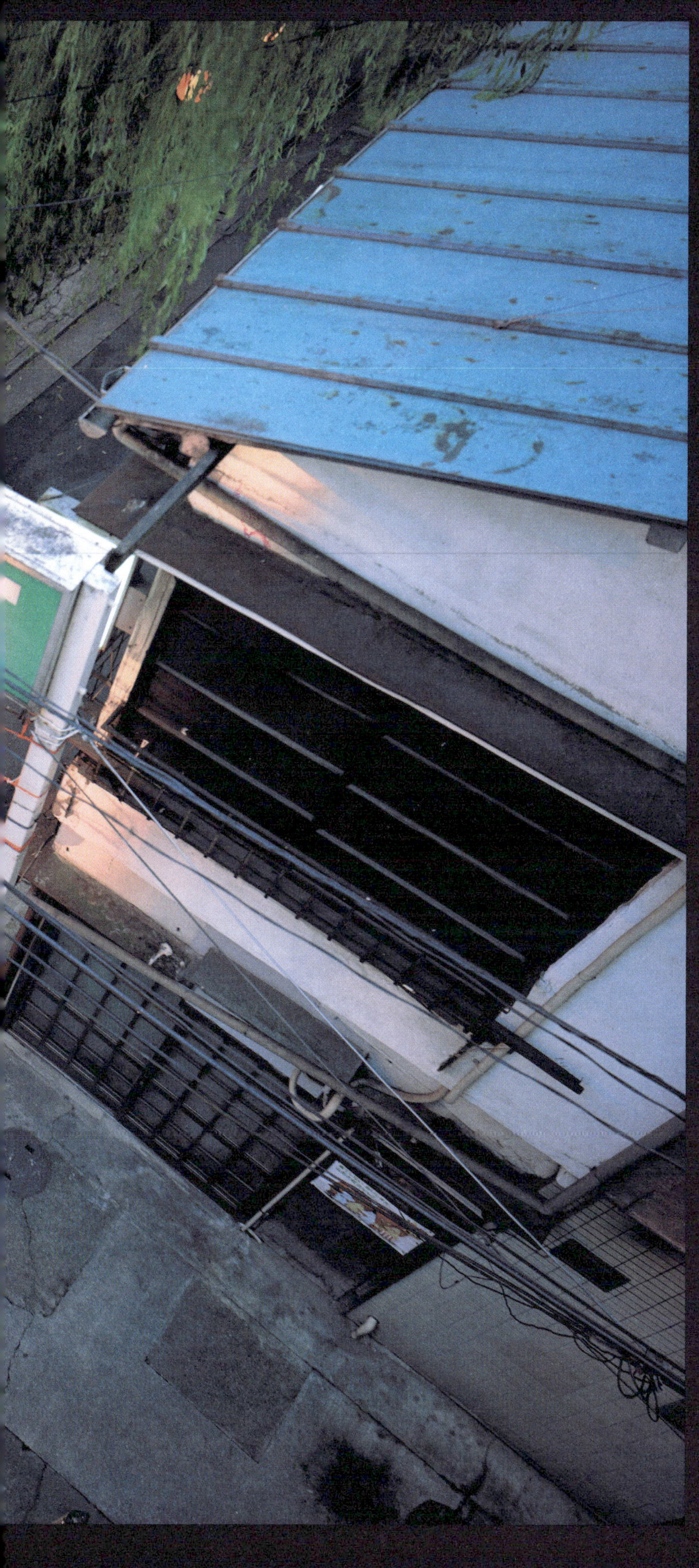

terence Koh

Ashes. Dead flies. Gold-plated excrement. Blackened urinals. Tar-covered drum kits with a train of dripping, semi-organic blackened detritus. Terence Koh often uses disturbing materials in his installations. One piece, *These Decades That We Never Sleep, Black Drums*, is made from a drum kit, paint, ropes from a ship found after midnight, black wax, plaster, vegetable matter, crushed insect parts and the artist's blood and semen.

Part of what makes pieces like these so disconcerting to look at is how the inanimate is made to look or feel animate. The train trailing off a static drum kit makes it feel monstrously living, a swamp-like appendage in a non-organic environment. For Koh, however, the universe is already alive. 'The floor, your nail clippers. You have to be open to the fact that there is no difference between the organic, the metallic, jewellery or gases. They are part of one picture that is constantly changing, a single beast teaming with life force. When I make these things, these long black strands, or objects or whatever, they are only to remind us that we all have the power to see this creature. This creature that we are all part of.'

Koh often limits his work to single colours – installations are solely black, gold or white. However, he argues that there is no intentional focus on this limited palette. 'There is no colour in this world. You have to believe that. It is our eyes clouded by inexperience, inexperience in how to understand the fundamentality of the universe that divides colours into colours.'

The Beijing-born, New York–based artist veers easily from poetry to bodily fluids.

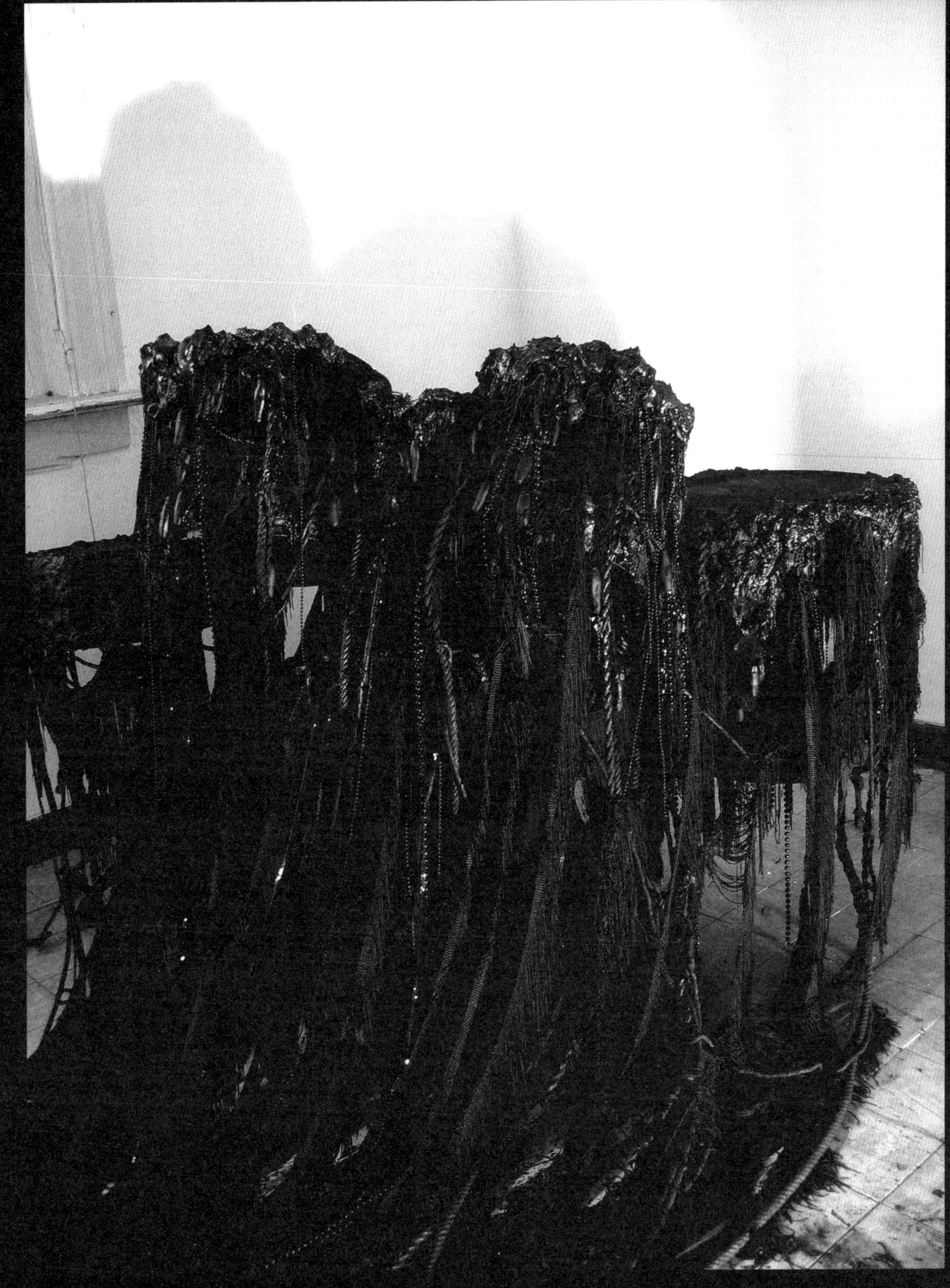

Sculptural chambers resemble black fusions of the confessional and toilets. There is something spiritual about his approach, but it comes out in a very visceral form. Alongside his sculptural installations, Koh began making work using an alter ego – Asianpunkboy. With this persona he explored performance, created pop and porn-infused publications (which sometimes came with soiled underwear) and online artworks at his websites kohbunny.com and asianpunkboy.com.

Throughout his work he explores a fascination with young male bodies. 'Young boys are full of power. Eventually we all become stone and they are still full of blood and tears.' He often uses young men in his performance pieces. The *Sprungkopf* installation he created for Peres Projects in Berlin in 2006 was part performance, part sculpture. The strobe-lit piece featured half-naked young boys playing overwhelming distorted music on tar-covered drum kits, while Koh screamed primal noises over the top. Even the remaining video footage is transformative and hard to watch and listen to. Koh's use of adolescent boys in his work is more collaborative than exploitative. Here he became the lead singer in a strange, art-world, death-metal band.

Music and drums are used in a number of Koh's pieces. 'Drum kits are magical demons, every single one of them – because they create repercussions that can open shifts in time. When you hit a drumstick to the surface, time bounces. It's not about going into the past or present or future. It's about time focusing into a point of space. When we play them, we as humans can, for a while, experience time as space. This is about being demonic; it's not some satanic evil thing. Being demonic means you perceive both space and time – and drum kits are portals into that.'

Koh has strongly non-conformist roots and never went to school. 'I was lucky enough to have incredible parents who taught me at home and didn't believe in the government or the usual rules of society. We travelled a lot, going to Africa and visiting tribes, visiting Buddhist monks in Nepal and Japanese master gardeners in Kyoto. I still continue to be a student by travelling the world.'

At times his work comes across as calm and almost spiritual – an interesting contrast to the black metal-influenced objects and imagery in many of his pieces. Sometimes the work resembles the aftermath of fire, chaos or violence. At other times pieces are minimal and wistful. 'I do not believe in violence. I believe in tearing. It's different. I do not want to harm an object, just to tear at its soul to reveal its vulnerabilities. This is not violence. It's letting the insides out, so that a rebirth can happen. There can be no rebirth without having shells torn. Blood, liquid, rain have to enter and kill oneself ever so slightly. Things I tear are always reincarnating. I have given them a second life.'

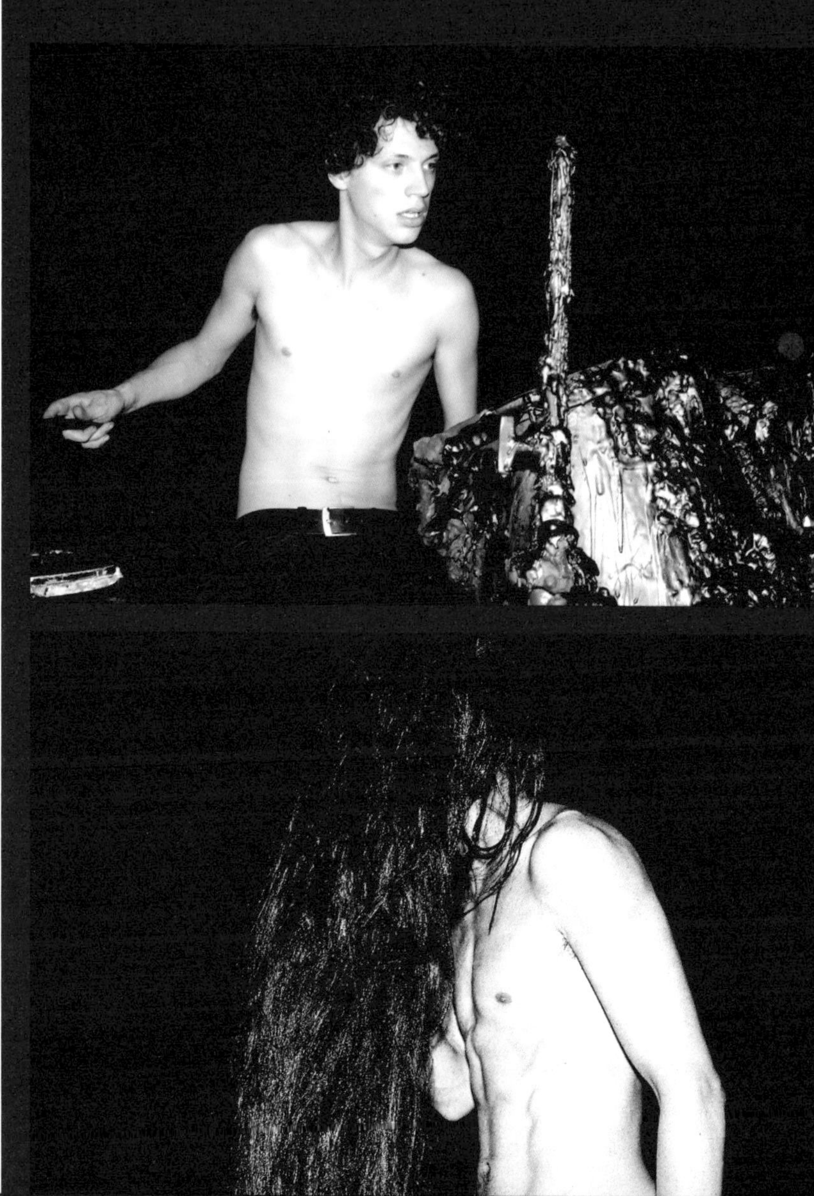

Below
*These Decades That We
Never Sleep*
2004
Drum kit, plaster, paint,
wax, pearls, rope, fur,
fabric and plastic
Dimensions variable
Courtesy Peres Projects,
Los Angeles/Berlin

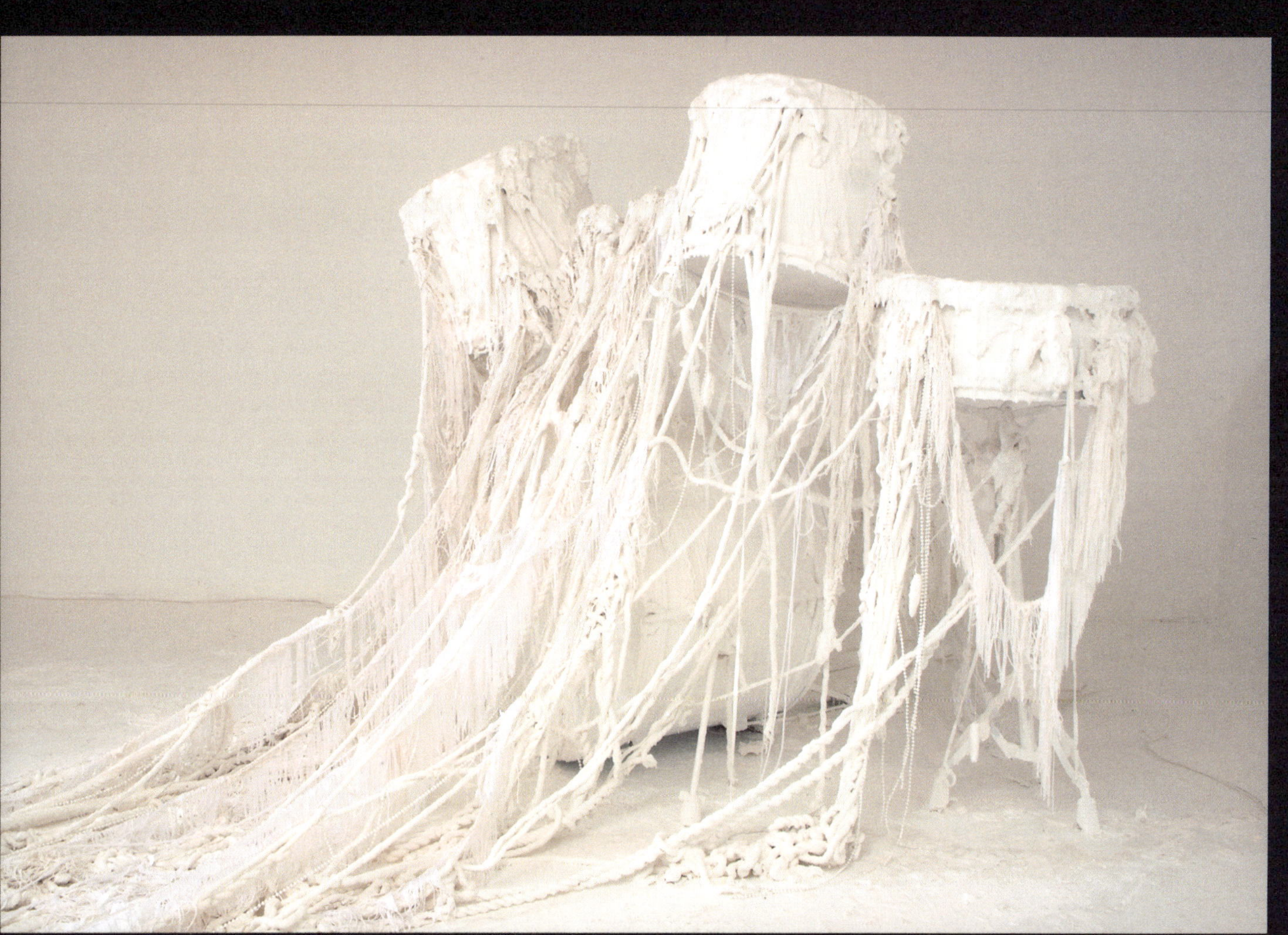

Right
God (installation view)
2007
Mixed media
Dimensions variable
Courtesy Peres Projects,
Los Angeles/Berlin

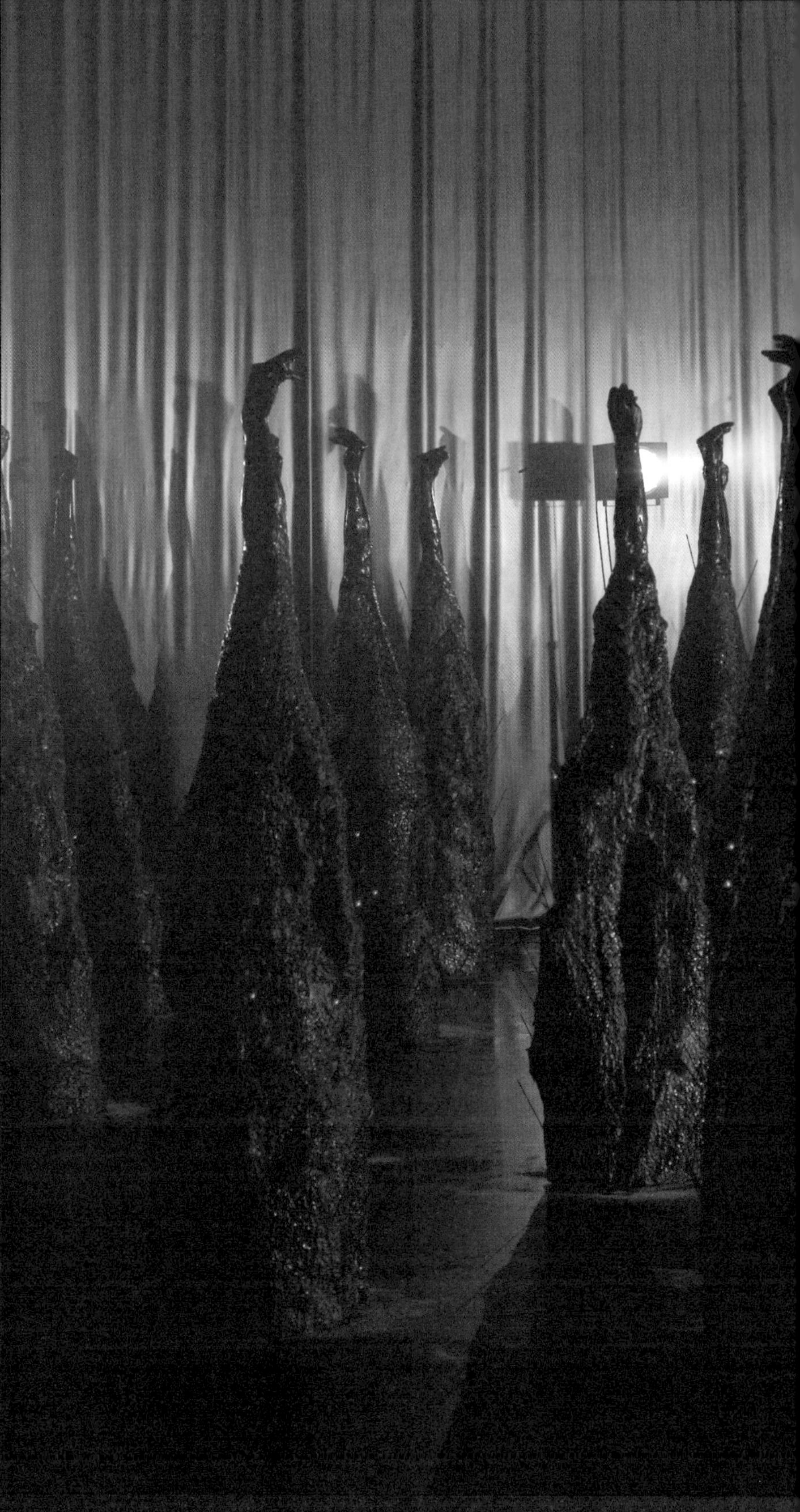

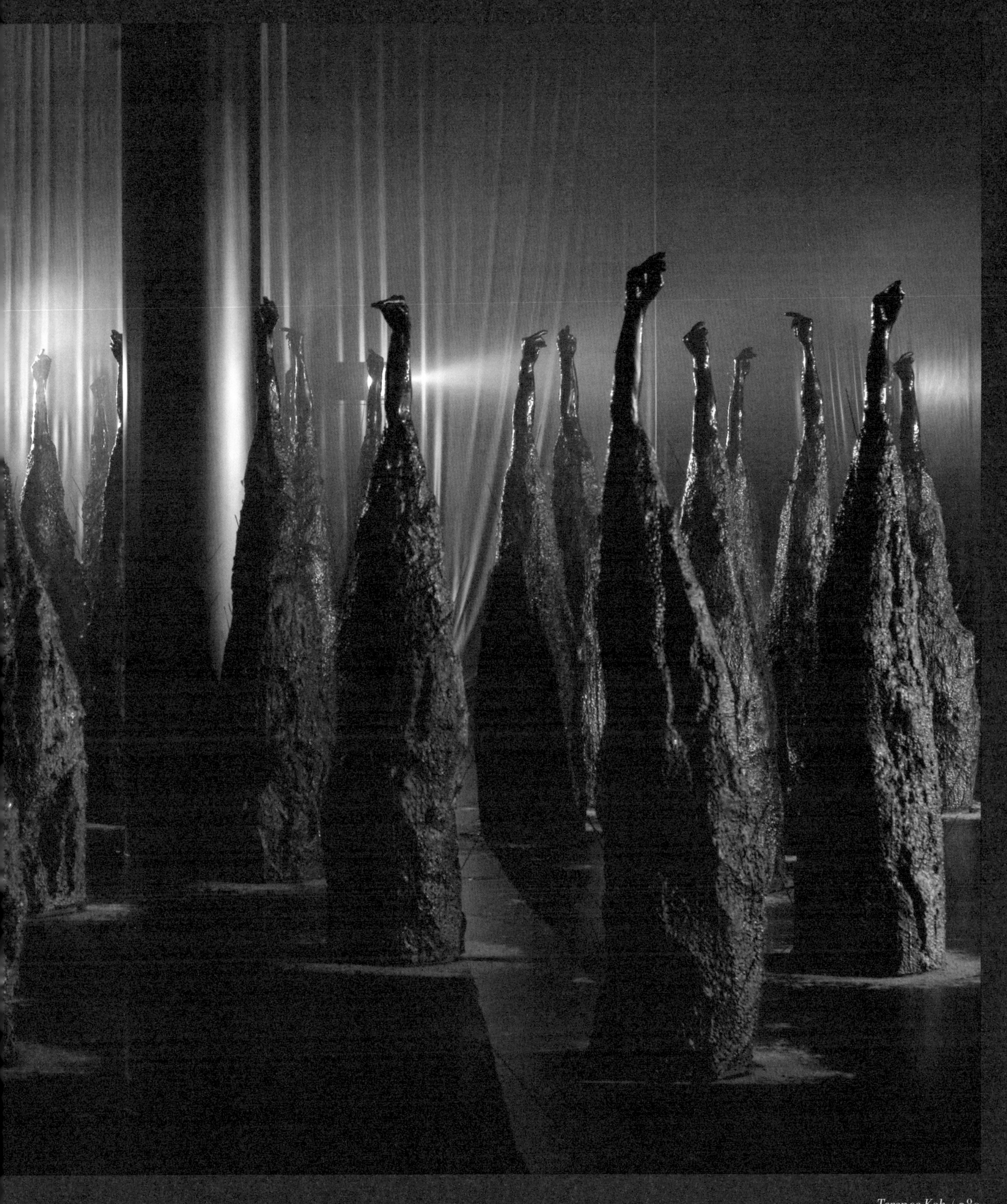

Terence Koh / 089

wes lang

There is a fascination with hidden American identity in Wes Lang's art. His drawings and paintings depict a side of the country that is hidden and disturbing: the racism, violence and rot. He explores the history of native Americans and slavery, the heritage that positivist, nationalist propaganda ignores.

It is fitting that Lang's work seems always to be executed on surfaces that are ageing. He started by drawing on old, browning paper left over from his grandfather's defunct printing press. 'It gives you a good surface to work on. Plain-old white paper is fucking boring. It has got to have some character. It definitely adds something to the pictures. It's already kind of worked on by time.' The pages themselves are in a state of decay.

His paintings grew out of his self-taught drawing practice. 'I don't really know how to paint. I just started taking what I learned from drawing and figuring out how to put it on the canvases.' He begins by creating a base that tries to resemble worn paper. 'I just lay the paintings on the ground and throw paint on them for ten minutes, see what they turn into and put something on top of it. I always work on old shitty paper, so I was working out how to get that quality on canvas.' Increasingly, Lang's experiment with airbrush painting, but not in an obviously airbrushed style. 'It's actually a great tool. It's almost the same feel as a tattoo machine. I've been really enjoying that. It's something that doesn't really fit in with the idea of what a fine artist can use.'

Lang's drawings and paintings are often covered in found images, and Lang's studio

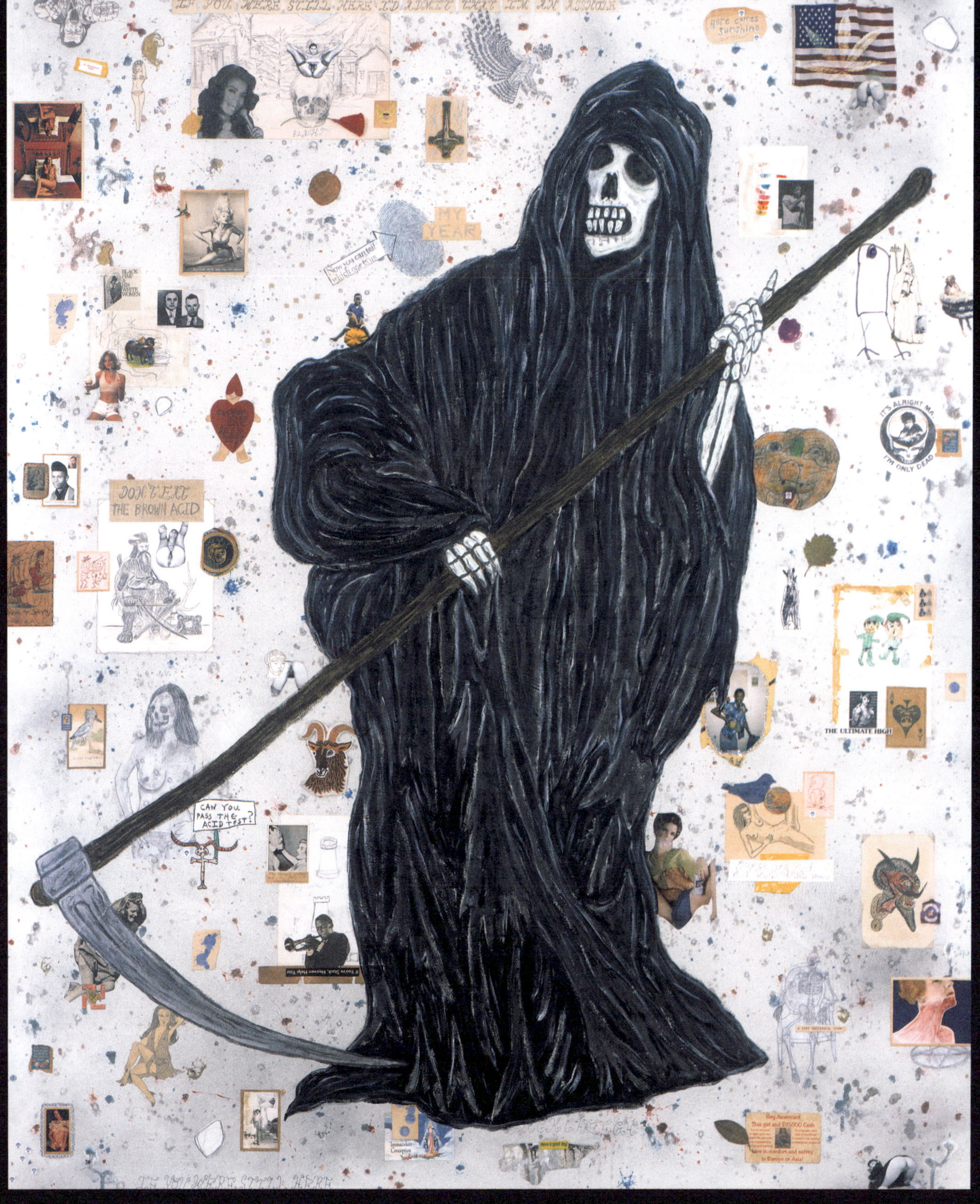

is filled with piles of research material. The narratives he creates from these found pictures are not precise or intended to be historically accurate. 'I buy a lot of books. I don't read too much about anything that I do. I don't pretend to know what I talk about. I just take elements of things and come up with a new story. Taking things out of context and making something new.'

Lang's work is often filled with sinister subject matter – pornography, the Grim Reaper, death, monsters, golliwogs. 'I'm talking about dark subjects, but I'm trying to add something positive to them. I'm not trying to take advantage of the hardships other people have had. I use a lot of text in my stuff – things about being positive and treating people nicely, but I'm using really horrible pictures. I'm sort of bouncing those two things off each other.' The work highlights a kind of cultural hypocrisy.

Another contrast in Lang's work is naked women and skulls. 'I usually put girls and death together. A really close friend of mine, this girl, died. I'm always doing stuff about her. A lot of what I do is about my friend passing away.' Many of his images of naked women come from porn, but Lang doesn't necessarily make them attractive. The canvas is soiled, so it looks like it has been covered in semen or tainted by something. The women can be ugly or in uncomfortable positions. Figures and found images are layered and layered to create something new. Lang often quotes his own school drawings within his pieces. 'I collage them in or redraw them. I want to be able to reuse them and reuse them. If I stick the original in, I don't have a second chance. I've been photocopying.'

He is beginning to work on a series about the Hell's Angels, using text from a Hell's Angels T-shirt. 'I have a romantic notion about how they began. They started out as guys who got back from the war and were totally disenchanted by what they came back to. Fighter pilots who got bikes, which were the closest they could get to an aeroplane. That freedom. They were also very American – and cared a lot about this country.' Lang is drawn to the more disturbing or repressed aspects of American culture: 'It's this great country, but it's filled with evil things I like to touch on.'

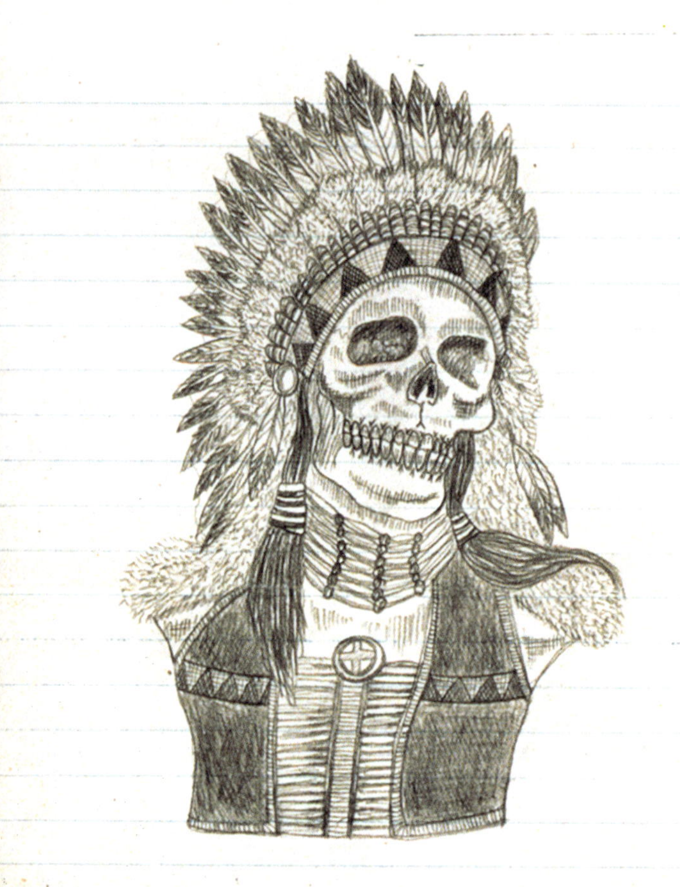

Below
*We Piss Eagles Around
Here* (detail)
2006
Acrylic and collage on
canvas
142 x 162.5 cm
Courtesy Galleri Loyal,
Stockholm

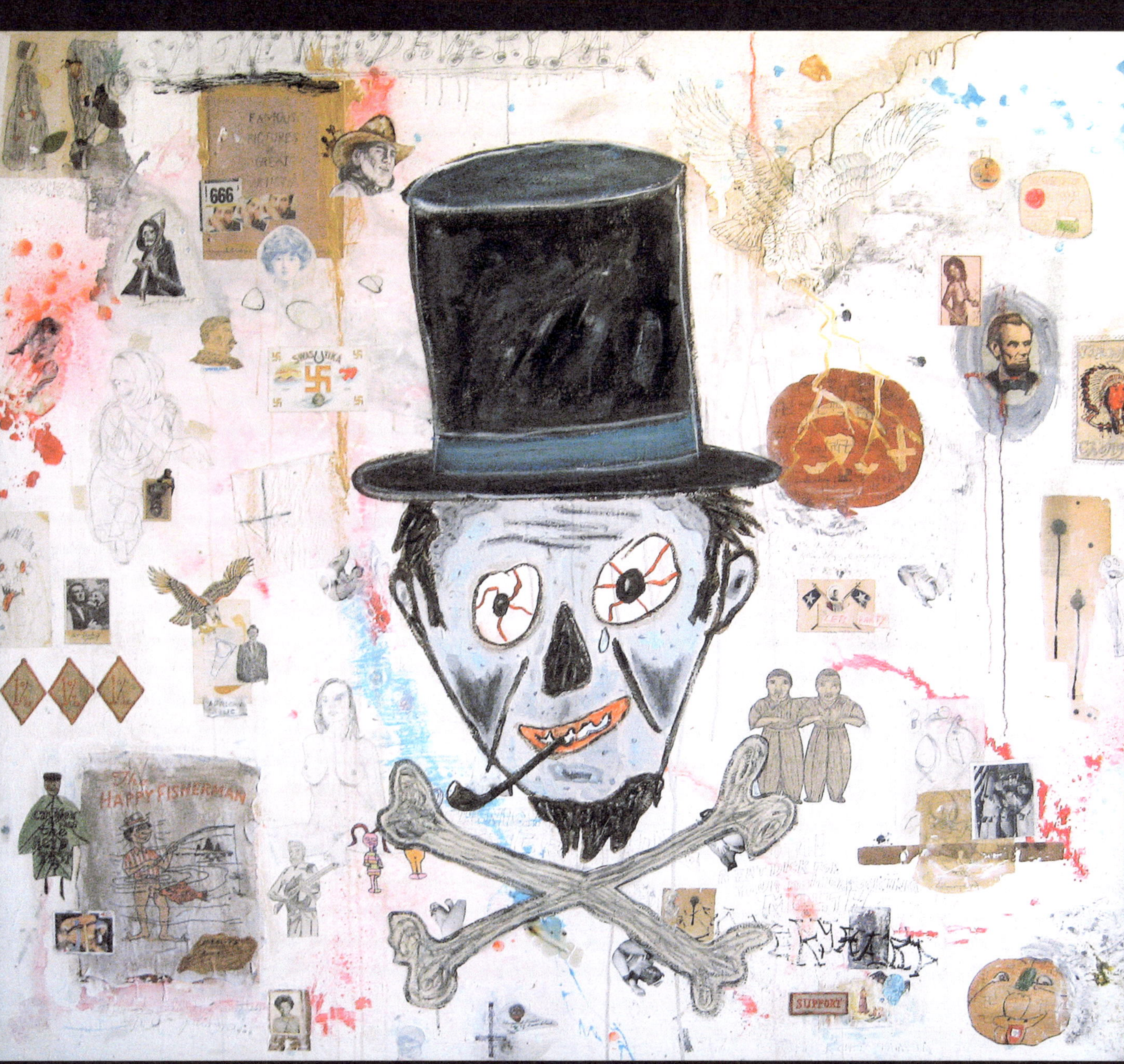

Below (left)
*Sometimes I Ride On
Your Horses, Sometimes I
Walk Alone*
2006
Pencil on paper
35 x 27 cm
Courtesy Galleri Loyal,
Stockholm

Below (right)
The Legend of Ole Shady
2006
Pencil on paper
35 x 24 cm
Courtesy Galleri Loyal,
Stockholm

Opposite
*'If You Were Still Here I'd
Admit That I'm An Asshole'*
2006
Pencil on paper
32 x 24 cm
Courtesy Galleri Loyal,
Stockholm

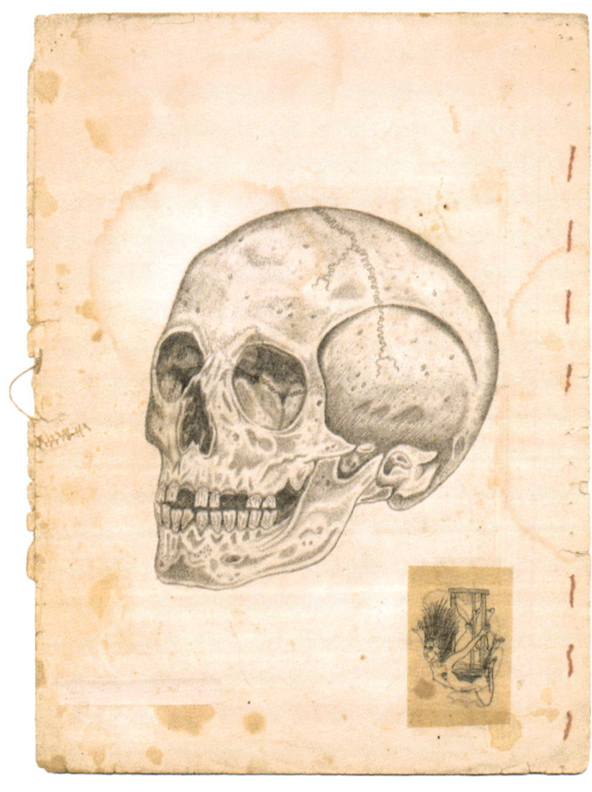

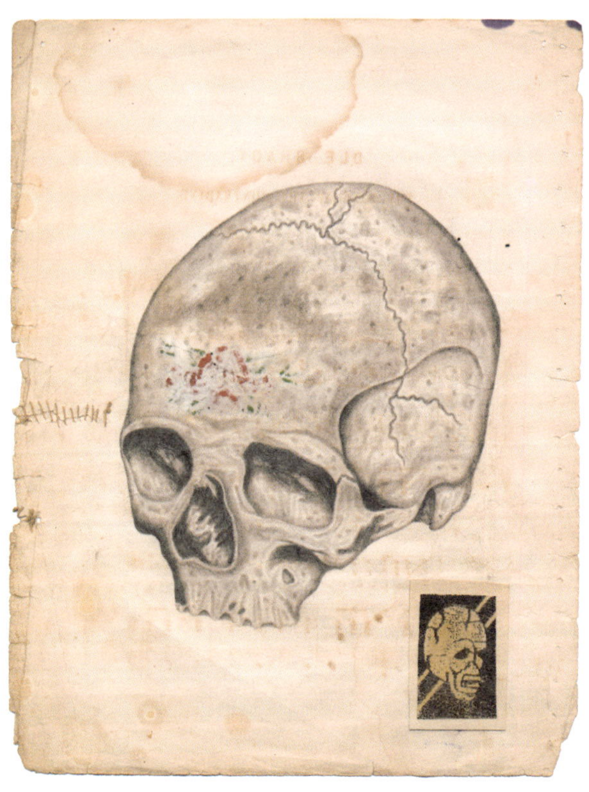

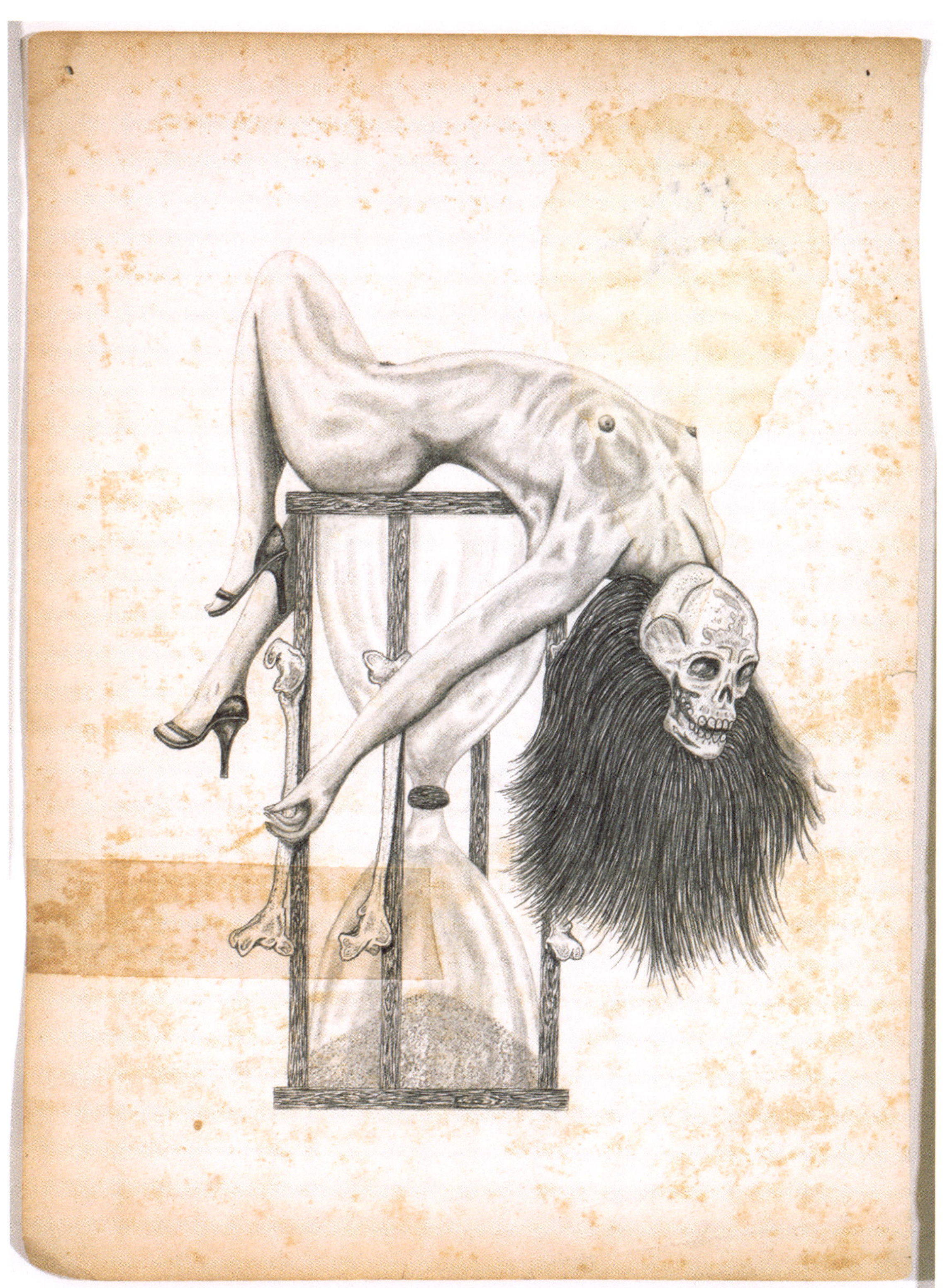

joss mcKinley

There is a ghostly Victorian edge to Joss McKinley's work. It is simply imbued with a sense of melancholy and the odour of death. The artist often uses dead animals and taxidermy in his photographs. His father was a taxidermist, which was an obvious influence. 'Death has always been something that's interested me. I grew up in a house occupied with images and items of death and curiosities, ranging from a Hogarth illustration of an autopsy to my father's vast collection of taxidermy. Some of the animals in the house are even stuffed to give the appearance that they are dead or dying. Hanging pheasants on the kitchen door and a sleeping fox on a chair in the front room. I was taught as a kid not to fear death.'

His series *Underneath an Abject Window* brought together images of found dead insects and animals. 'I'd find drowsy wasps in or near my bedroom window. I used to sit and watch them for a bit, staggering about waggling their antennae, until they eventually stopped and died in front of me. I imagine that there was a nest in the chimney. Over time I had a collection of about 20 or so wasps and at that point I thought I should do some work about these insects.' In a way the work was a memorial to the last moments shared with the dying creatures. The project was put together slowly over a year as the artist came across the carcasses of wasps, spiders, frogs, birds and mice. There is a bittersweet texture to their transient beauty. Death falls effortlessly under his lens. Nothing here is forced or murdered. 'I never want my work to come across as being callous, like I'm throwing a dead animal in front of the viewer's face to shock them.'

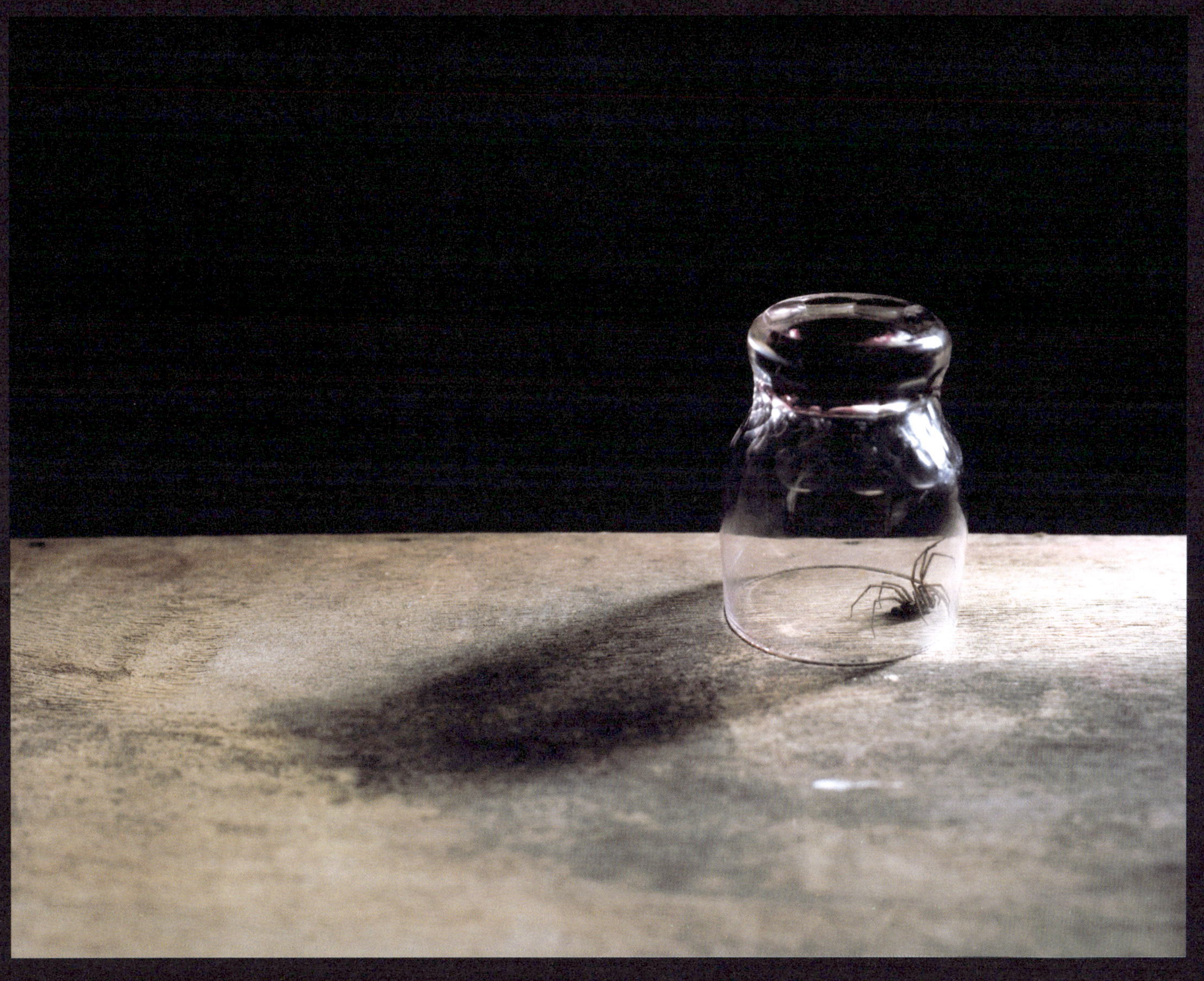

Although McKinley uses natural light, there is a strong chiaroscuro in his images. He makes every-day light appear dramatic or intensified, creating a haunting atmosphere. At the same time, there is something soft about his light. In the *6 Rue de Vaux* pieces, cobweb-filled rooms are misty and gentle. There is something slow and haunting about these images. McKinley's vision of death reflects the slow passing of time.

McKinley worked indirectly with animals again when photographing the *Moonlight Rooms* series, which depicts the nocturnal rooms in London Zoo. Animals themselves are absent. Instead we are left with dark and looming landscapes. The rooms sparked off the artist's childhood memories of looking into the nocturnal spaces, searching for an animal, unclear what it was or if he saw one. 'Most of the time, as kids do, I'd end up just using my imagination. This is something that I wanted to show in this series. When you see them at a large scale, you find yourself staring at them for ages trying to work out what the image is of, where it is and even when it is. I like the idea that you're looking into an almost black, lost world and the viewer is required to romanticize and come to their own conclusion.'

There is something specifically black about these pieces – something harsher than other works. The small light we do see only makes the void at the centre of the works more disturbing. There is a strong sense of an abyss or something hidden. The lack of clarity is central to the photographer's intentions. 'I get pleasure from pieces of work that lure you in to use your imagination, whether it be in music, art, film or books. Too much of what we see today has an ending or a conclusion. It's interesting to have a break every once in a while when you're drawn into doing this yourself.'

His work focuses more on decay and loss than full horror. These are images capturing the aftermath of something, the romantic loss rather than the action of violence. 'There's enough of that in the newspaper and on the television every day. I want people to look at my images and feel comfortable with what they are looking at. I know this is not always the case.'

Previous spread
From the series
Underneath an Abject Window
2005–6
C-print
50.8 x 60.9 cm
Courtesy the artist

Below
From the series *6 Rue de Vaux*
2006
C-print
60.9 x 50.8 cm
Courtesy the artist

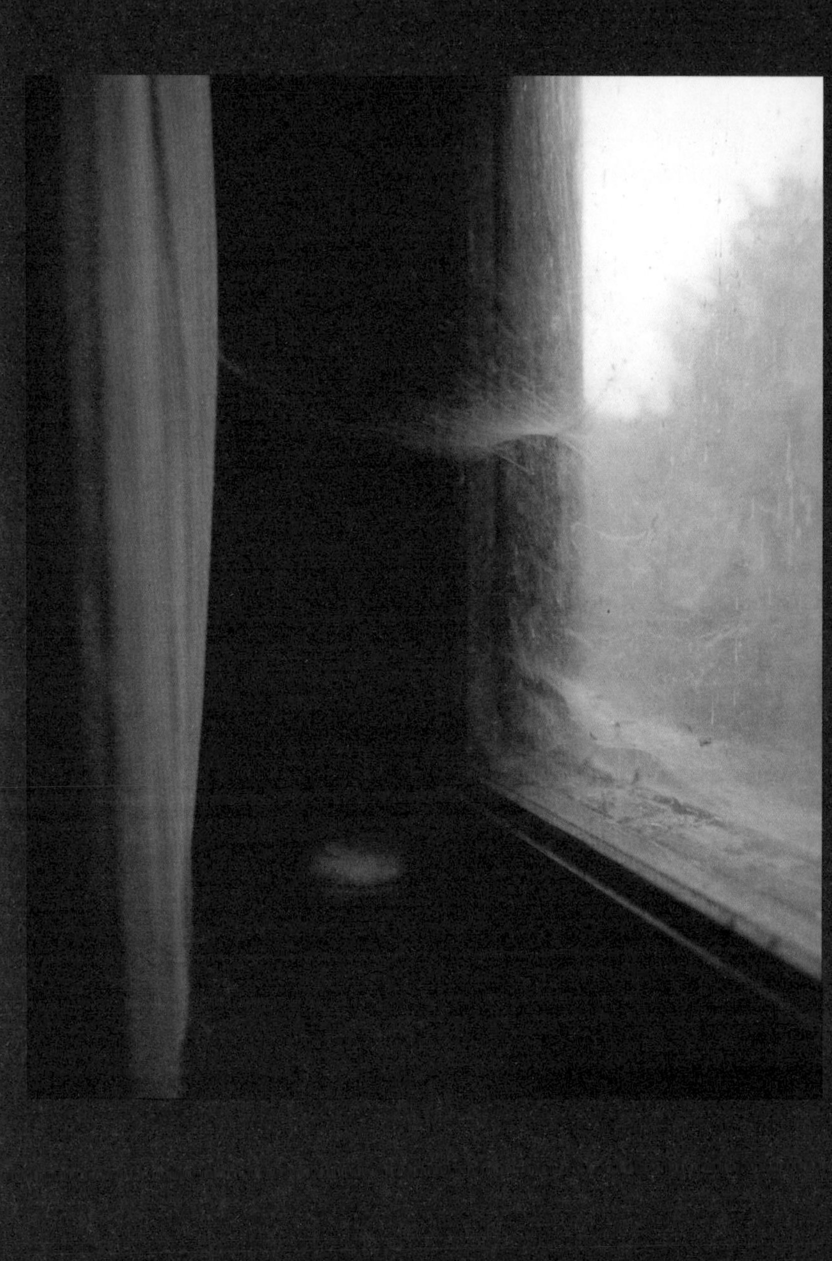

Below
From the series *6 Rue de Vaux*
2006
C-print
50.8 x 60.9 cm
Courtesy the artist

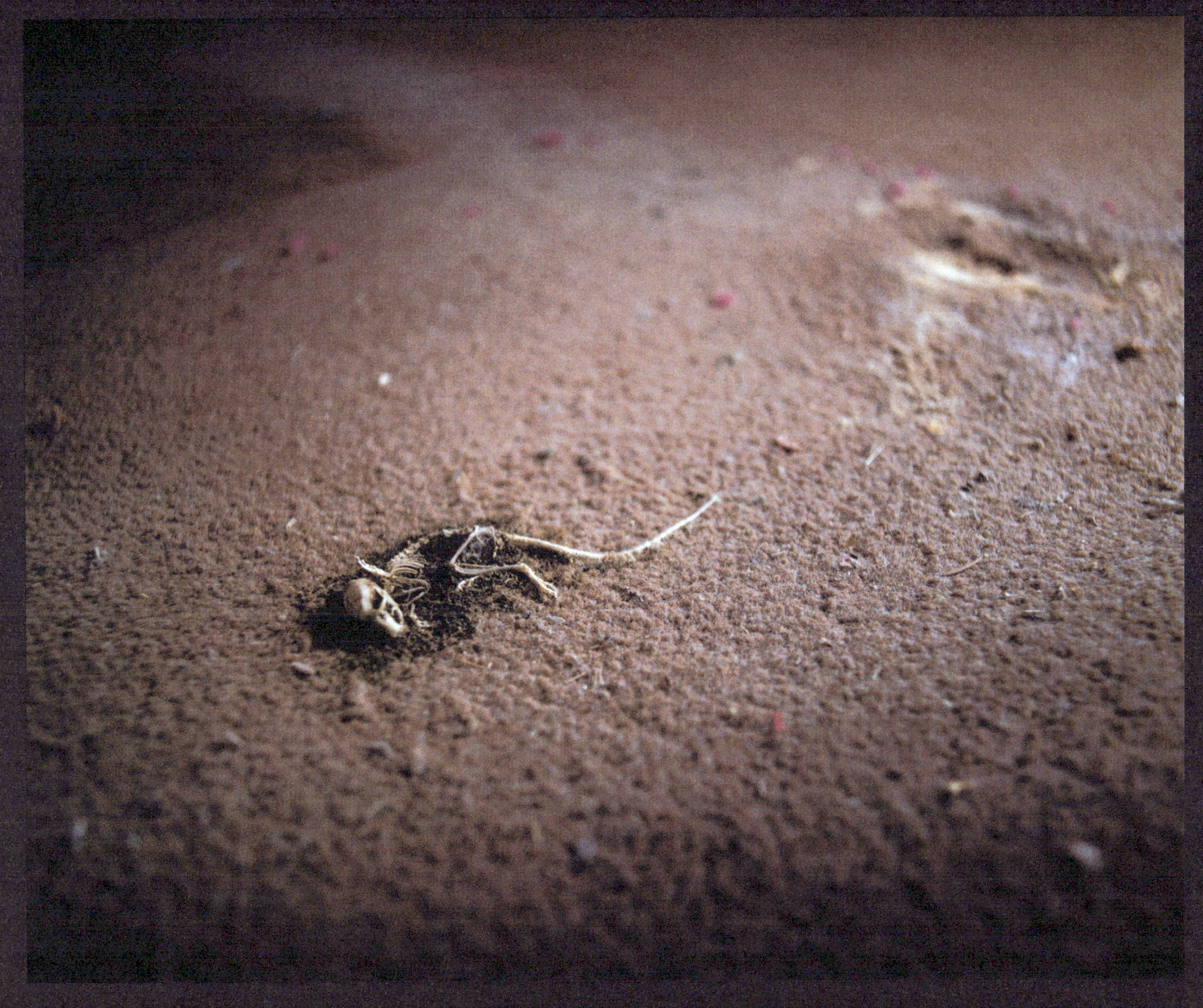

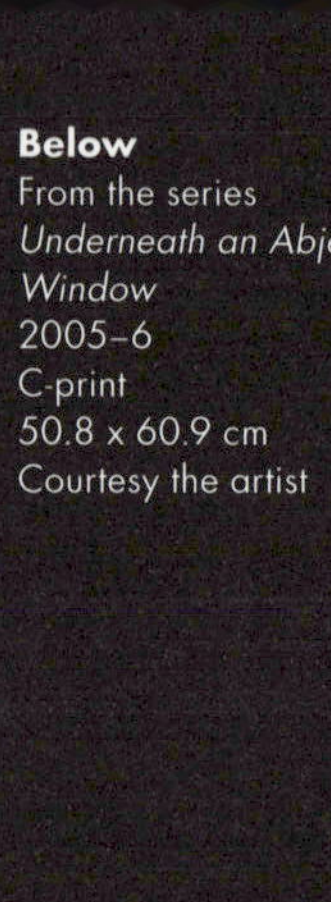

Below
From the series
*Underneath an Abject
Window*
2005–6
C-print
50.8 x 60.9 cm
Courtesy the artist

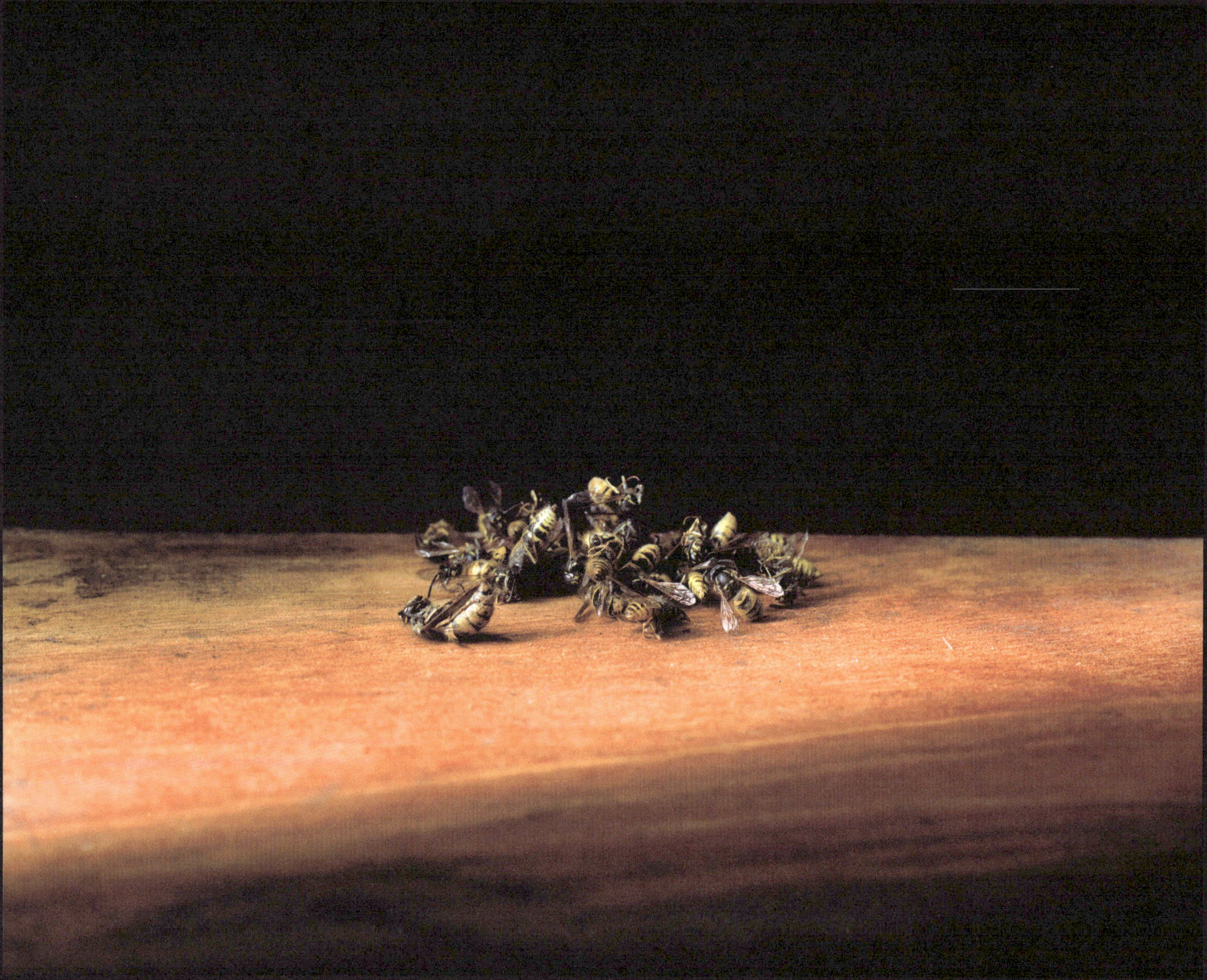

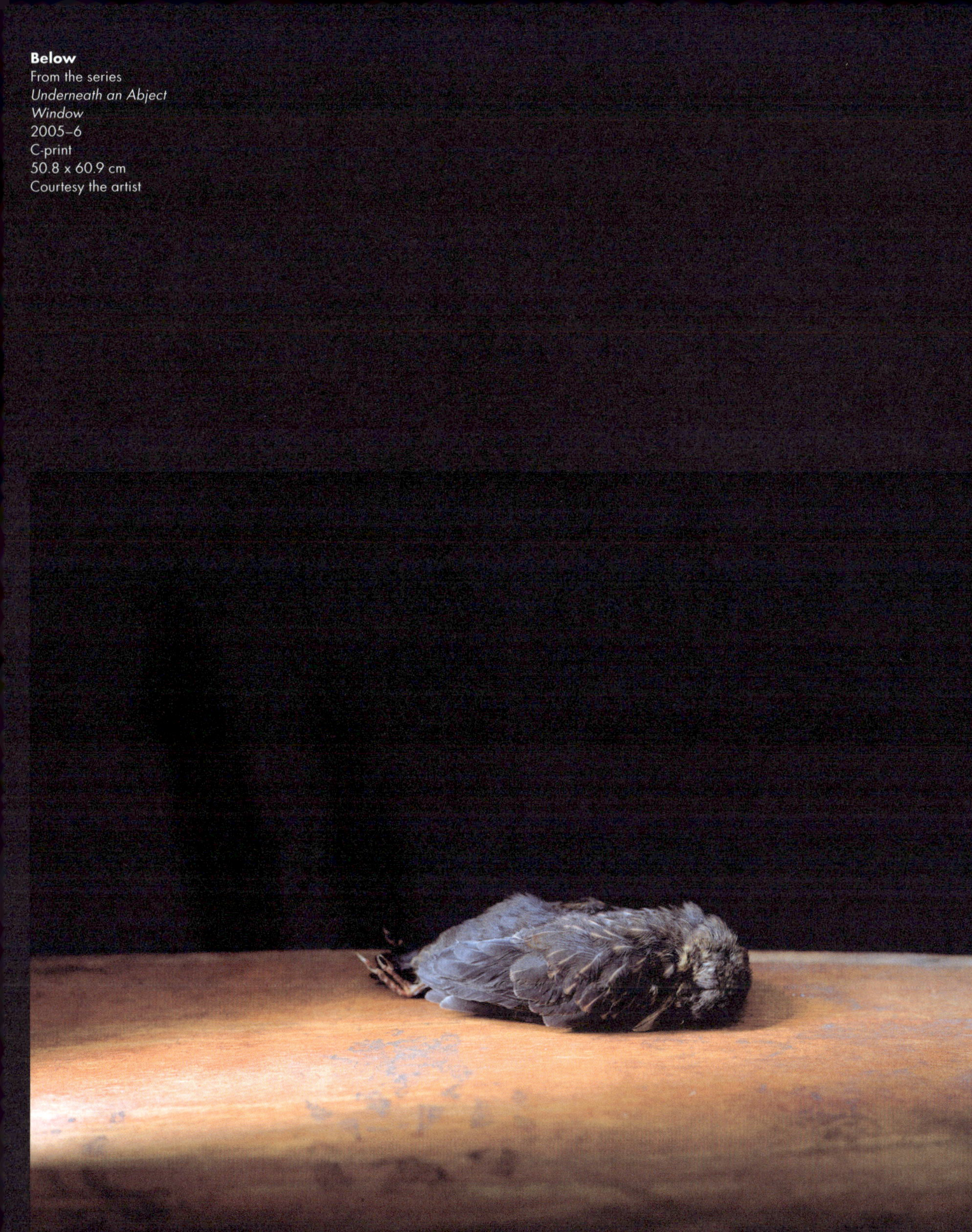

Below
From the series
*Underneath an Abject
Window*
2005–6
C-print
50.8 x 60.9 cm
Courtesy the artist

jonathan meese

There is one word to sum up Jonathan Meese's practice: chaos. The artist is impossible to pigeonhole, but his work exudes an intense, pulsating energy. Meese actively uses disturbing and transgressive imagery throughout his paintings, sculptures, installations and large-scale performances. Yet he speaks about art as if it were something almost passive. 'If humans create art, they do so in humility and with absolute neutrality. I simply let things happen. The necessities occur as they want to. Caligula, the Moomins and Ben Hur are great artists.'

Meese creates a world of visual excess. His performances overflow with props and junk. His thick paint is applied with notably violent strokes. 'Actions are always about vitality, esprit, radicality, hermetism and neutrality. Brutality and violence belong on the stage, therefore in art, not in human reality.'

Sometime his aesthetics veer towards the monstrous or grotesque – particularly his bronze sculptures. In the *Soldier of Fortune* series, skull-like forms with militaristic details emerge out of hard, painted metal, like primordial monsters in slime. They appear both solid and in flux. 'The incorporated skeleton parts are like the levers and instruments of a new era. These skeletonized tools are the keys to the future. Skeletons are like primal glands. Skeletons are never cowardly or self-fulfilling.'

Many of his past performances have also included skeletons as props. These bony figures flank the artist on stage or are scattered around his installations. They appear like a DIY artistic army rather than sinister comments on death. 'Skeletons are very good partners, since they

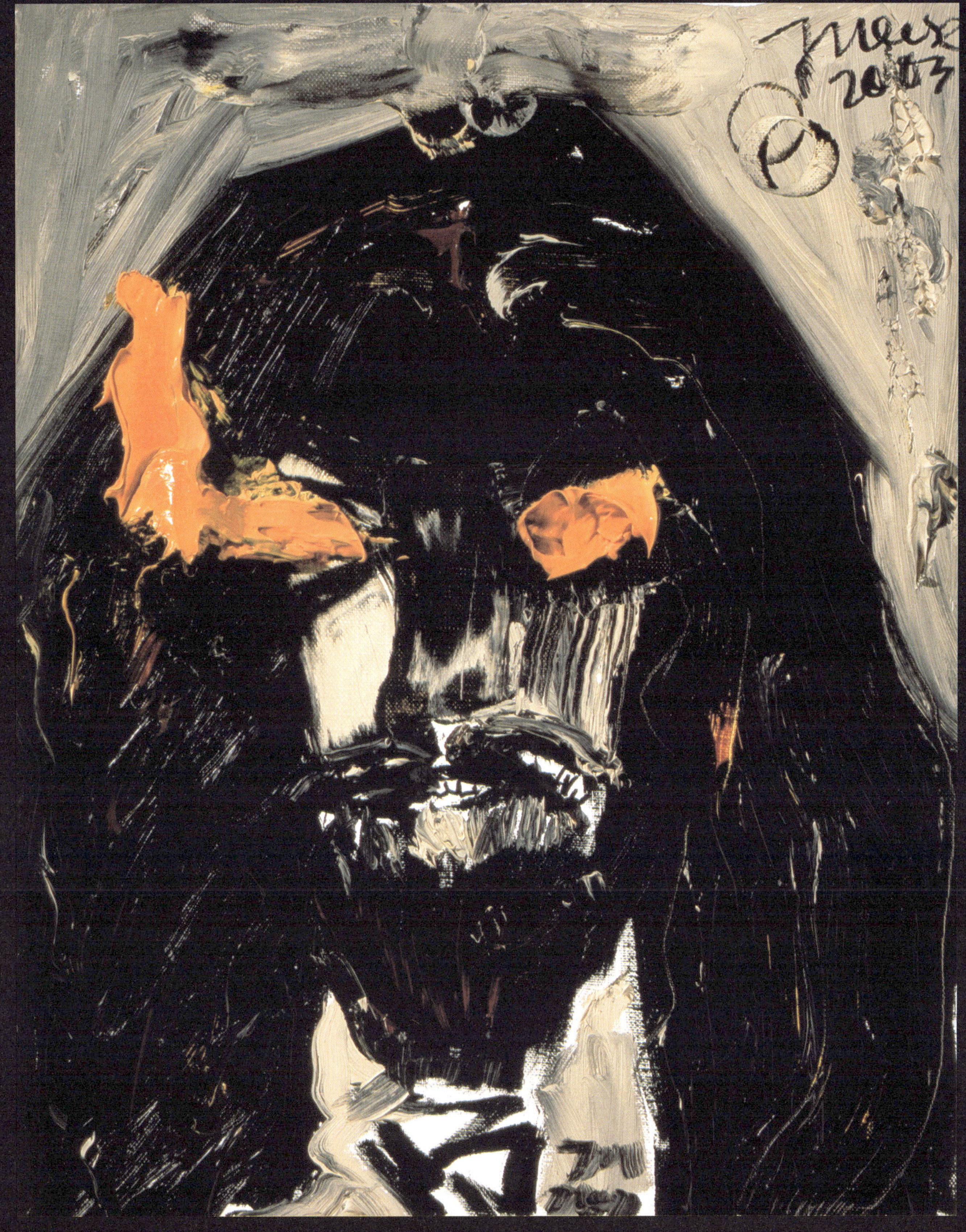

do not act as though they are "individualists". These skeletons are like ants, like baby animals. Skeletons are the humans of the future, absolutely revolutionary and unique. They are the system of rule of the future.' Sometimes Meese's performances can be intensely personal. He once brought his mother on stage to discuss his appropriation of Nazi imagery in some of his work.

There is a sense of hysteric comedy in Meese's work – something dark and often funny, in the same vein as artists such as Paul McCarthy. 'There is no real difference between "humour" and "darkness"; both are equally neutral. Art is always in a good mood, because art is the revolution of the object. The Devil is overstretched by art. He becomes see-through, then he is very funny. The Devil is like Punch. Take the Devil, Lady Satan, on your arm and sing a goodnight song to the harmless, Lolitaesque Devil.'

Despite all this chaos and violence, Meese can come across like a big child – an individual who creates work with the free enthusiasm of a toddler playing in its faeces. There is a wild edge to his approach. His self-portraits are jagged and violent, echoing the German expressionist approach to paint. He often depicts himself with demonic red eyes. There's lots of black and red paint in these paintings. 'The flaming eyes are the optical equipment of the Art Revolution. Perhaps I am the Hagen of Tronje, the Dr No, the most affectionate Rasputin, Lady Macbeth, Ivanhoe of art….'

The artist often draws on military imagery in his pieces – largely connected to Germany's own controversial history. At one performance he provocatively enacted Nazi salutes on stage, alongside the gesture for wanking, while shouting 'Adolf Hitler'. In some ways his actions and his appropriation of images have dispelled their power in the cultural consciousness so they lose their impact.

For Meese, his militaristic, sexual and medical references are things that have precise meaning. 'They concern instructions, clear language, symmetries, hall geometry, oracle, uniforms, rules and discipline. I love uniforms; I love crystalline forms and geometrical formulas. Art is always a neutral-military, revolutionary act.'

Meese speaks about art in pointedly revolutionary terms. For him, art should never be about self-expression or conceptual navel-gazing – despite the fact that he often features in his own work. He argues that he has much more sizeable considerations. 'Self-fulfilment fanaticism is abhorrent, disgusting and always anti-revolutionary. Never confuse art with your own life. Art is a different reality. The next big revolution will not come from the street, but from art.'

Previous spread
Pharao de Mees mit ausgesudetem Auge d'Orange
2003
Oil on canvas
50 x 40 x 2 cm
Courtesy Contemporary Fine Arts, Berlin
Photography Jochen Littkemann

Below
Soldier of Fortune 'Humphrey' (day)
2003
Bronze
56 x 27 x 25 cm

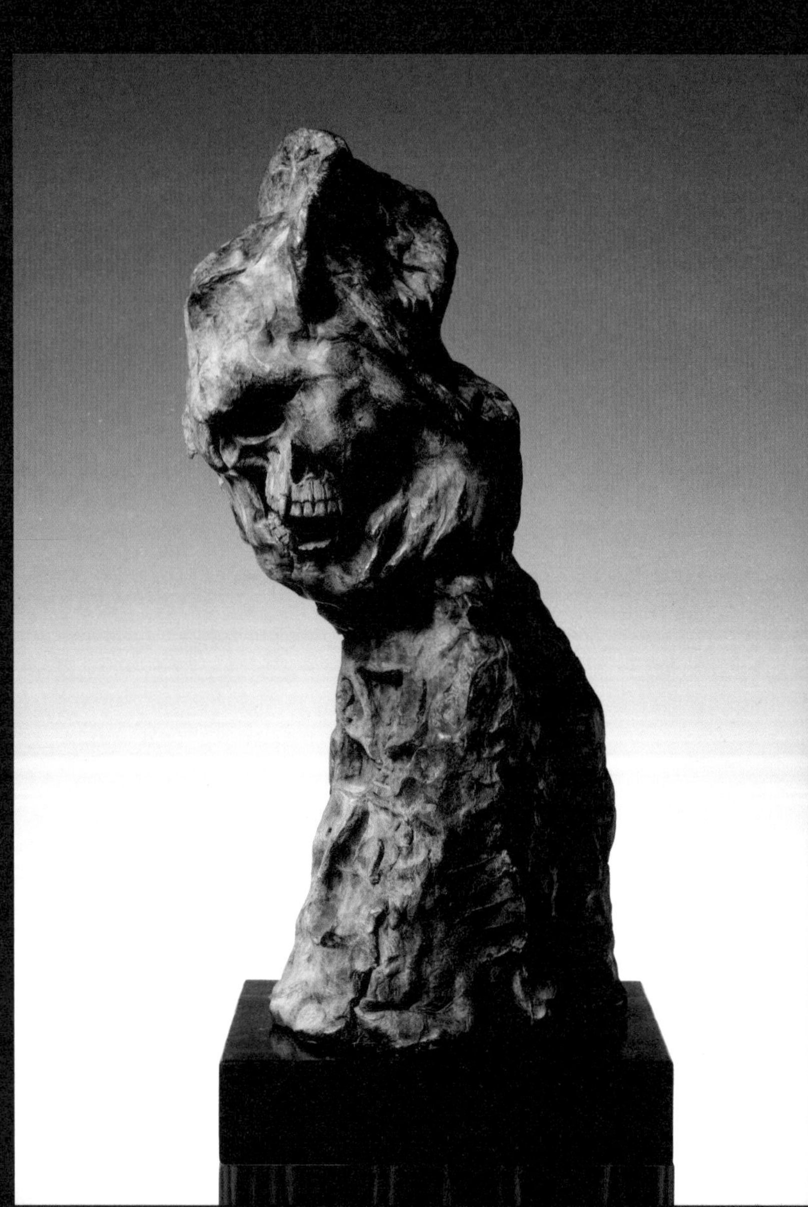

2006
Oil on canvas
270 x 140 x 4 cm

2006
Oil on canvas
210 x 140 x 2.4 cm

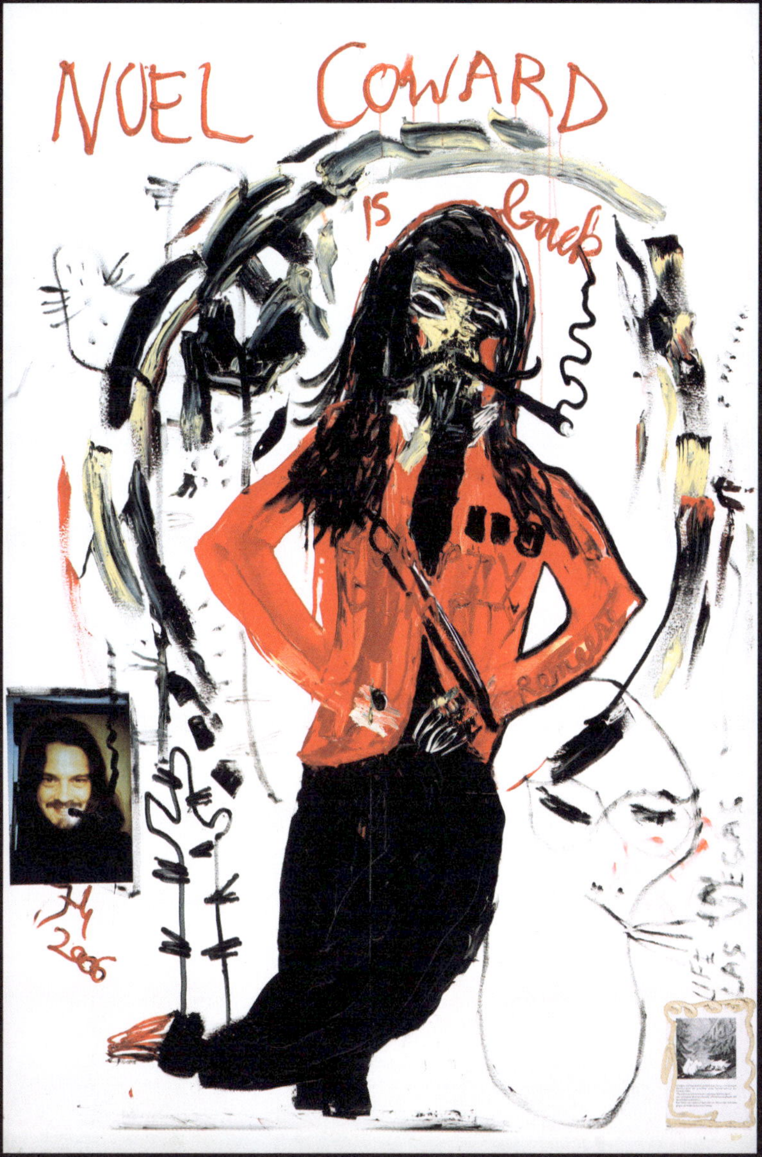

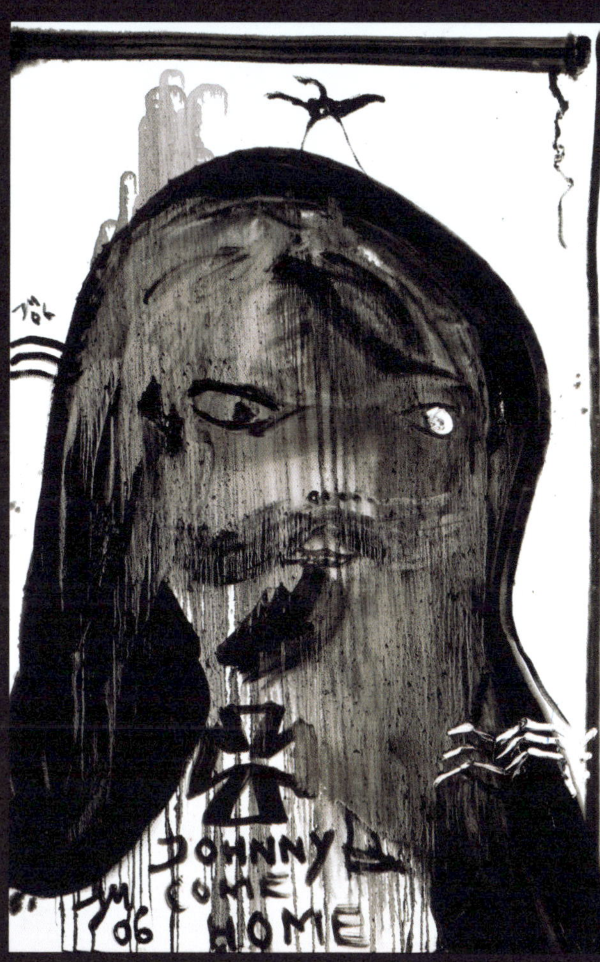

elina merenmies

Watercolours and ink gain a supernatural texture under the hand of Elina Merenmies. The Finnish artist's paint seems to blur and spread in an almost viral way. The fluidity of her use of water spills over the lines of her monstrous subjects, creating an atmospheric aesthetic that seems to cross the boundaries of reality. 'In literature, I've always been more interested in decadence than realism. For me, horror and the supernatural are part of everyday reality.'

There is something almost melancholic about her paintings – an arguably Scandinavian sense of ennui or sadness. 'Those things stem from a subconscious need to create a comforting image. You could perhaps compare it to sad songs. I often shed tears while working, and only then do I know that I'm suffusing the theme with something mournful.' Her palette is often limited – images that are just shades of red or nuances of grey. Her drawings and ink pieces stick to a dark monochrome. 'I've always liked it [monochrome] because of its simplicity and austerity. The most important book of my childhood was a Bible full of Gustave Doré's etchings.'

The imagery in Merenmies's work veers from portraits of slavering dogs that resemble monsters to wild forest landscapes. She often creates portraits of malformed faces, which seem to quote stern-faced medical drawings. Other pieces focus on skeletons and skulls. 'These symbols point to the transience of this life. For me, they're above all a grotesque and humorous motif.' The more gothic imagery is often the most light-hearted. An ink drawing of a person alone on a hospital bed is given

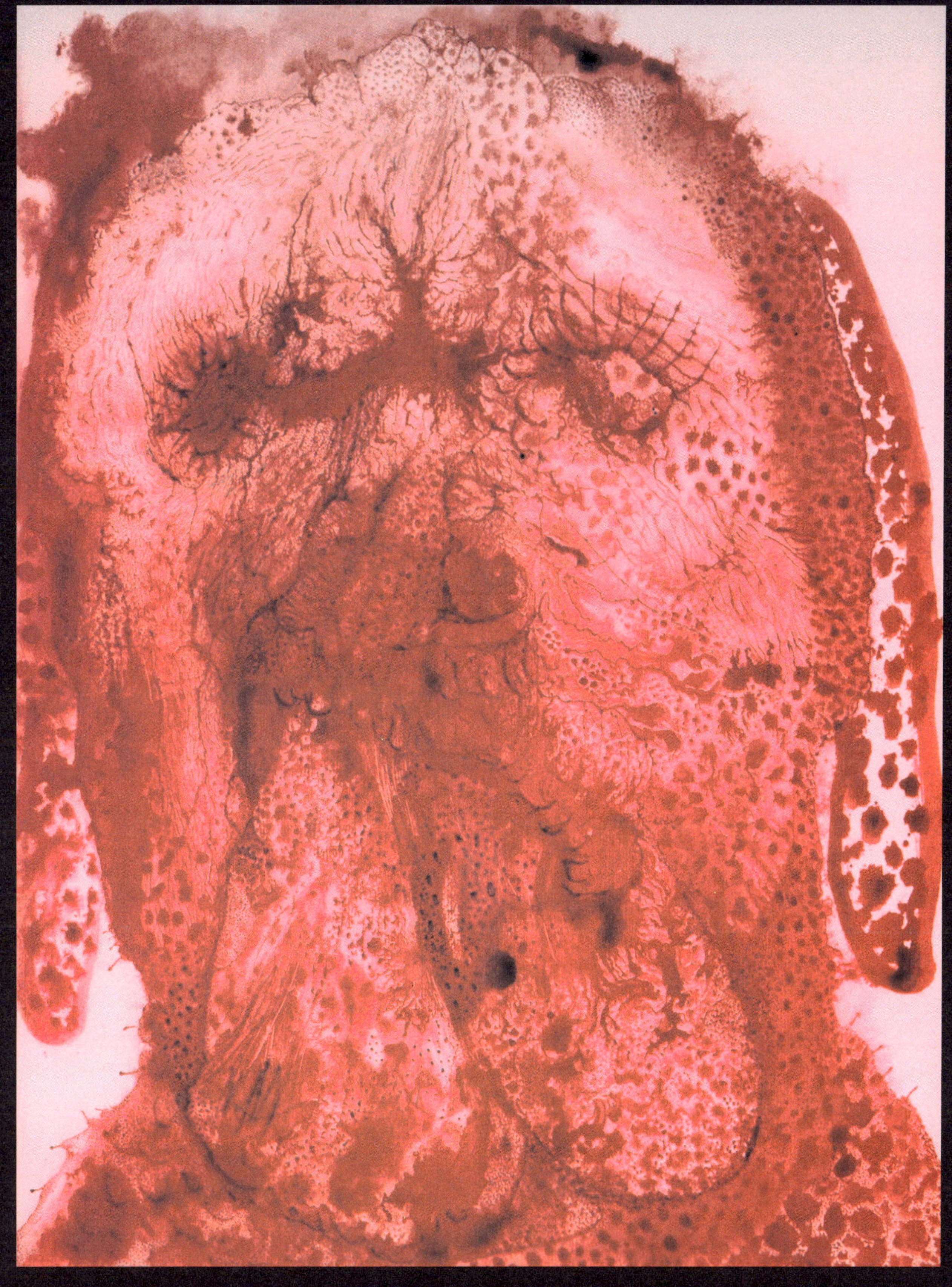

the teasing title *There Must Be An Angel Playing With My Heart*.

Some of her paintings and drawings lean towards something wilder – consciously adopting a childlike scratchy style and more extreme colours. Pieces like *Ampiaset* and *Death Disco Look* depict red-faced, half-human monsters, being attacked by swarms of bees or insects. The figures scream out at the viewer in a visceral way. There is a sense of chaos in her quick use of paint. 'It's always so good to scribble. I felt a similar joy when I was young – I used to create page upon page of completely illegible scrawl, a kind of madman's automatic writing.' She describes pieces like *Death Disco Look* as both sad and funny at the same time, like a desperate and ridiculous last dance. That wildness is a reflection of her desire to break away from the central restriction in creating any artwork – the contact between the mind and the hand. A sense of chance is innate to her approach. 'A series of catastrophes leads to something simple and I feel that my drawing hand is a misfortune in its own right. I've never considered my own gesture to be an important element in my images.'

Nature is a central theme in Merenmies's work, as she explores the influence of the Finnish landscape. But this is nature without colour. Instead, trees, clouds and leaves are shown in deep mournful washes of grey. Her world is permanently in decay. This is the land of swamp and tornados. There is beauty here, but it is a brooding loveliness.

Although there is something eternal about her pieces, they still explore and reflect a contemporary zeitgeist. The seeping black ink in her depictions of forests, for example, seems particularly disturbing in the context of environmental fears. Here, horror is projected on to the natural landscape. For the artist, the most frightening things are those that appear to be benign. 'I see horror in half-pornographic advertisements and other commercial material. For example, the McDonald's clown is the most blood-chilling creature of all time in all its impersonality. It expresses unwitting horror in an interesting way.' In her work, this sense of daily horror is transformed into poetry.

Interestingly, Merenmies relates the process of looking as something innately linked to death – or rather the avoidance of death. 'I've always noted that looking at pictures also involves the fast and uncontrollable instinct of self-preservation.' For her, we respond to art with the primitive, animal aspect of ourselves.

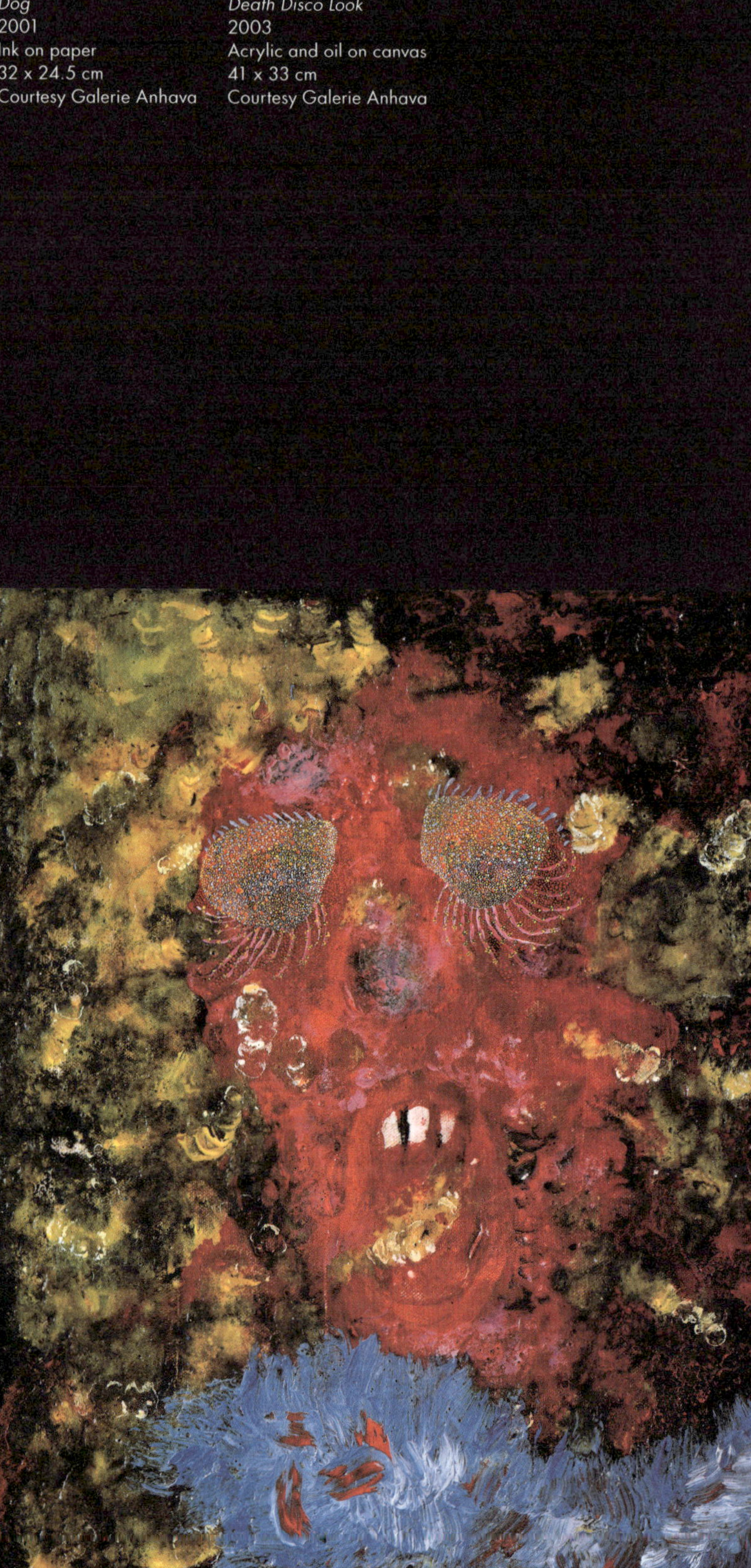

Below
Potato
2001
Ink on paper
31.5 x 24.5 cm

Right (top)
Birthday Party
2005
Ink on paper
22.5 x 18.5 cm
Courtesy Galerie Anhava

Right (bottom)
Trees Dancing
2006
Ink on paper
18.5 x 22.5 cm

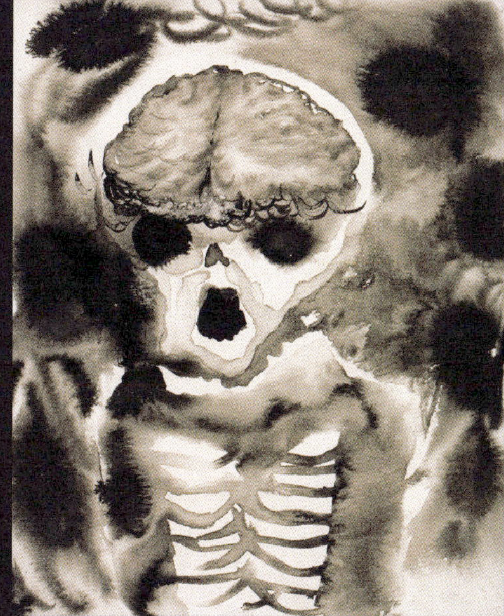

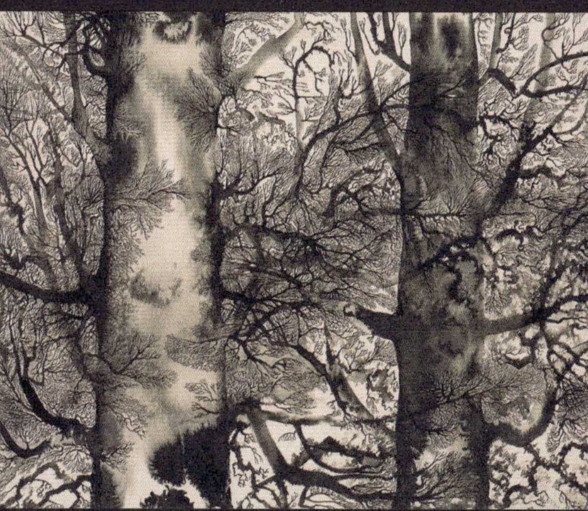

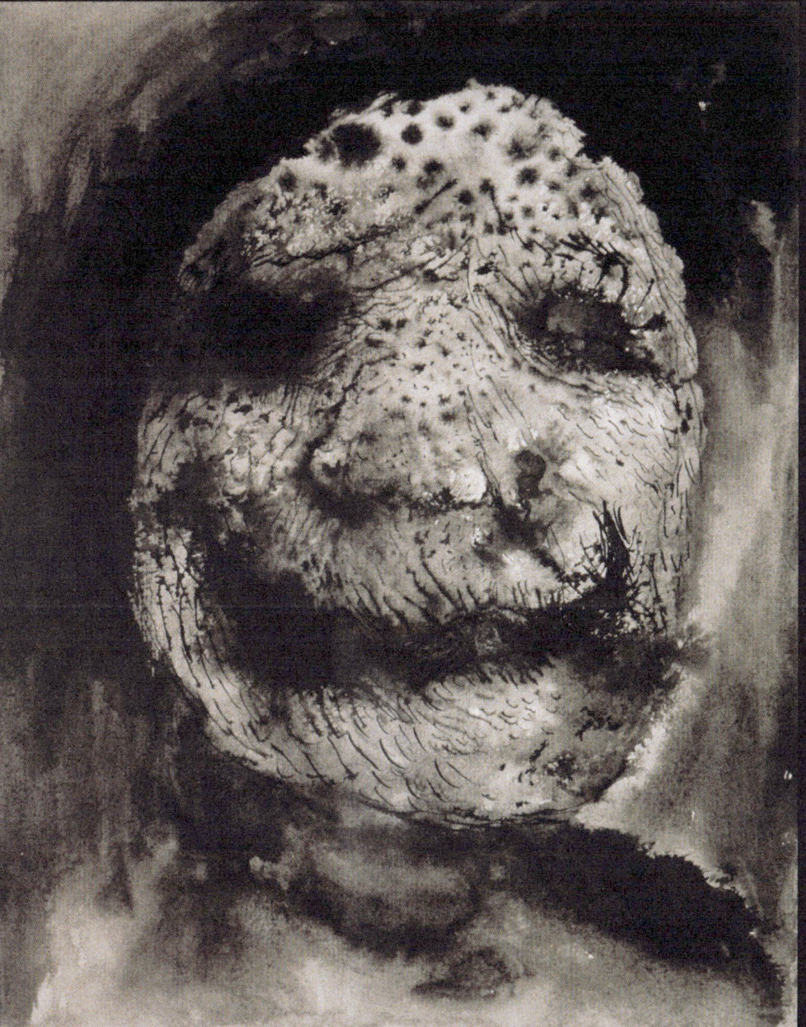

tim noble + sue webster

im Noble and Sue Webster began by making seemingly positivist neon-light pieces. As their work developed, they were drawn to the underside of their glowing brightness. They began to experiment with shadow. They made sculptural objects that left figurative shadows, often portraying the artists themselves. Their pieces are intensely worked and fiddly. 'Nowadays you find someone to fabricate your ideas. The YBA [Young British Artist] thing was very much a movement of that. Our thing is much more frustrating. When we started we didn't have a gallery or money. You mess around with whatever's around you.'

As their careers developed, their work grew increasingly dark. The shadows from their objects revealed the hidden inner meaning or the artists' minds, what Webster describes as a kind of third dimension, or, according to Noble, 'the closest thing to the truth.' In an attempt to kill their own image, Noble and Webster started working with dead animals. The first piece using taxidermy was called *British Wildlife*. The animals in this piece were taken from Tim's father's house after he died. This evolved to *Kiss of Death*, which is made of macabre birds and rats – old English flesh-eaters. It reveals a shadow portrait of the artists' heads kissing, while impaled on spikes. 'We're going through a phase where we are trying to get rid of our own self-image. We're making that evaporate.' They are now working on a sculpture made of mummified animal corpses – the next stage in decay.

Noble and Webster's most gothic exhibition was at the Freud Museum in London, Sigmund Freud's former home. One piece, *Black Narcissus*,

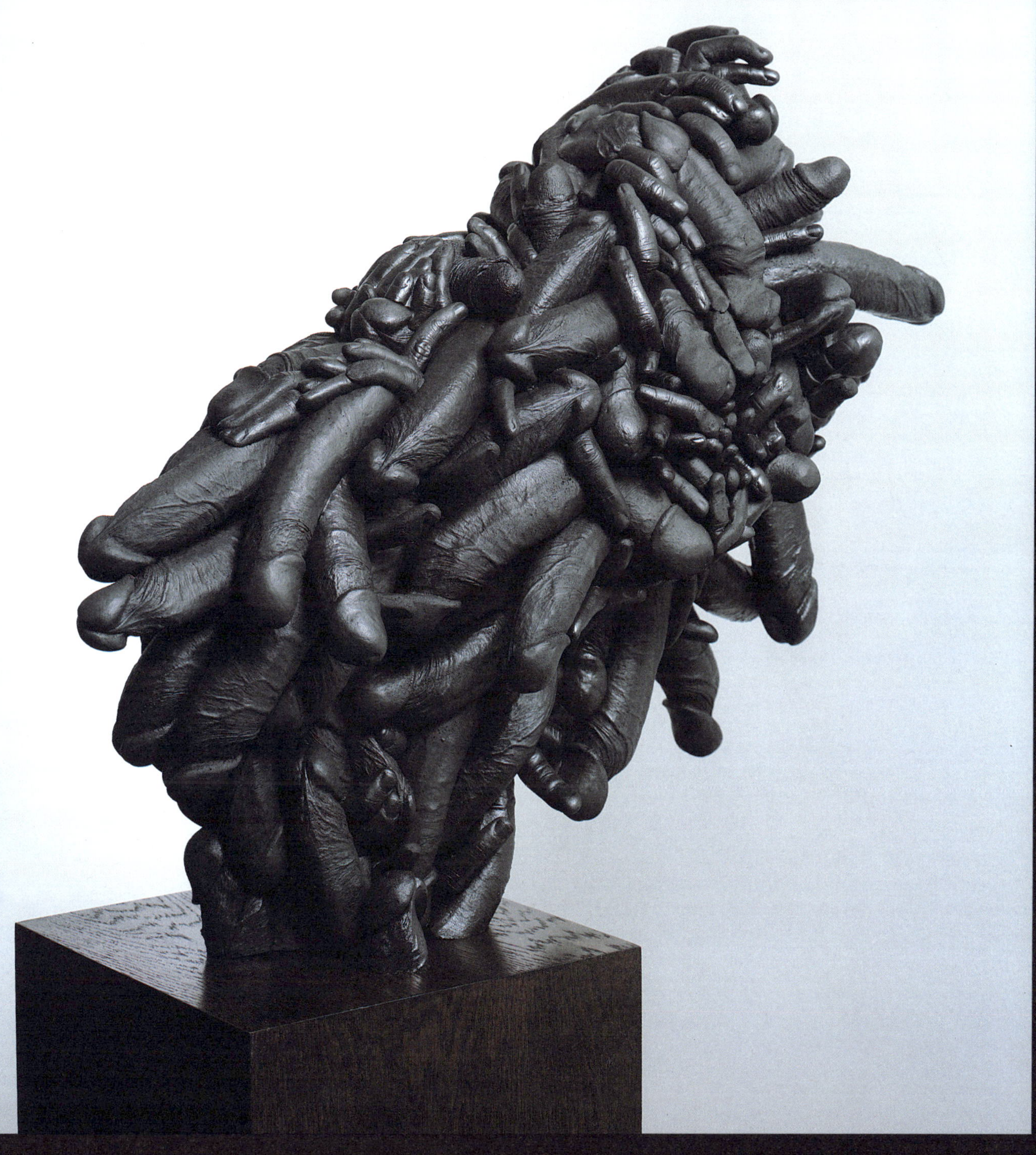

is a mound of black rubber penises and fingers that create a shadow of the artists' profiles. Part of what makes the sculpture so hypnotic is its blackness — a kind of swarming, unearthly mound of physicality. 'It tricks your senses slightly. It works as a mass, like a void you are sucked into.' The piece was inspired by a hard-core gay sex shop in East London, near the artists' home. 'They have a cabinet of dildos. We were overwhelmed by them. We set about buying them in bulk to make a sculpture. We realized the rubber was inferior, but there was an amazing rubber used in art-casting that was really strong, and we used that.' The piece is made of casts of Noble's penis and Webster's fingers, the difference in scale giving the sensation of a swarming mass of worms. 'What we didn't realize was that in the morning, it started secreting. It would be sweating. This whole shape took on this other form, like a giant slug.' The piece was displayed in a low-lit room in the Freud Museum on a dark wood plinth, looming out of the shadows.

The central piece in this show was a mesmerizing, moving installation called *Scarlett*. The piece was formed naturally on workbenches that had been made for Noble and Webster's studio. It consisted of a large number of intersecting objects made from dolls, old tools and found objects, sometimes covered with dirty plastic bags. These pieces moved and juddered, were penetrated, cut up and impaled.

They started making the kinetic, moving contraptions more than 15 years ago, and slowly objects grew. 'Its beauty was that it was perpetually unfinished. It very much existed because it was a little thing we were doing on the side, not our main project. It was something growing out of the corner.' In the exhibition, the piece was located in Anna Freud's room — a space devoted to child psychology. Some of the actions were hard to decipher. 'Tim put a plastic bag over it all, so the movements were still there, but you could only just sense what was going on. It diffused it a bit.' The Freudian context brought out layers beyond the object itself. 'It's not just about art — it was about how all the objects seemed to resonate with people's imaginations. It keyed off all these things going off in people's heads.'

There is something alchemical about the creation of illusion in Noble and Webster's works. 'There is an element of magic to it,' Webster agrees. The process of creation is hidden and made obtuse. Throughout their career, they have been greeted with disbelief — as if the objects they create are somehow faked.

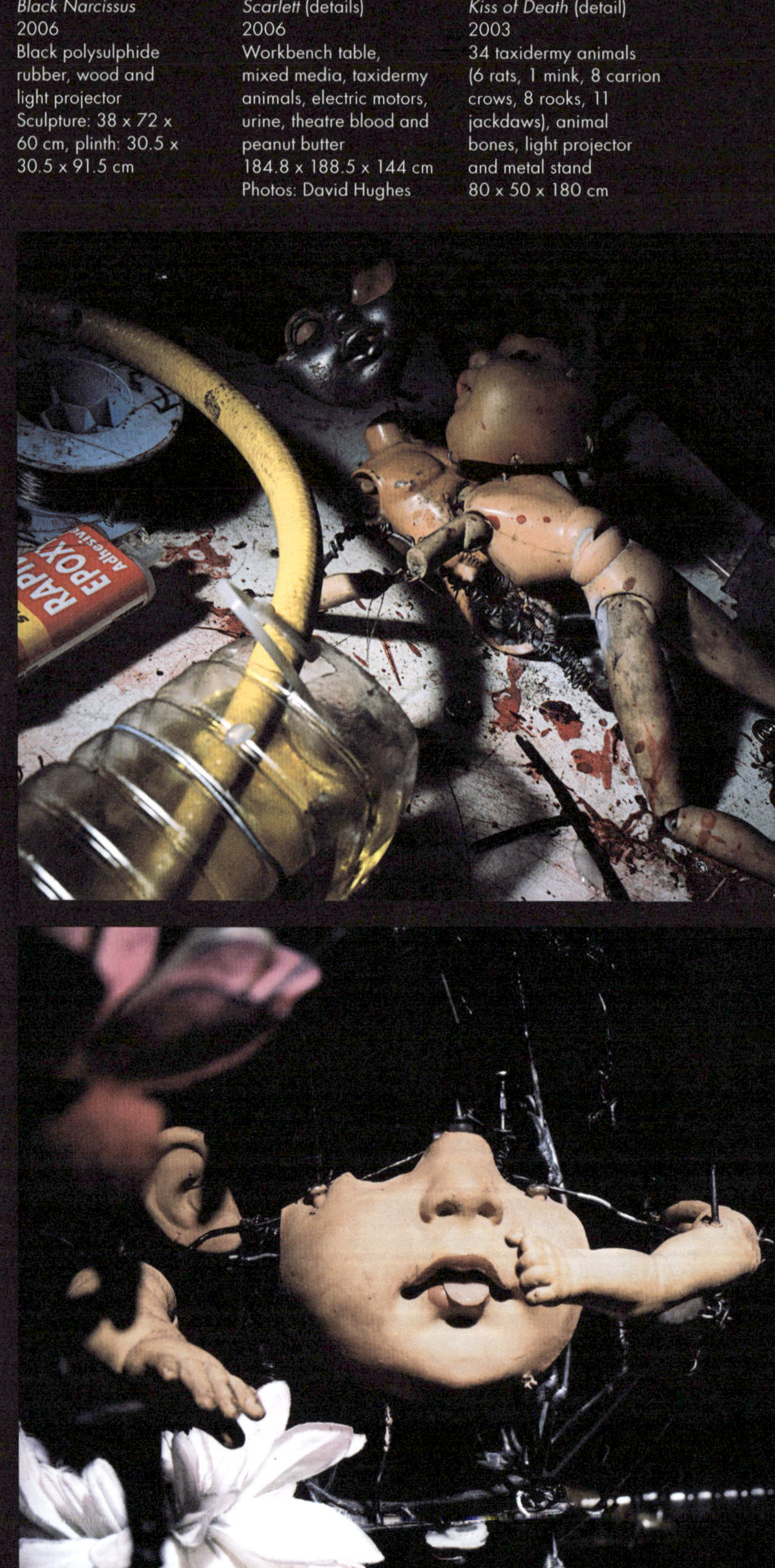

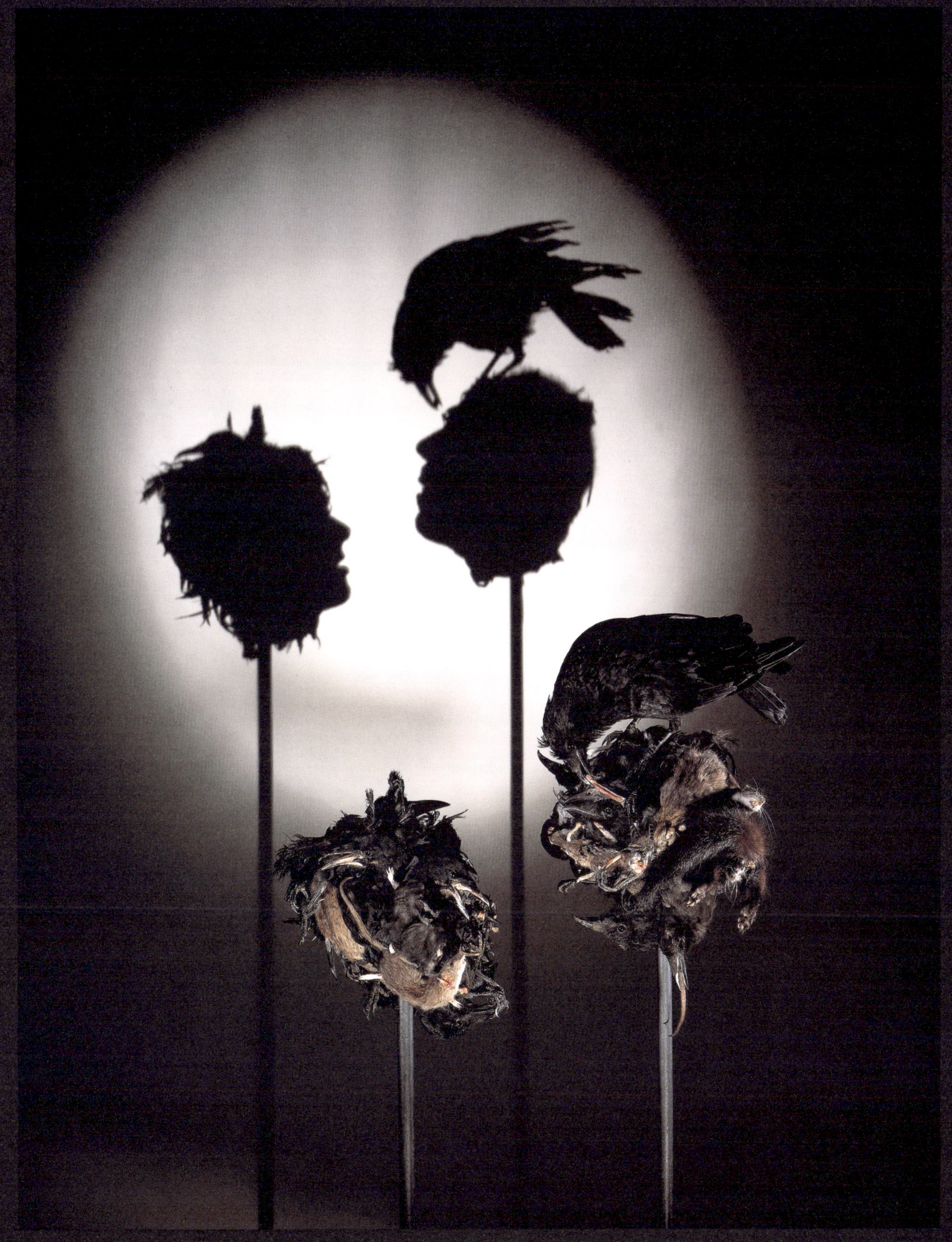

Below and right
Scarlett (details)
Photos: David Hughes

Opposite
Metal Fucking Rats
(version 1)
2006
Welded scrap metal
and light projector
51.5 x 53 x 19.6 cm

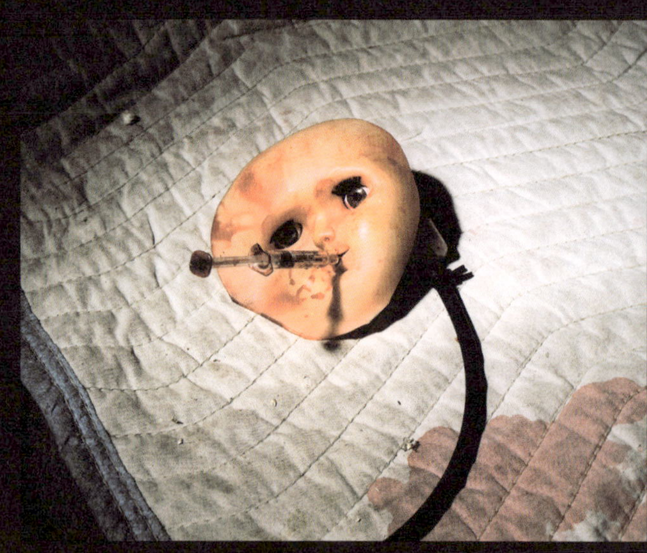

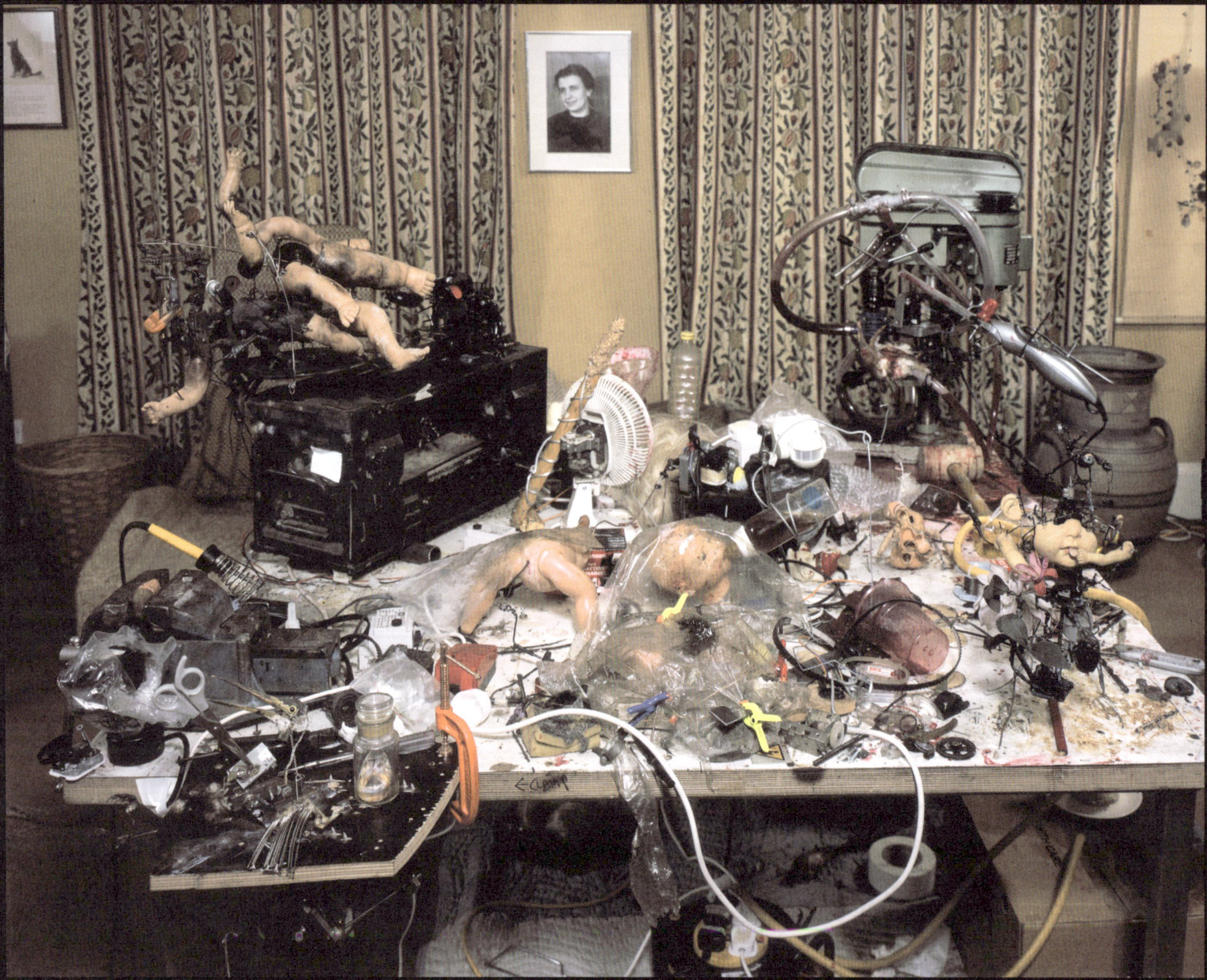

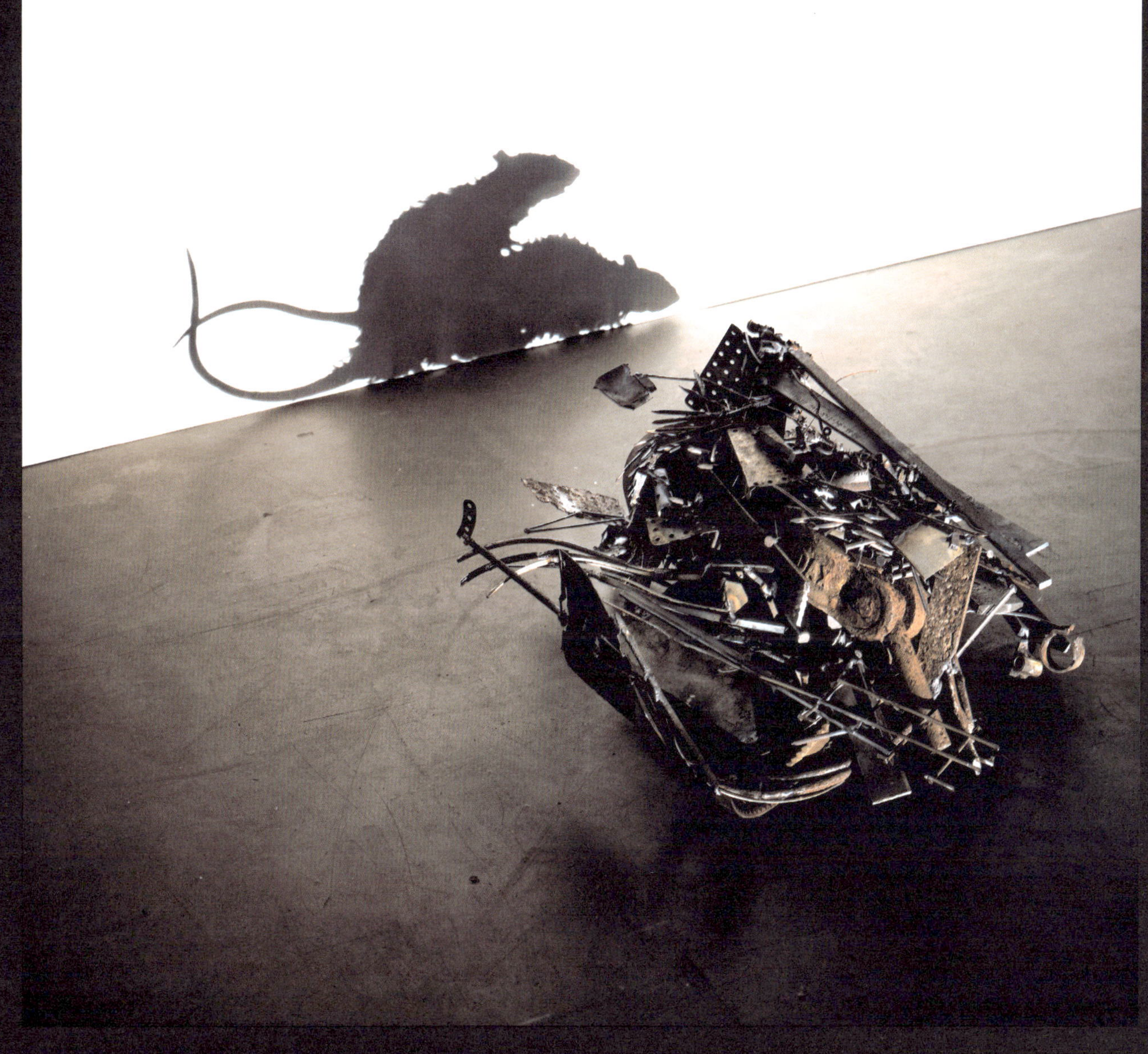

david noonan

avid Noonan seems to be consciously seeking ambiguity in his sense of narrative, his use of colour and his imagery. He creates work full of strange rituals and unexplained performance. Nothing is obvious. Events are unveiled but cannot be completely read or understood. His work is filled with a sense of mystery and melancholy.

The Australian artist's interest in ritual may have grown out of a teenage interest in mysticism and his early years spent in an Indian ashram, but this connection is not something Noonan emphasizes. He is more interested in looking at and transforming imagery from avant-garde 1960s performance theatre. 'The Russian constructivist theatre we studied at art school was probably what first interested me in the aesthetics of that kind of experimental theatre, when costumes and props were as important as the plays themselves.' He found theatre magazines from the late 1960s in a charity shop when he first moved to London and became intrigued by the images. 'I started collecting more, not knowing what I would do with them. Montage and collage became the way I used these found images. I am interested in the representation of performance, the way the body in dance or performance can become abstracted. Often the action takes place in a purely fictional scenario, particularly a play with extreme set design or costumes.'

There is a very interesting tension in Noonan's work. He depicts active, live performance as something frozen and still. Taking movement and making it static creates a kind of inner conflict to the images. His visual layering of photographic imagery makes the

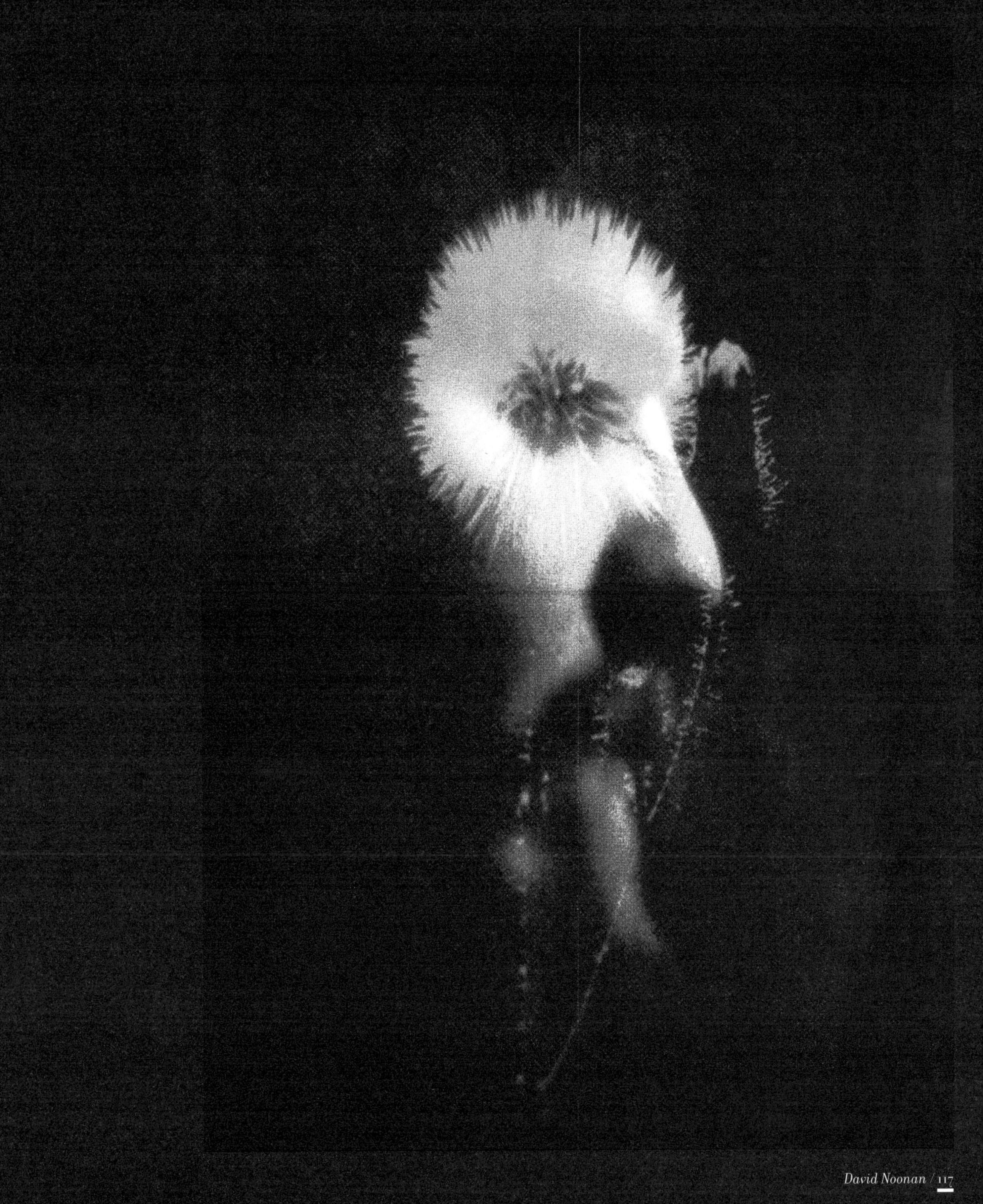

events appear even more unclear and inexplicable. Noonan trained in painting but has worked with techniques and processes ranging from oil painting, gouache and watercolour to sculpture, etching using bleach and screen-printing. 'I still use a lot of those processes. The screen prints I have been working with lately happened to be a good way of superimposing two different images on to one picture plane. It is a way of presenting a montaged image.'

Much of the work is monochrome. Colour rarely infiltrates the images. 'It makes images feel less locked into a particular time – or less of this time, perhaps. Also I like the simplicity.' His smaller collage pieces fit squares of opaque black together with smaller highlights of black-and-white photographs. Layering in particular is a technique he uses to take images and create something entirely new. Noonan removes the original narrative of his found photographs and fits the imagery together, in varying degrees of opacity. 'I am interested in the collision between two different images – the unexpected narratives that can occur when two disparate images are combined. It is almost like a planned accident – putting the conditions in place.' There is no set scale to the images – distant full-size figures are layered over uncomfortable close-ups. Noonan takes groups of images and intuitively or experimentally combines them to see what happens. 'Sometimes you arrive at something, often you don't.'

Noonan has an interesting lexicon of imagery within his work. His images include unseen men in cloaks, seated characters with strange masks, shadow puppets, characters dressed as clowns and children in period costume. Groups of people join together in almost religious processions. Birds, especially the owl, are a recurring theme. 'Owls come with such strong and ambiguous associations already.' He has made owl paintings, sculptures of white plastic or rustic wooden owls and has used photographs of the birds in collage.

The pieces employ the language of mystery, making the figurative into something abstract, hiding all meaning. He often uses images of people in masks to underline this sense of concealment. 'I think all cultures have used masks for many different reasons and functions. I like that it is really a ready-made. Every person brings their own baggage and experiences to these images. I like to play with that.' The artist creates a strange world of weird juxtapositions. His layered pieces resemble stills from an occult silent movie or the remnants of a strange, underground cult. Although black and white, there is something psychedelic about the pieces. Here, imagery overflows and recombines.

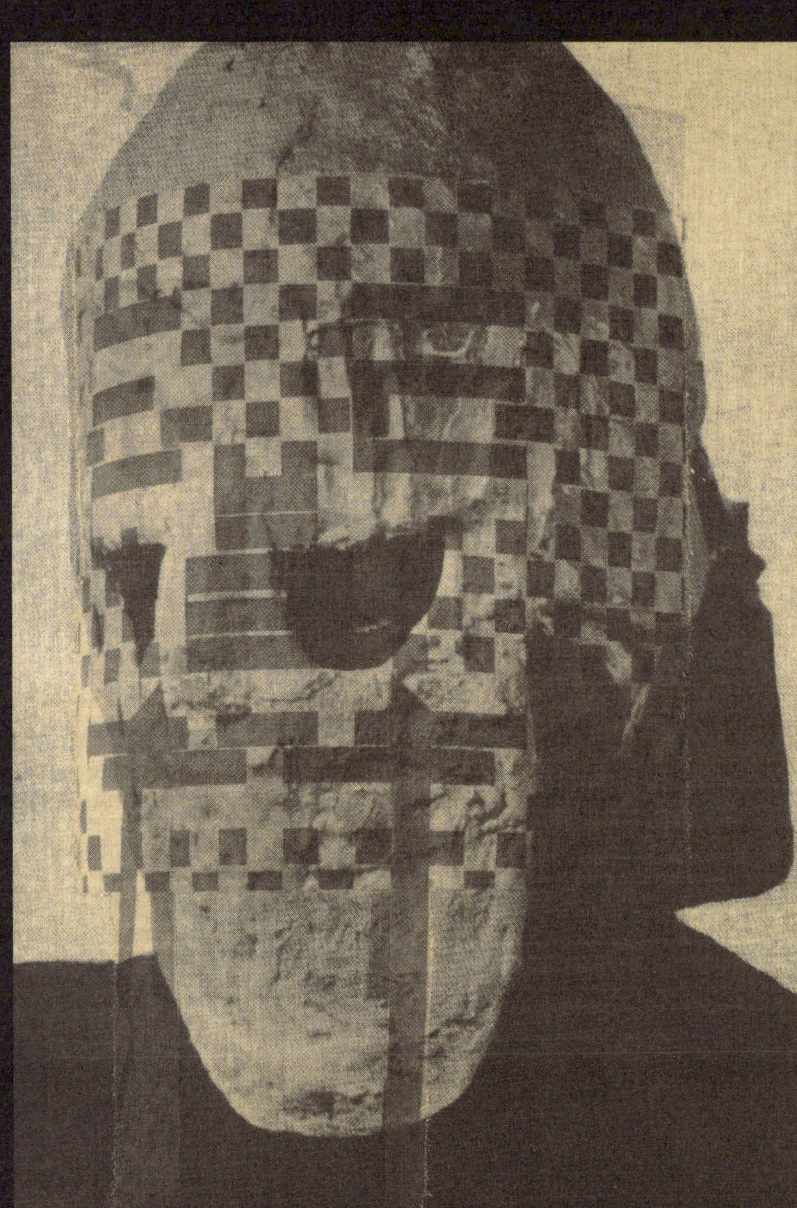

Below
Untitled
2007
Silkscreen on linen
213.4 x 304.8 cm
Courtesy the artist and
Foxy Production

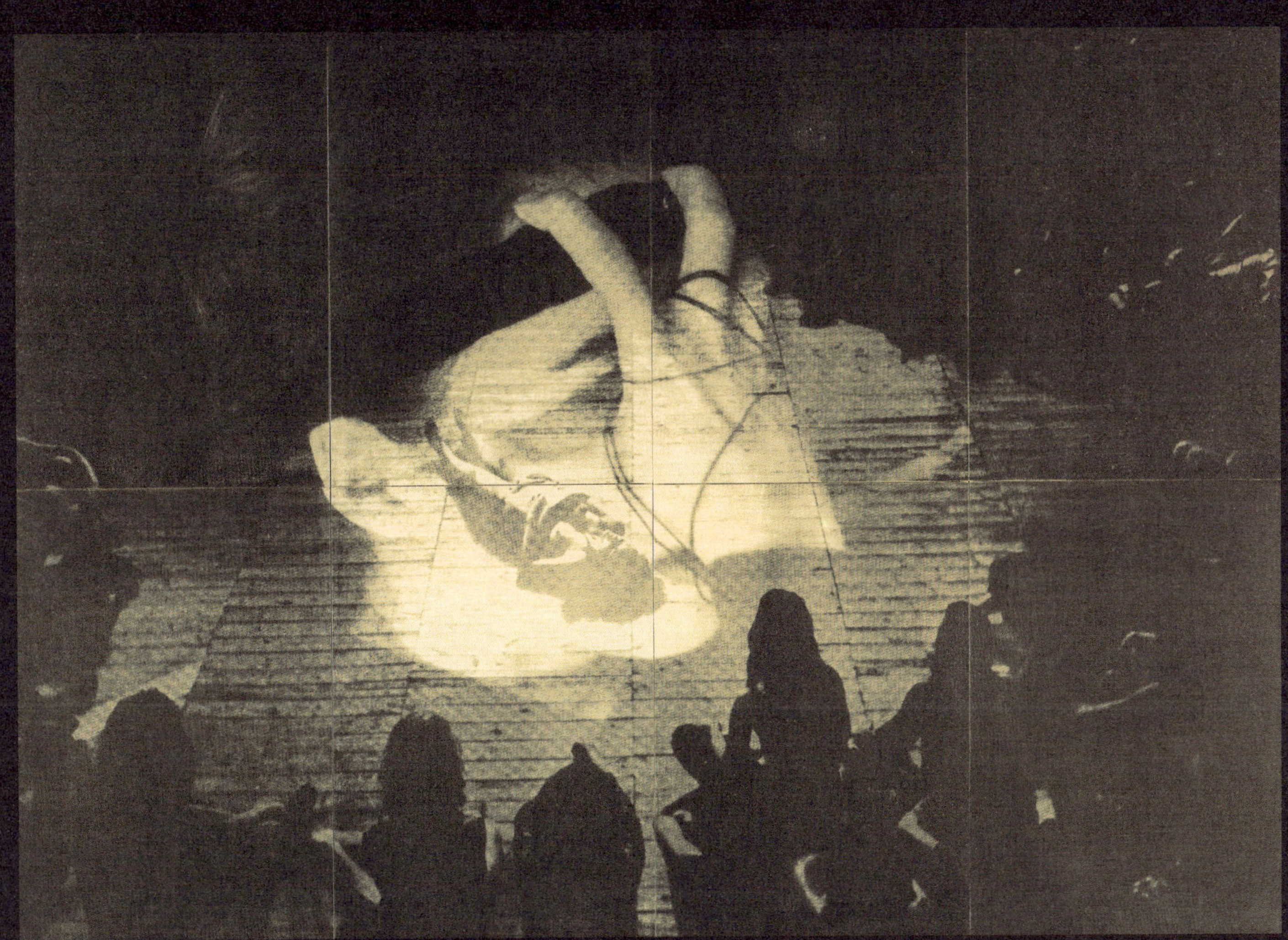

Right
Untitled
2006
Screen print on laminated
plywood
188 x 266 cm
Courtesy the artist and
David Kordansky Gallery

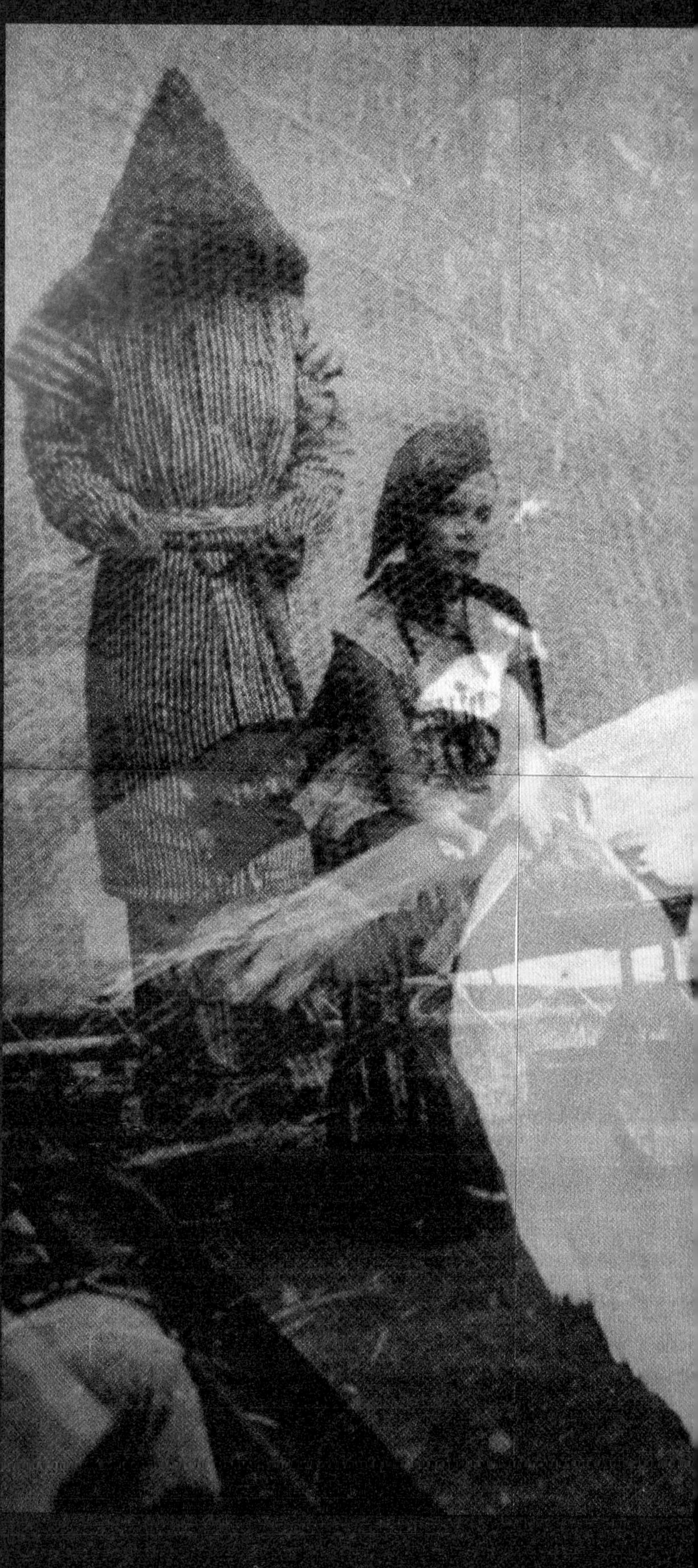

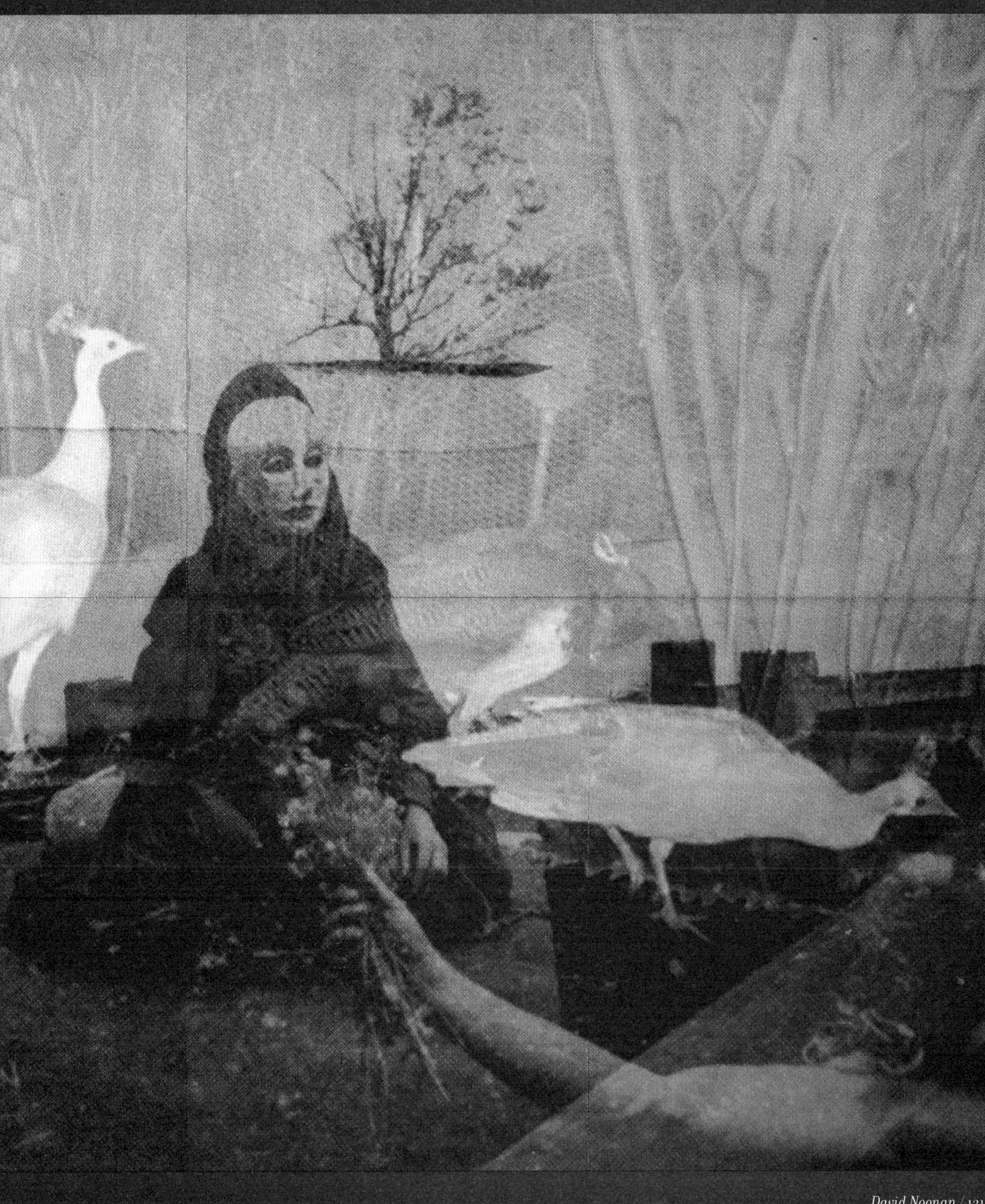

chloe piene

The horror in Chloe Piene's drawings and films is not inspired by the darkness of modern iconography. Instead, it reflects a fascination with the Northern Renaissance. 'Dark skies, hellfire, open graves, death prancing around with his guts hanging out. Horror movies might seem influential but there's a historical precedent that is way bigger and meaner than all that American teenage date stuff.'

Her film pieces are truly disturbing. *Black Mouth* focuses on a mud-stained child set against a black background. The figure looks as if it is in extreme pain, escaping some horrifying situation or writhing in primitive fear. At one point the mouth of the child opens too wide and releases an unnatural scream through a gaping black hole. The speed of the film is slowed down so the child's actions are made more disturbing than perhaps they would be in reality. Something that could be playful becomes infused with terror.

Piene's use of children in her films is twisted but fascinating. They veer between victim and monster, the inflictor of pain and the pained. 'Their energy is very direct. They play. They aren't burdened so much by appearances.' Often the artist distorts her use of sound to increase a sense of discomfort and horror. 'A whole episodic power can be rolled into the force of a single cry, shriek or call.' She uses sound in a very different way in *The Dwarf*, an installation in a gallery closet that consists of a video screen on a shelf and the use of disembodied sound. The screen is largely black, accompanied by the sound of high-pitched giggling. At intervals a dwarf appears and disappears on screen in an empty hallway – like a digital apparition.

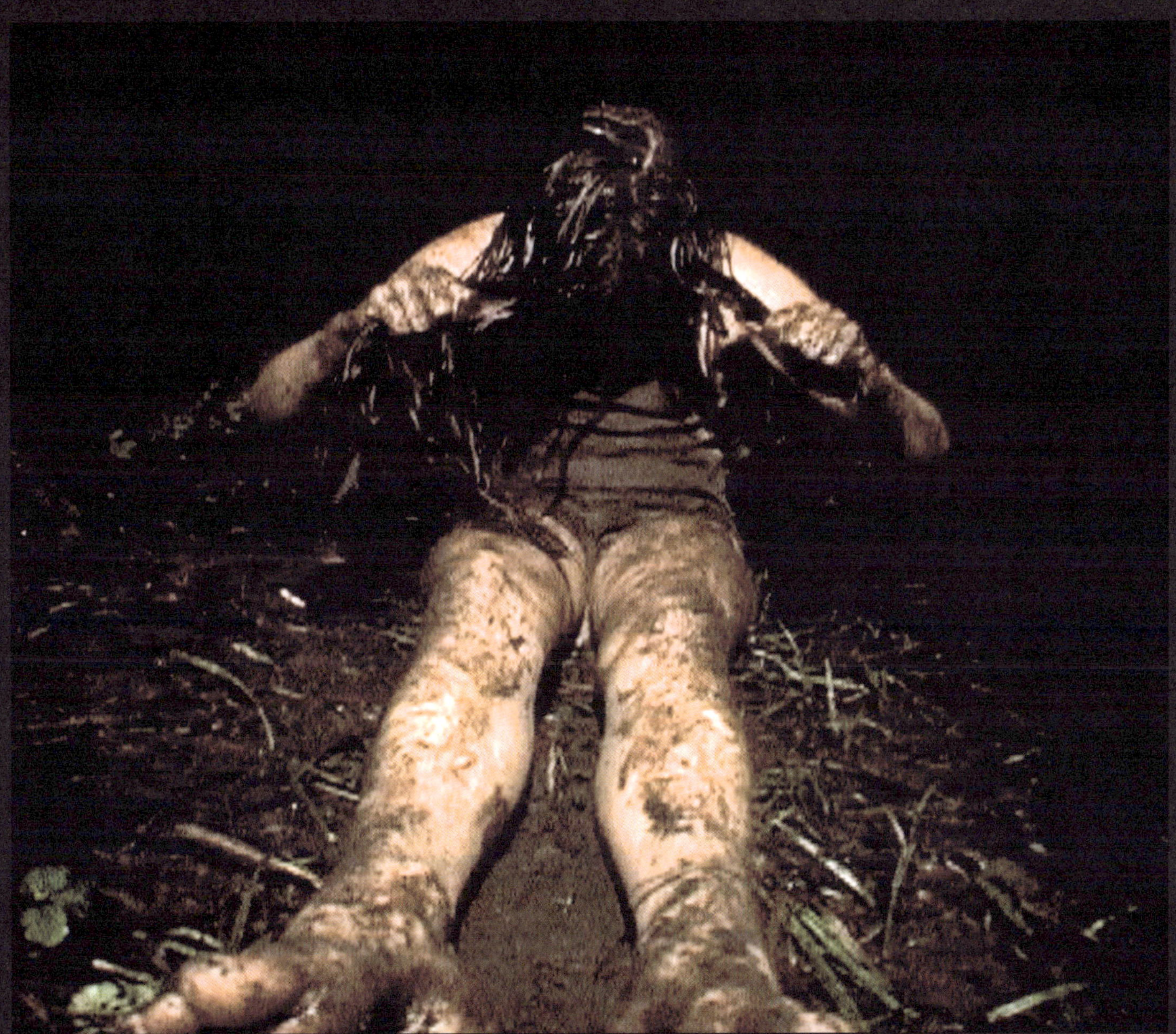

Piene's interest in creating art grew out of an academic one. 'I have always drawn, but I studied art history in college. It allowed me to pursue the things I love and admire, in a very open and analytical way. I would spend hours at the art history library, looking up medieval bestiaries, anatomical charts and mythologies, things on alchemy. I felt it was a privilege to be able to pursue images, which no one was paying much attention to, but which seriously interested me. I still feel that way. As an artist I am always in dialogue with things that intrigue me endlessly, relentlessly.' Her influences include artists like Hans Baldung Grien, Albrecht Dürer and Matthias Grünewald, as well as the aesthetic quality of dead languages and the imagery of old-school metal bands like Pantera.

In addition to her film work, Piene creates fascinating pencil drawings on vellum. These images are often very large and surrounded by cream-coloured space. There is a fluidity to the texture of her pencil on the smooth parchment, with its curled lines – as if drawn with intense speed. There are glimpses of a skull or a bony hand in the scrawled pencil marks. 'I don't always work on vellum, but as a material it's a bit unusual, because it's not made for charcoal drawing.'

These pieces are often described as 'automatic drawings', although the practice is something Piene has always done consciously. 'I've drawn since I can remember. Even when I was a girl I drew animal and human hybrids, monstrous creatures, naked women. When I was about seventeen I did a nice portrait of my horned self in a corseted, Tudor-style dress. I got teased in school for drawing naked women absentmindedly in class. I think I was just contemplating my own body, wondering about it. Knowing that the body was the love object of a lot of fairy tales – a lot of articulated fantasy – I was looking for a connection, and identifying with Snow White and the hag, the bewitched princess, the fairy, the elf and the magical creature.'

The process of creating the drawings is an essential part of their make-up. 'Drawing is a process, you have to work to get to a point where things come together, and start to make sense on their own. It always involves a kind of silent progression towards some degree of perfection.'

Previous spread
Black Mouth (still)
2004
DVD NTSC Video
Running Time: 00:02:51

Below
Consolation 01
2006
Charcoal on vellum
30.5 X 22.9 cm

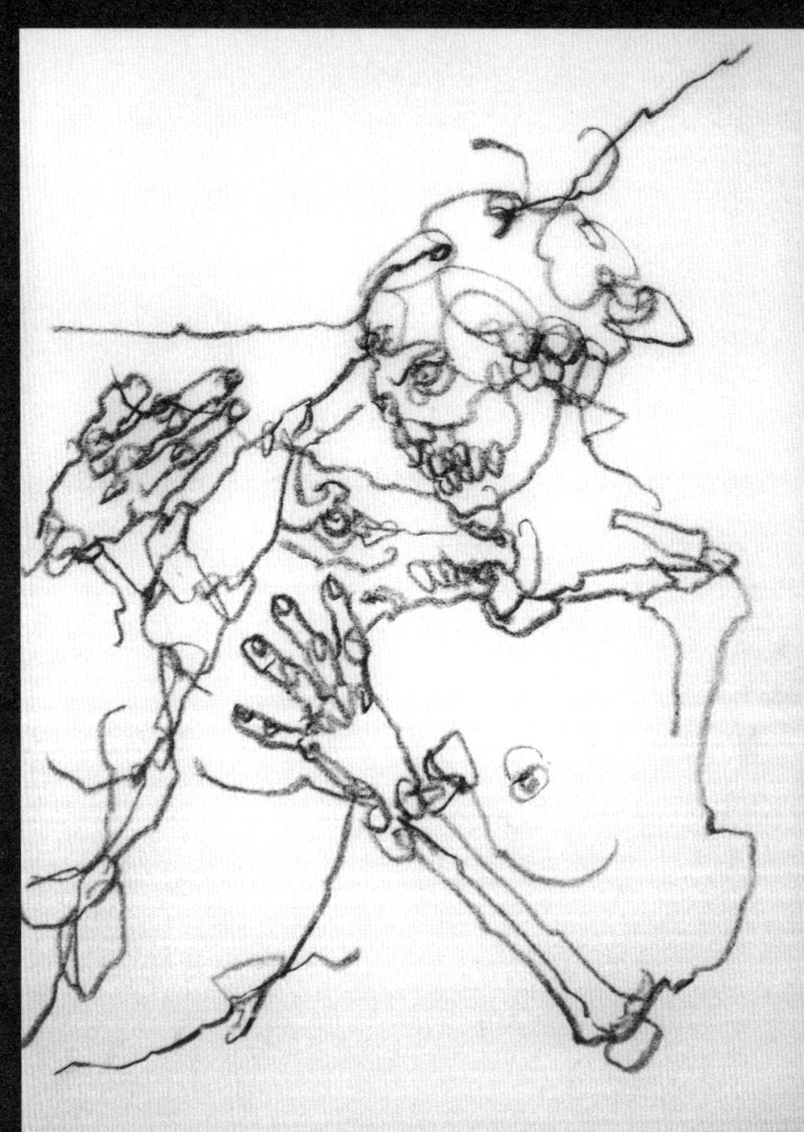

Below
Untitled CP #3
2003
Charcoal on Vellum
122 x 115 cm

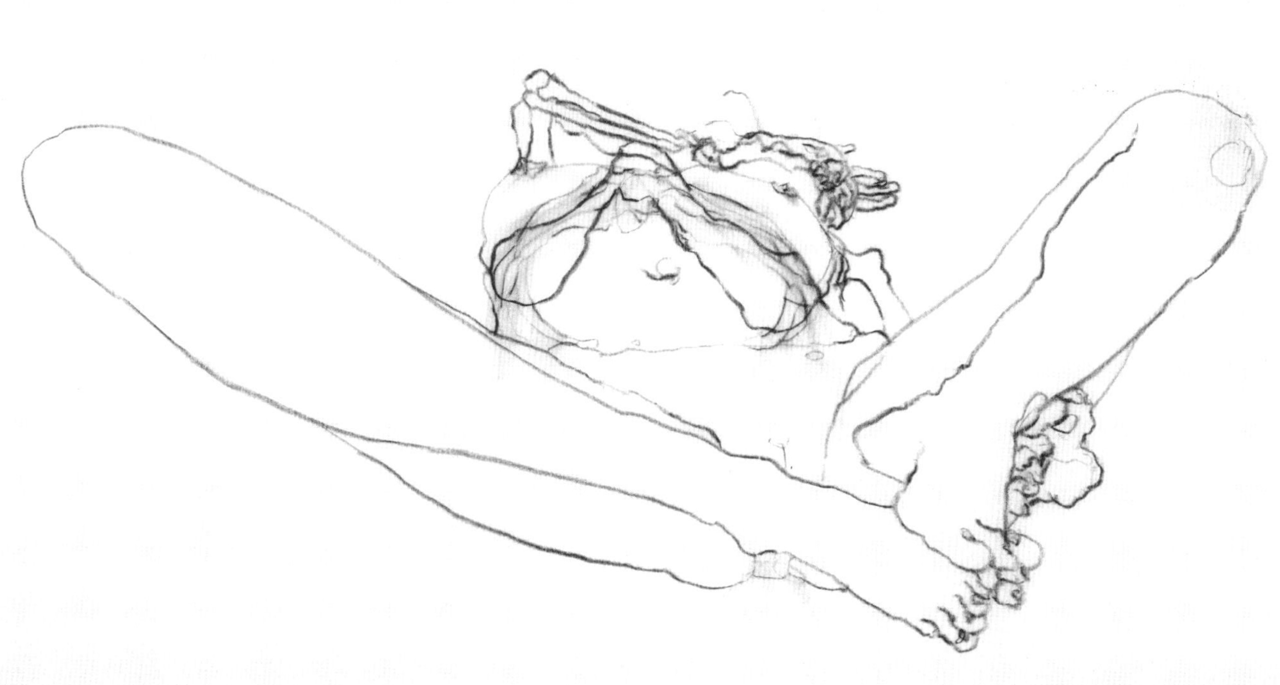

pure evil

The etymology of the word 'evil' is similar to that of the English 'over' or German 'über'. To be evil is to cross the line and transgress into a very unethical way of being. The artist Pure Evil brilliantly explores the many manifestations of the word. His moniker grew out of a dark childhood experience. 'I shot a rabbit when I was ten years old. My relatives gave me a shotgun and told me to go out and play with it. I went for a walk and played the *Deer Hunter* game. I saw two little bunny rabbits who were looking a bit *Watership Down* and I glassed them with both barrels. I thought I would shoot the gun and the rabbits would run away and that would be the end of the game. But I walked over and a rabbit was lying there with a little bead of blood coming out of his mouth. Pure Evil is the rabbit – the soul of the rabbit – that's come back to knock me out. It's like an alter ego for me. I think I'm a really scary, evil person, whereas I'm just not at all scary and evil.'

The Welsh artist originally started by creating street art. He gained notoriety by stencilling or spraying a simple scrawled image of a bad bunny with fangs on the streets of London. Yet his visual background was in pop art rather than graffiti culture. The image had accidental echoes of the San Francisco underground poster artist Frank Kozik. However, Pure Evil was also influenced by a bunny character used to advertise the Barcelona Olympics. 'I'd go out and do the bunny rabbit and "Welcome to Hell", which is something I'd read when I was going to Belgrade Station in Yugoslavia. Taking things I had experienced and placing them in a different context, like going into a church with a gun and shooting it.'

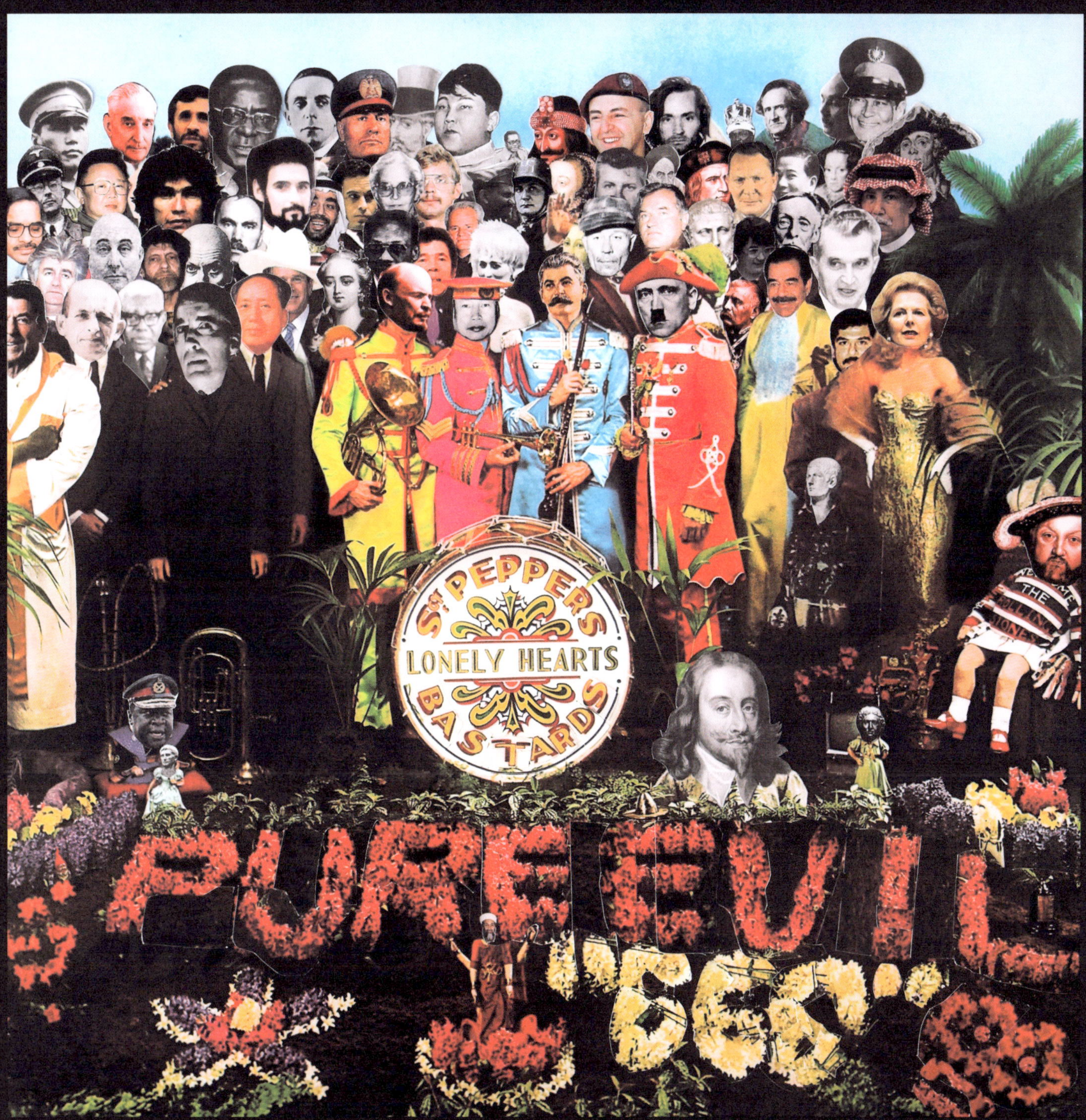
Sgt PEPPERS
LONELY HEARTS
BAS TARDS
PURE EVIL
"666"

His current work pushes these early street interventions into far more complex directions. He decided to develop the dark themes of living in the universe right now and exploring 'why people are so oblivious to a lot of things that are happening'. Pieces include neon works, marker-pen drawings on canvases, collages and paintings. All the work plays around with the idea of evil. One print combines the image of earth seen from space with the Star Wars' death star. Another disturbing collage reworks Peter Blake's album cover for The Beatles' *Sgt. Pepper's Lonely Hearts Club Band* into an image of the evil bastards throughout history. Some of his most skilful works – marker drawings on canvas – include a skeleton growing in a post-apocalyptic jungle scene. His inspiration was partly the nineteenth-century artist Félicien Rops, who created a disturbing engraving to accompany the 1866 edition of Charles Baudelaire's *Les Epaves*. Pure Evil added the names of different humanitarian disasters (Iraq, Somalia, Kosovo) in the barren landscape depicted at the base of a skeleton with outstretched, branch-like arms.

Other works play around with Banksy's model of factory paintings based on images created by the artist. In particular, Pure Evil creates humorous montages with fantasy art. Here bunny characters atop black horses prepare to fight dwarves and demons. 'I get them done in an oil-painting studio in China. I was looking through eBay and finding out a lot of places that were copying Jack Vettriano. Factory-style fine art. Fine art for the masses.' This fantasy-art series includes images of a bunny man in a loincloth coming out of a swamp of floating skulls. Another fantasy painting, entitled *Ikea Riot*, was full of trolls and monsters on the verge of violence.

Pure Evil infuses imagery of death, evil and menace with layers of comedy and humour. 'That's my way of dealing with how insane things are. With *Sgt. Pepper's Lonely Hearts Bastards*, I was putting all the heads together trying to find the biggest bastards. I had to read up on about 80 of the most horrible despots, dictators, serial killers. At the end of it I had an eerie feeling of dread from doing the actual piece. I went out and bought a UV security pen for documents and started doodling – giving Margaret Thatcher droopy boobs, writing on Pol Pot's head.' The layer of humour was only visible with a UV wand, used for scanning money. Knowing that the laughter was just under the surface was part of the pleasure. 'You got all these faces. No matter how pompous or self-important they think they are – no matter how important Mussolini thinks he is, you can always doodle on him.'

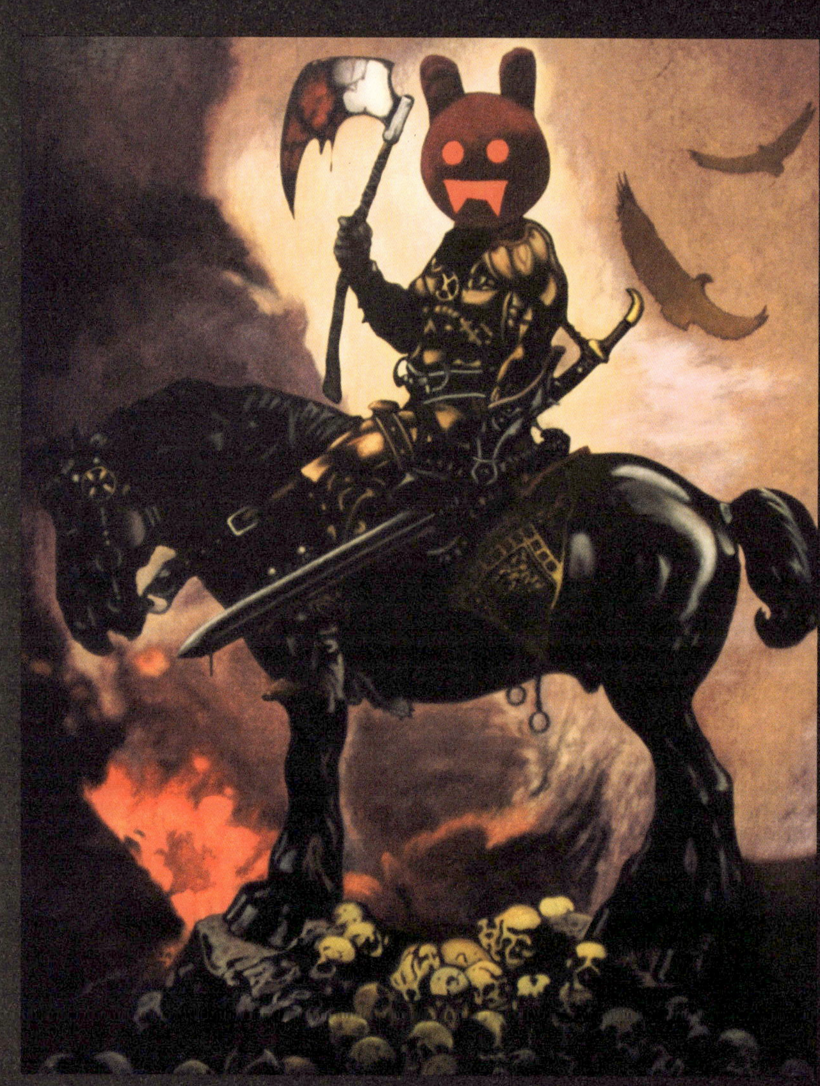

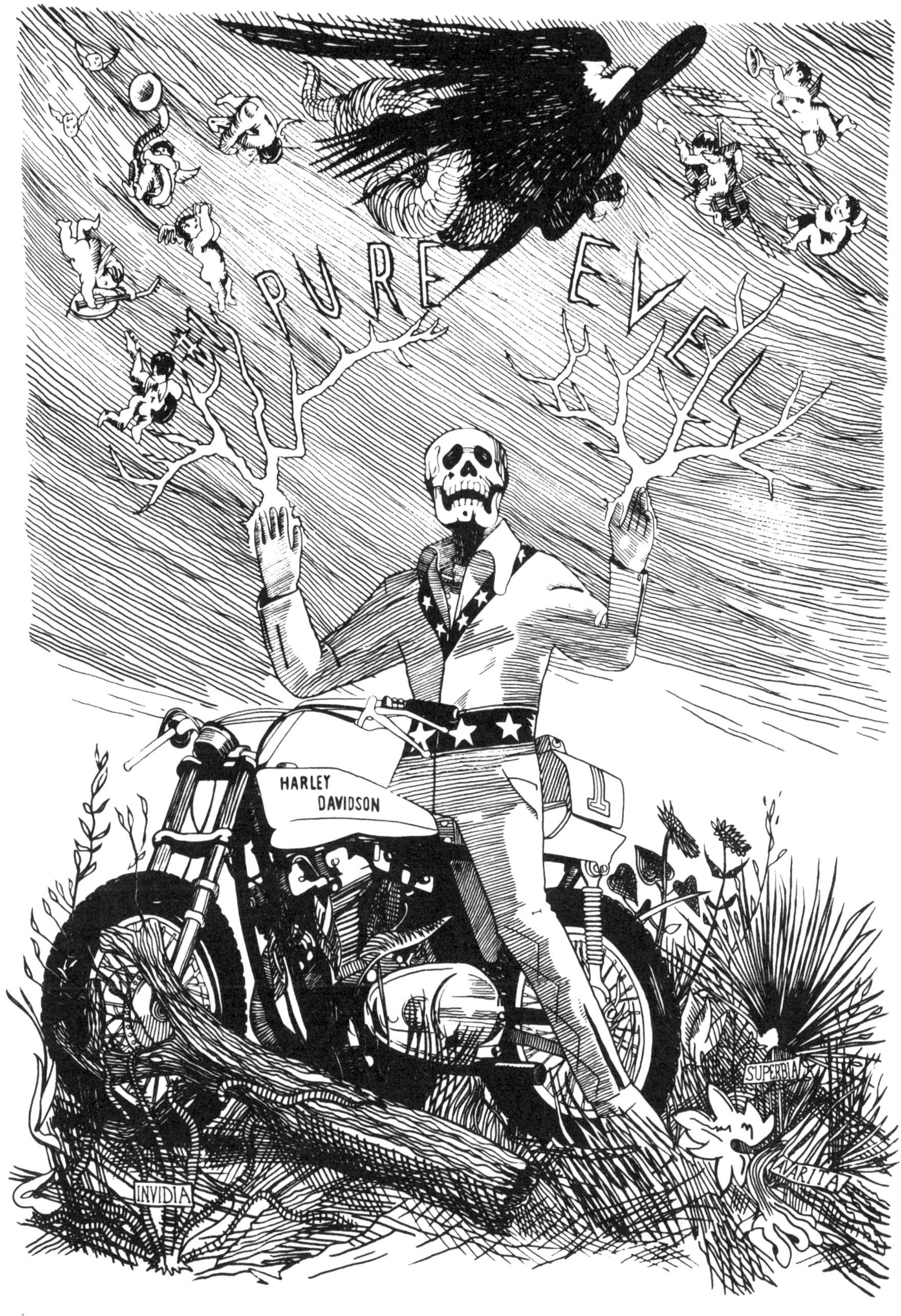

PURE EVEL
HARLEY DAVIDSON
INVIDIA
SUPERBIA
VARITAS

putrid

Sometimes a name says it all. Putrid's art is the epitome of smelly, rotting gore. The American artist's drawings follow a strong tradition of horror comics and heavy-metal illustration. The single-name moniker was part of that heritage. 'A lot of my favourite artists had a sign name and I always thought that was real fuckin' cool. My favourite comic artist Graham Ingles signed "Ghastly", which is perfect – because his work is just that. There's Pushead and Artgore. Mine came pretty naturally from a drawing I did entitled *Putrid Zombie Intercourse In Rancid Leuchorrhoea and Mephitic Chyme* – kind of my version of a Carcass song title. The first anti-hero skateboard graphic I did used this drawing and it got shortened to the Putrid board.'

His drawings have been themed around violence, gore and horror from a young age. Initially, as a child, the film *Jaws* influenced his pictures. He became obsessed with depicting sharks ripping human bodies apart. This developed into illustrations of other horror films. 'I grew up watching horror movies so every time I would watch one I'd have a string of drawings following each movie. I probably wouldn't have pursued art as enthusiastically if it had not been for the horror genre's constant bombardment on my little brain.' His work was filled with scenarios from classic horror films, including *Friday The 13th*, the *Alien* and *Predator* movies and John Carpenter's *The Thing*. The artist watches ten movies a week for inspiration and new ideas, and is specifically drawn towards 'sleazy, splatter flicks' and exploitation film from the 1960s onwards. Sometimes he works directly from

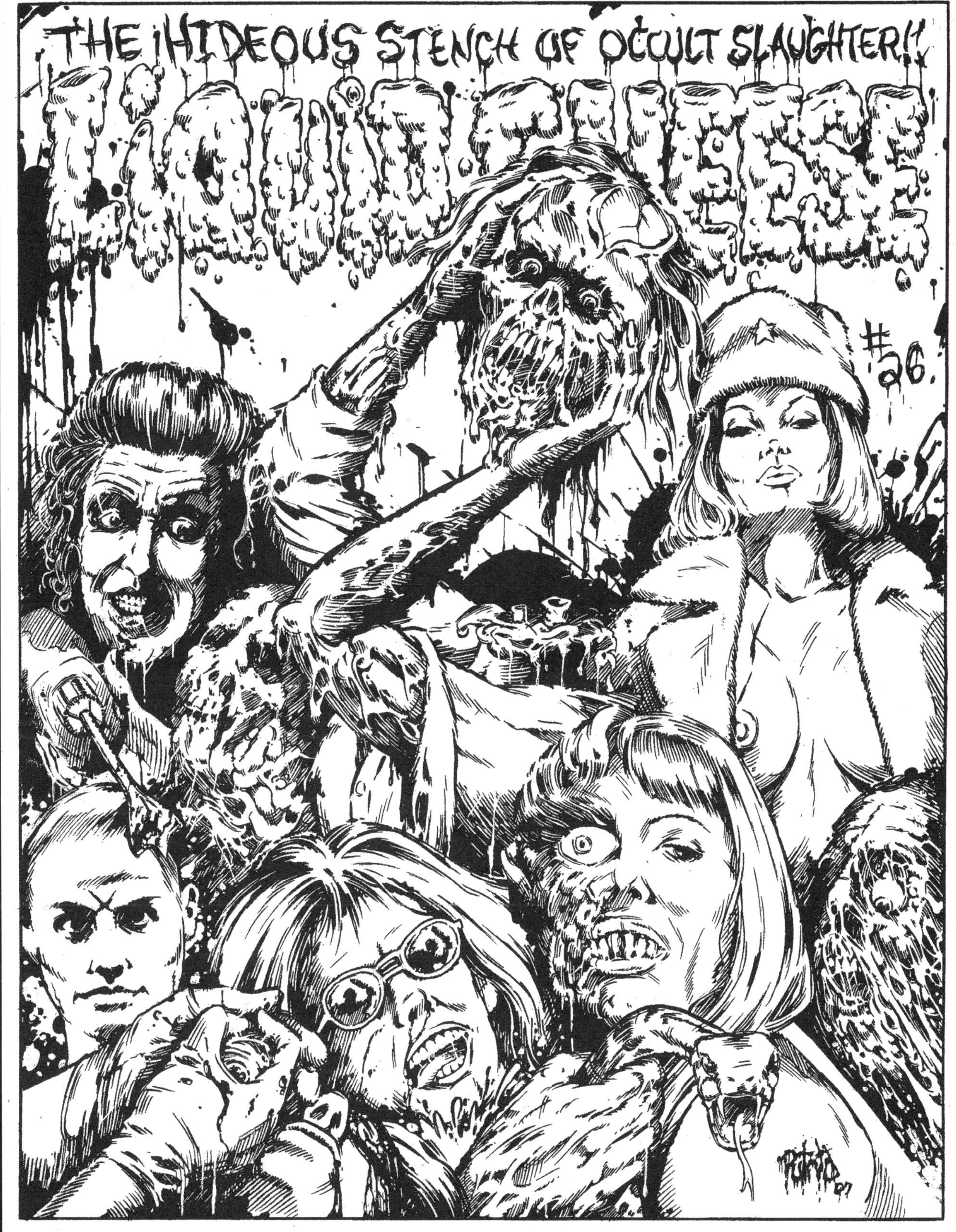
THE HIDEOUS STENCH OF OCCULT SLAUGHTER!!
LIQUID FLESH
#26.
PUTRID 07

stills, or he works from his imagination, filled with the imagery he collects on screen.

Putrid is essentially self-taught, but his work is not just a reflection of horror films. He is fascinated by the expression of horror in art, music and literature. His work fuses horror comics, the more extreme end of skateboard graphics and death-metal band cover art and T-shirt images. Much of his work is for death-metal bands with delightfully violent names, including Blood Freak, Frightmare, Razorback Records, Fondlecorpse, Cardiac Arrest, Bowel Stew, Plerosis, Ghoul, Reeker and Impetigo. His work focuses on full-on gore and violence, rather than fear or dramatic tension. In particular, he is drawn to pictures of people decomposing or being disembowelled. In his work, people are literally falling apart. It could be interpreted as an interesting vision of contemporary humanity and the collapse of personal identity. 'I've been drawing this stuff for so long it's just what I like to draw and know how to draw. If I didn't draw gore I wouldn't even know where to start.' He enthuses about the pleasure of drawing guts, entrails and especially the large intestine. That 'bodiliness' is what makes his drawings so effective. The body is ripped apart, exposed and shoved in the face of the viewer. 'I get a laugh out of someone telling me I'm weird, but most of the time I'm not shooting for shock value. Some pieces I wanted to do just to see how gnarly I could make them, but for the most part I draw what I like and if you like it or not it doesn't really matter.'

The artist is currently working on his first short horror/gore/porn comic for *Sleazy Slice* – a small publication from Robin Bougie, the creator of the exploitation porn film zine *Cinema Sewer*. Horror comics are a major influence on his sense of narrative. Often monochrome, Putrid's pieces are brilliantly extreme: heads are decapitated and held aloft as their skin melts; limbs are cut off; everything seems to be in a constant state of dissolution. Often there are medical references in the imagery, such as an insane 'Doctor Gore' attacking patients and turning them into bloodied carcasses. This is the B-movie horror of slasher films and underground band culture.

There is nothing serious about this imagery. It is drawn with skill and imagination and brims with acid, extreme humour. 'If I'm drawing a zombie dude fucking and cutting a girl's tits off, it's all in good humour – albeit slightly deranged to the "normal" person.' His work is consciously pushing the boundaries of what is acceptable. The aim here is still to laugh at how extreme and ridiculous his scenarios are. These are the bad fantasies of humanity at their most vile and outrageous.

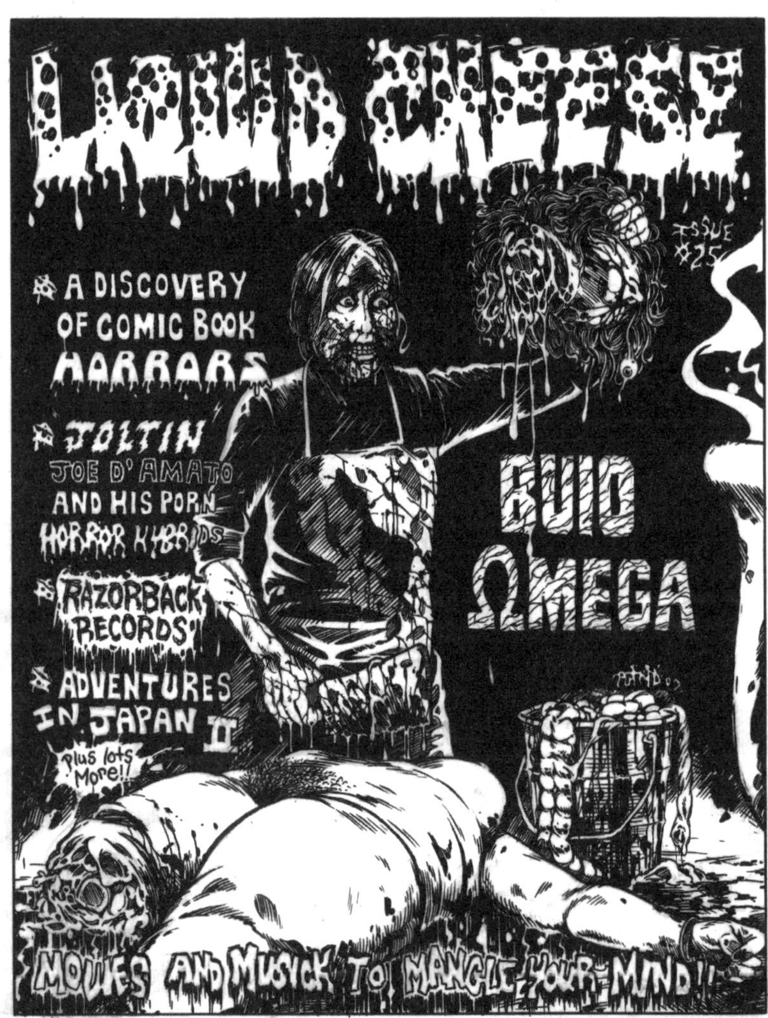

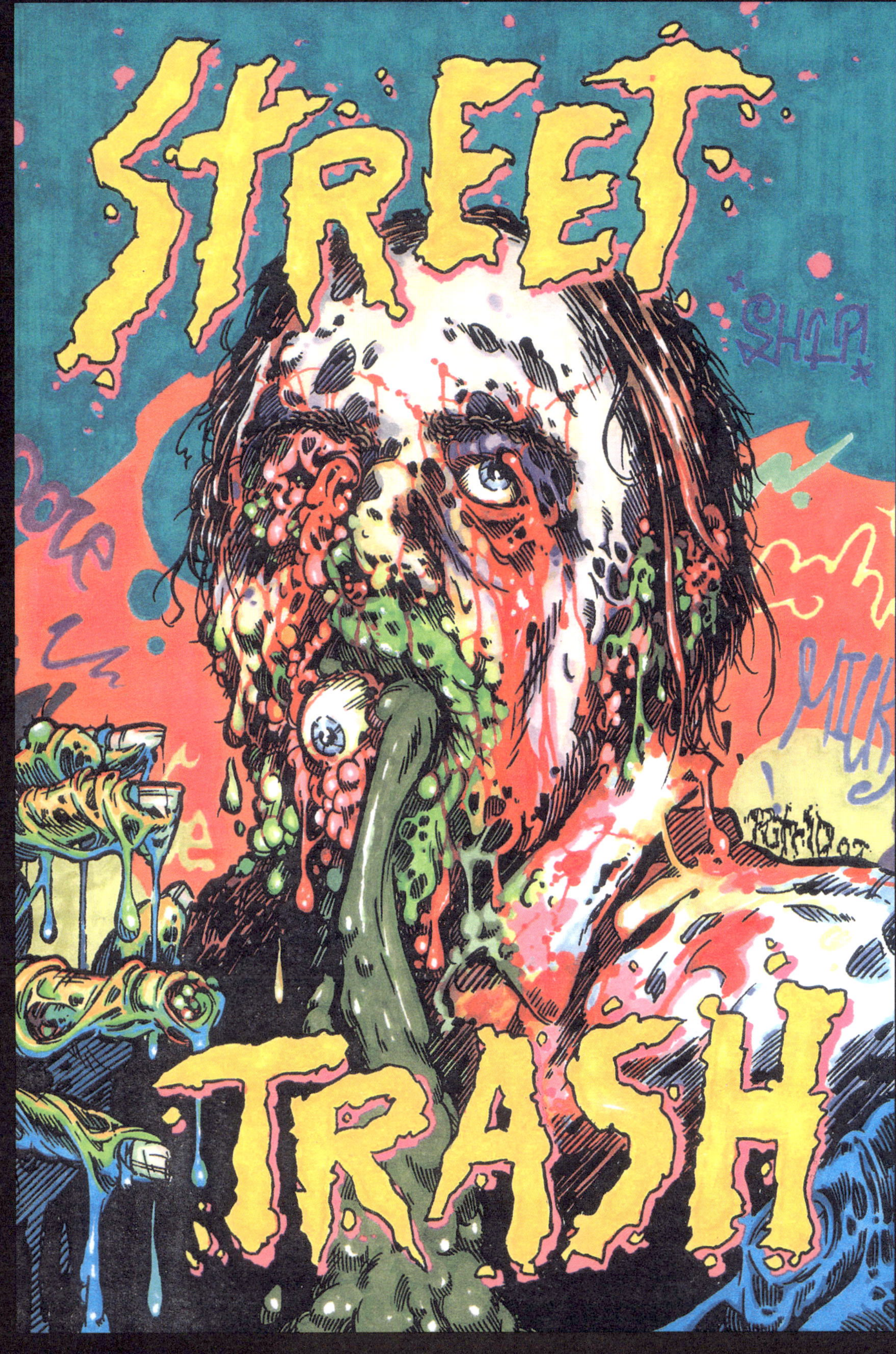
STREET
TRASH

boo saville

oo Saville seems to be constantly searching for answers as to who we are. Her early work focused on animals and monkeys, but she has moved on to look at the history of humanity itself. She makes images of bog men and mummies, bodies preserved in death. Often they are created in pencil. A sense of closeness is central to her approach to drawing. 'It enables me to concentrate on the surface in a more intimate way. In drawing, I can focus on the materiality of the drawing, which can be as interesting as the image. It is a good vehicle to explore the content in my work.' Initially, she made works on paper as preliminary sketches for larger paintings, but increasingly the sketches themselves have become the final results in their own right.

There is something fluid about Saville's approach. Her images seem to melt or drip. It makes sense that her influences include Francis Bacon and Marlene Dumas. Like the work of these two artists, her pieces have a sense of blurring or bending, a fluidity between violence and pensive emotion. For Saville, it is about the contrast between horror and the sublime. 'I am interested in both the polarity of life and the beginning and the end of things. When working with extreme feelings and states of being, you inevitably find unnerving, intense imagery. Looking at a dead body can be either fascinating or terrifying, but it is always compelling. I think the imagery I am currently using is very gothic, although I don't look at things in these terms. Some images just demand to be seen. By taking it and drawing it, you fetishize the surface and it becomes more provocative. I like that there

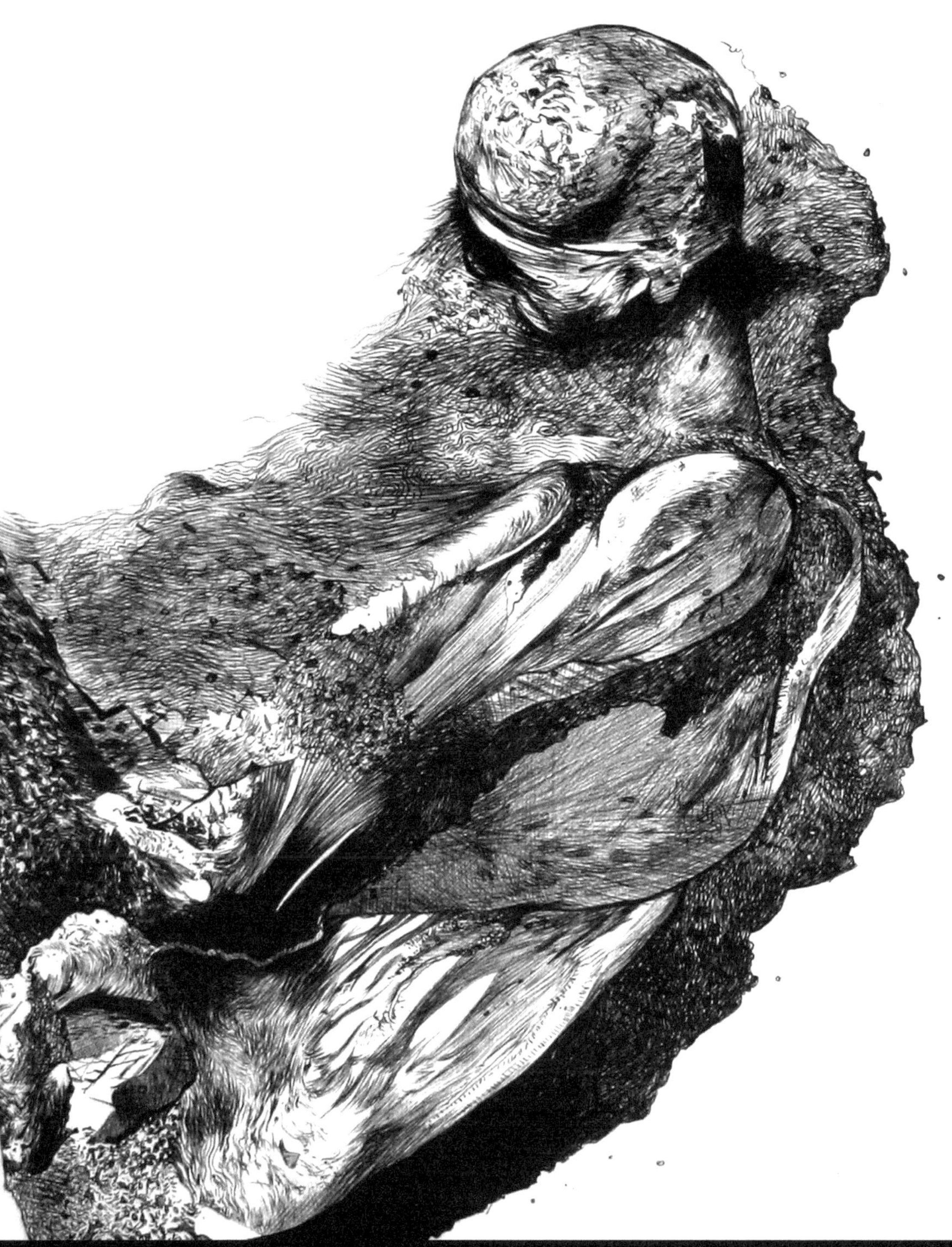

is a contradiction or battle between images, which are both terrifying and beautiful.' She argues that beauty and horror cannot exist except in contrast to each other.

Bog men and mummified bodies often feature in her work. 'I found a book on the Lindow Man in a charity shop a few years ago and I was fascinated by it. There was so much mythology and beauty surrounding this ancient figure. It was literally frozen into the ground – his moment of death had been captured. I remember being in Italy and seeing the bodies of the people who perished when Mount Vesuvius erupted at Pompeii. The people had been killed running away from the lava, frozen and screaming. Since then, I have always wanted to make work about this.' She often researches her work at the Wellcome Institute and Natural History Museum in London, as well as at the Pitt Rivers Museum in Oxford. A process of cultural archaeology informs her approach.

Her figures are frozen in perpetual action, arrested at the moment of death. For Saville, these bodies echo the crucifixion. 'An image of Christ dying on the cross is both soothing and frightening. I am looking for some evidence or proof of life. If a person is sitting in a chair and gets up to leave, the chair continues to stay warm. I believe life can often be determined when there is an absence of it.' Many of her figures are curled up in a foetal position, a common position as death approaches. There is an ambiguity to these figures, which inhabit a space between sleep, death and birth, and could be in all three states simultaneously.

Moving away from the bog men, she is now looking at mummification and burial rituals. Her work is focusing on more monstrous representations of the human form. Her figures are increasingly drawn from behind, their faces hidden and unseen. 'The image of the man's back was so mysterious to me. There is something amazing and horrible about being squashed face first into the dirt – becoming part of the earth.'

Saville's work touches on visual disintegration. In some pieces a face looks as if it is melting. In other works, a body is being torn and ripped up. 'I believe creativity is in part destructive. I can never tell how a picture is going to end up. You can play with an image and remove or add parts to make it more or less interesting. Things become more beautiful at the point of destruction.'

Previous spread
Flat Man
2006
Ballpoint pen on paper
40 cm x 40 cm

Below
Bogman
2006
Ballpoint pen on paper
100 cm x 180 cm

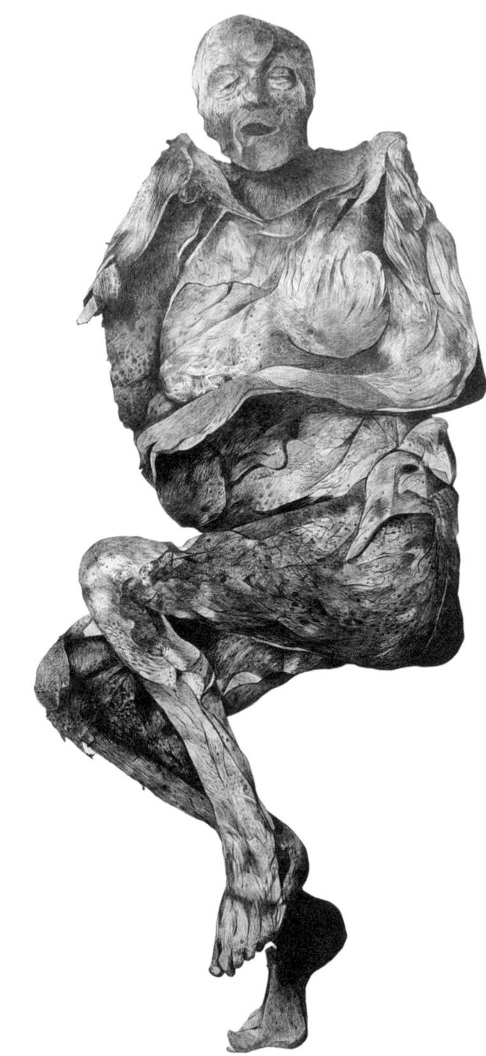

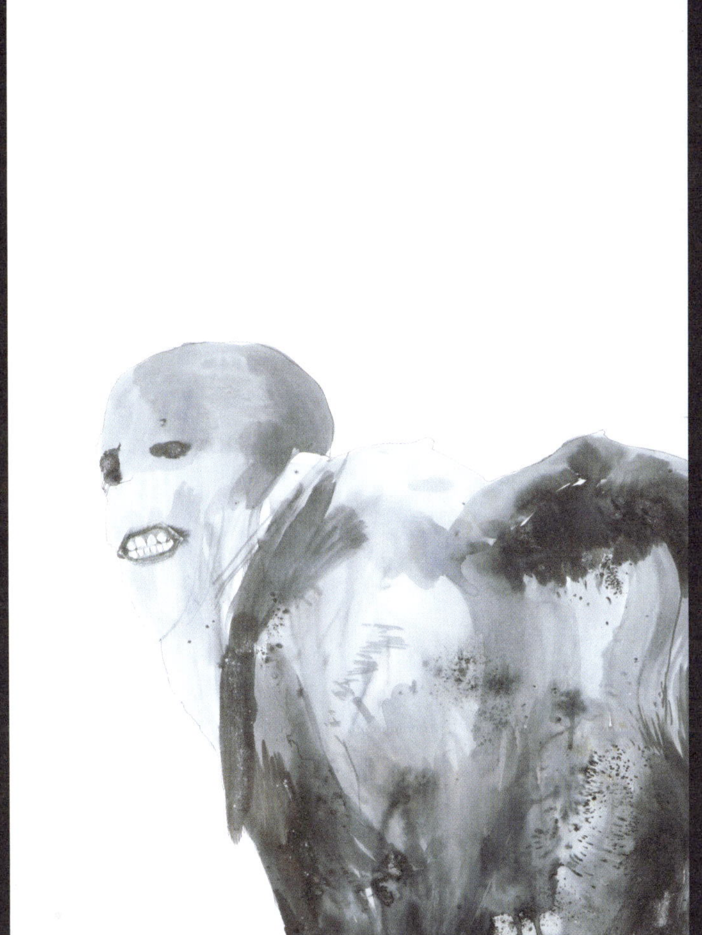

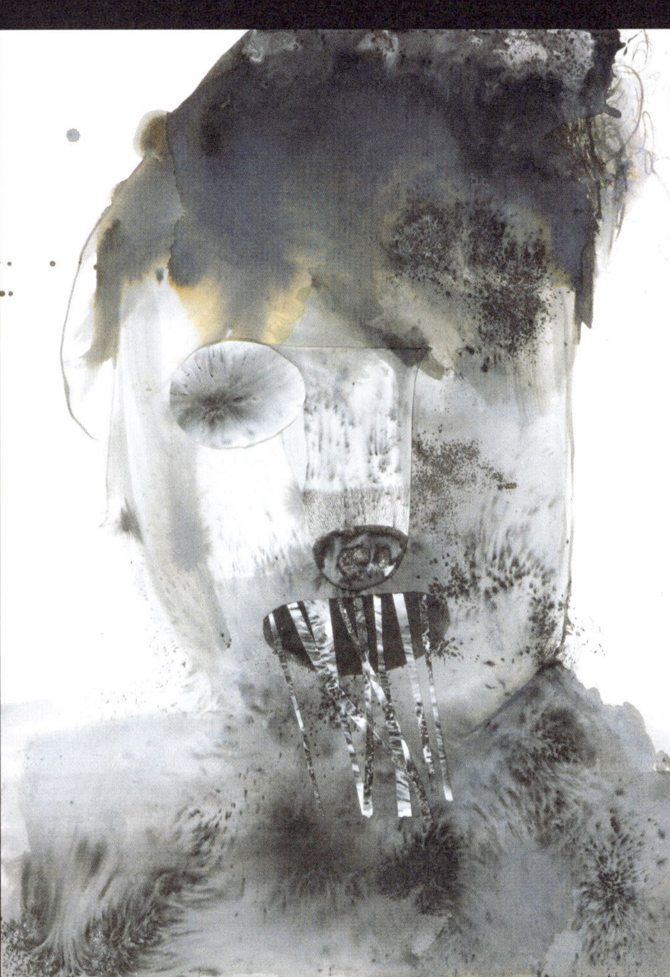

bill saylor

ill Saylor's upbringing was a strong influence on his approach to art. 'A big part of my creative background was growing up next to my grandfather's farm, which he converted into a road-construction business just outside Philadelphia. The whole family had connecting properties and all my aunts, uncles and cousins had serious hobbies – woodcarving, ceramics, motorcycles, hunting. My mother's was painting; my father's was pigeon racing. So I grew up with a lot of things going on around me. Turning a Volkswagen into a horse trailer was no big deal.' At eighteen, Saylor moved to California to study drawing and painting. After travelling in Europe, he settled in New York where he worked in the studios of the artists Ross Bleckner and Julian Schnabel. He then began to exhibit.

Dark imagery has always been central to Saylor's work. 'I've always had an element of blackness to my work. I guess it comforts me. While I was in school, a visiting professor from Germany gave me a copy of Joseph Beuys's book *The Secret Block for a Secret Person in Ireland*. It's an incredible book of delicate drawings and was a big influence on the way I pursued my image-making – mixing elements of death and nature, while hopefully keeping a great deal of mystery and beauty.'

There's an interesting contrast in Saylor's work between a preoccupation with the imagery of death and a colourful approach using bright and vibrant colours. His painting of bats shows them on a background of delicate yellows and turquoise. Monstrous hybrids are depicted in dazzling reds and blues. 'I've always had a natural tendency towards rich colour. I spent

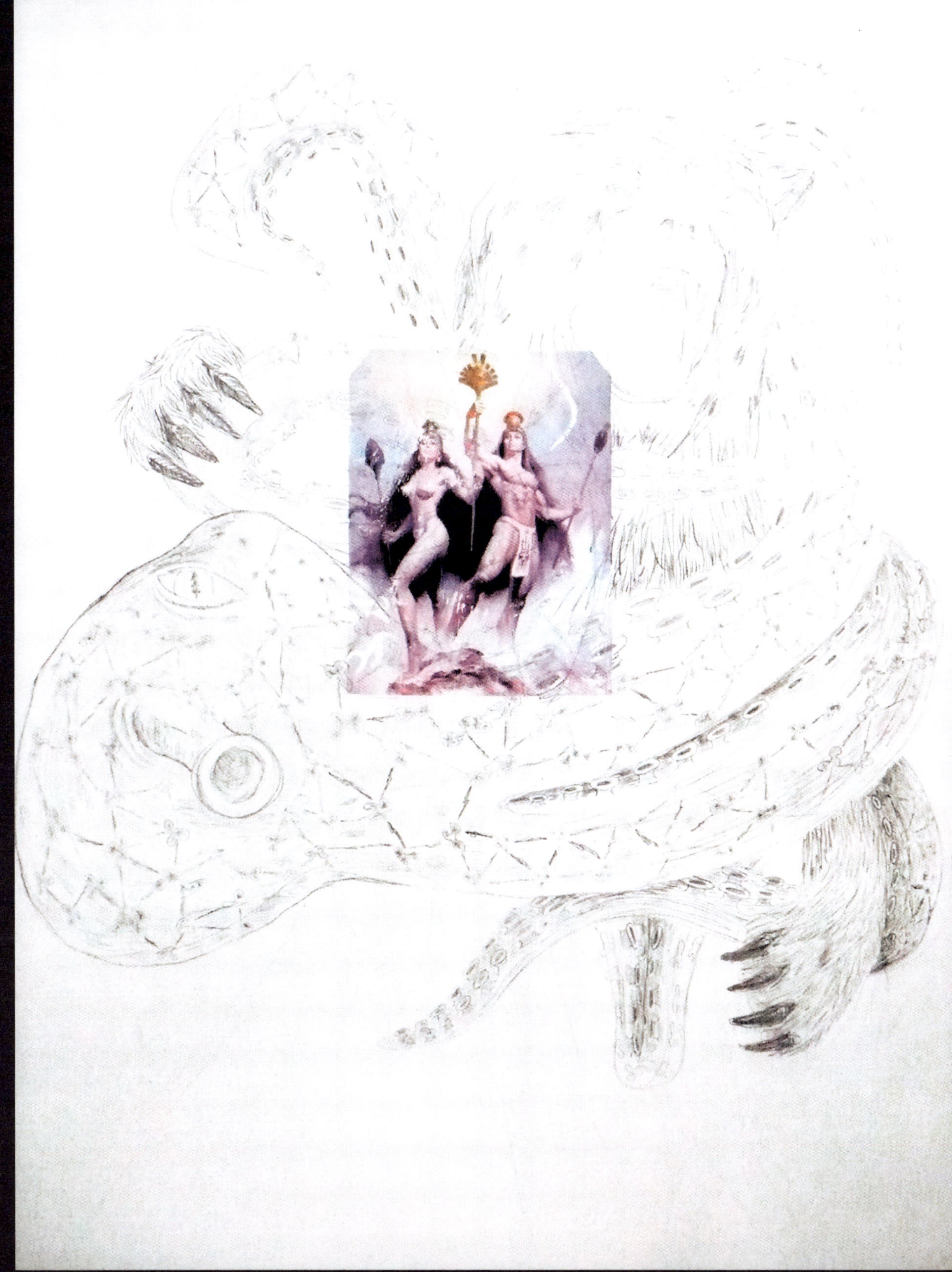

a lot of time in the ocean off Santa Barbara, surfing and diving. I remember the marine life there being very psychedelic – the drugs there were also very psychedelic.' The vibrancy of his palette is an interesting foil to Saylor's darker imagery and outlook. 'I do like the complexity it brings into the visual language, the tension created and the balancing act needed to keep it from imploding on itself.'

There is a sense of freeness in Saylor's work – something wild and unrestrained about his brushstrokes and lines. 'I like a bit of speed when I work. It keeps you honest. Not thinking; just working with what's at the tips of your fingers.' Saylor largely uses oils for paintings and gouache or watercolour for his drawings. 'I make a lot of drawings. Some are just like notes that I leave on the floor for reference when I work. Others are larger and more involved.'

He often quotes directly from found images in his pieces. Sometimes he places a photographic image at the centre of the page and draws around it. A reproduction of a fantasy painting of two heroic figures in loincloths, for example, is surrounded by a drawing of a giant bear wrestling a snake. His research comes from books and magazines on natural history, science or movie-making. Or he searches the Internet for taxidermy and costume shops. There are many references to natural history, especially to animals associated with violence or decay. 'I see vultures and snakes all the time in Pennsylvania, where I still have a small house. The vultures fly over, looking for road kill or fish. You see them eating the deer that get killed by cars. They look so prehistoric – it's like going back in time.'

Motorcycle and biker imagery are also recurring motifs. Saylor's interest grew after reading Sonny Barger's and Hunter S. Thompson's books on Hell's Angels. 'I just got interested in how they developed as a subculture in America and represented an end to the 1960s – to now becoming some dark undercurrent in America, like the mob. Plus the older choppers are just sexy. Real blue-collar sculptures.'

Despite this strong imagery of male icons and violent animals, Saylor's paintings can be almost ethereal. Many pieces are often faint and distant. Saylor taps directly into a child-like doodling approach and a sense of unrestricted imagination. There are skulls or roaring bears, but there are also topless women, robots and even innocuous pet birds. Often the organic and the mechanical sit side by side in almost psychedelic crests or coats of honour.

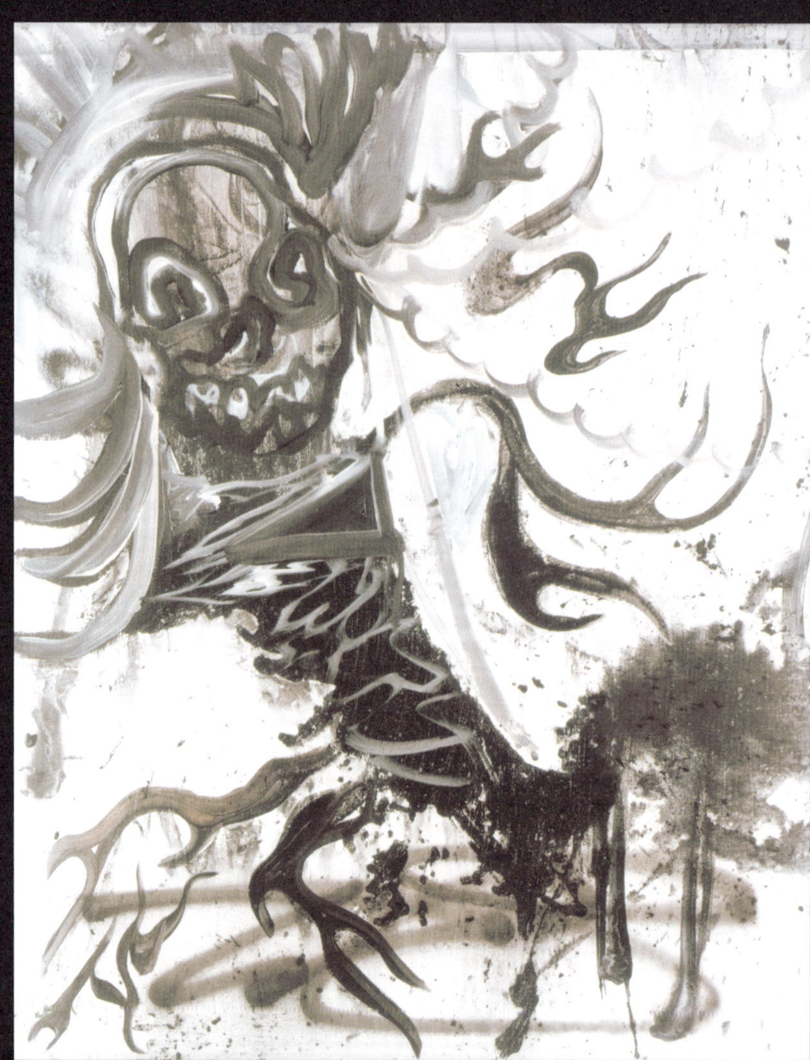

Right
Untitled
2003
Watercolour, graphite
and collage on paper
98 x 75 cm
Courtesy Galleri Loyal,
Stockholm

Below (left)
Anti Siesta
2007
Oil on canvas
160 x 130 cm
Courtesy Galleri Loyal,
Stockholm

Below (right)
Chill Seeker
2007
Oil on canvas
152 x 122 cm
Courtesy Galleri Loyal,
Stockholm

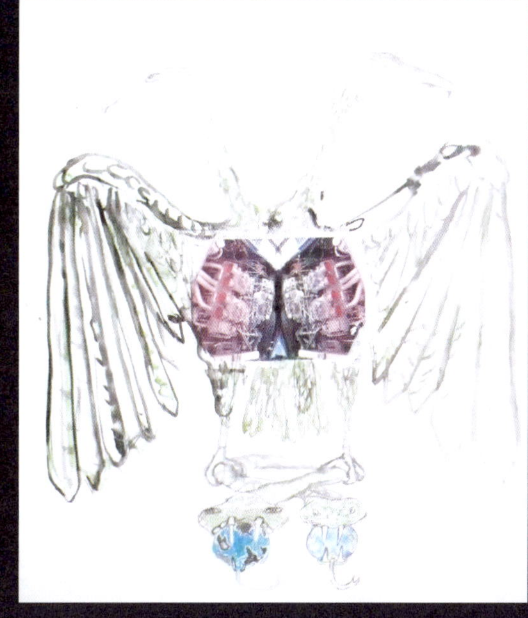

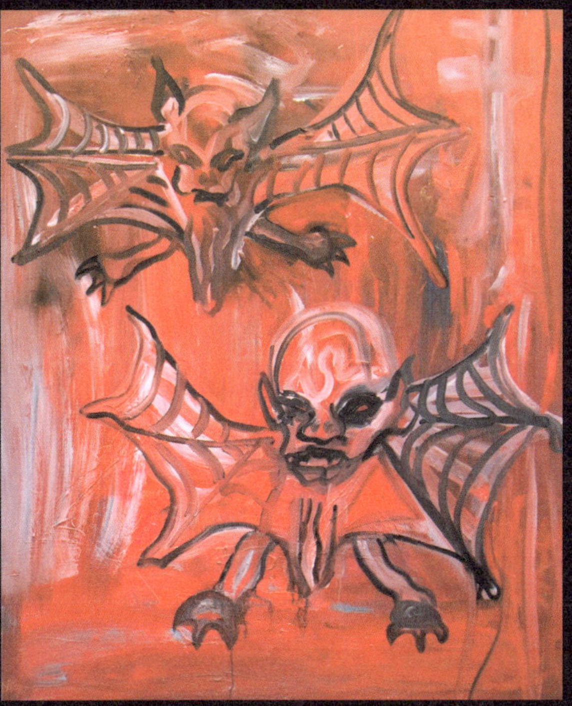

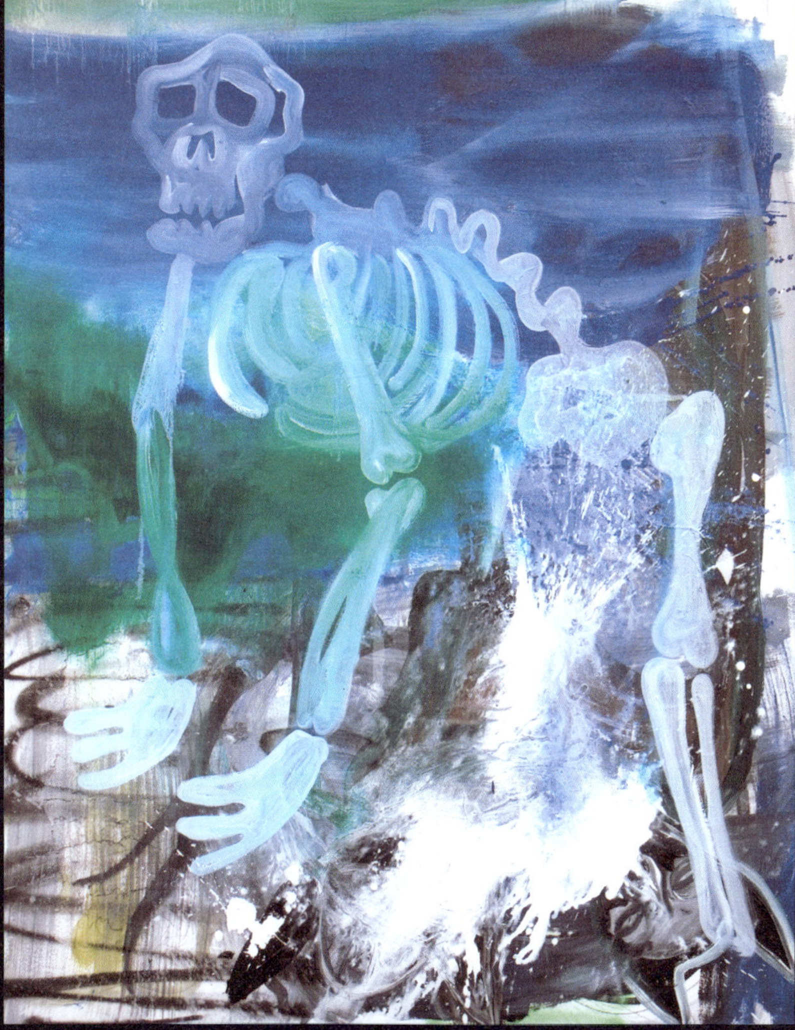

noe sendas

The image of the outsider has always been an object of fear and suspicion in Western culture. Noe Sendas's sculptural figures harness that sense of distrust and force the viewer to address it. The Portuguese artist, born in Belgium and raised in London, began creating his life-size figures as a by-product of making work using found film footage. 'I found myself filming uncanny every-day situations, mainly more exposed people, street wanderers.' He edited these images so they had no context. 'I only had these strange lost actions. I was relating these situations to known characters taken from paintings and literary works.' He began to mould characters around his own body, rather than film homeless people in real life. 'It was like having a football in my hands and turning it inside out. I built these characters from within and I can do whatever I want with them, just like a writer.'

Sendas's 'characters' are often alone and entirely still. 'It was like a duel; I had to take the floor from under their feet. I had to create situations where they would not look stiff, but rather restrained or exhausted.' The outsiders are often hunched over as if in physical or emotional pain or intensely exhausted. Nameless and faceless, the characters would be named after a location or action. 'I relate to these figures exactly as a writer or a filmmaker relates to his characters.'

There's something very disturbing and tense about being able to come so close to a figure, trying to sense if it is dead or alive. *Versus* is a hunched, long-haired loner surrounded by many small mirrors. The installation reflects the creature, but he has no face. 'I had been dealing with the idea of impersonating, but it

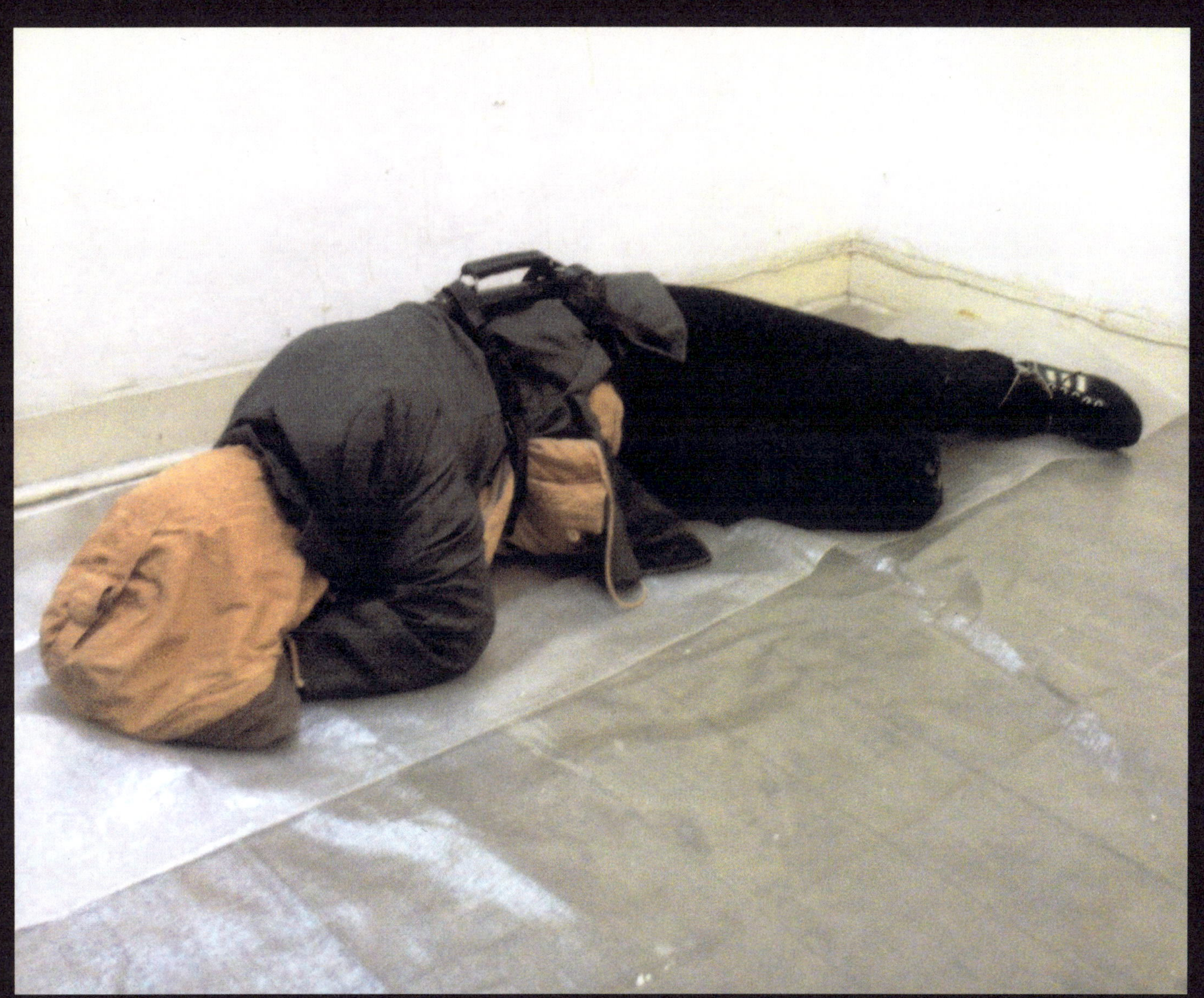

really started when I found a photo of Bruce Nau-
man impersonating Samuel Beckett, who was, in
turn, impersonating Antoine Artaud, the king of the
impersonators. *Versus* was my own impersonation of
them. This character is really a frozen impersonator
of an artist in a creative moment.'

The bodies are made in different ways – some
slickly, while others are stuffed with 'bits and pieces
that were lying in the studio', before being coated
with resin. They are often dressed in classic John Doe
anonymous outfits – the trench coat or the forgettable
suit. They are abandoned on shelves, squashed into
suitcases, hunched over on benches or hiding with
their heads in buckets. 'One of the decisions I made
when I started thinking of these characters was that
they were in a given situation because of their own
will, and not out of exterior social pressure. Like the
figure in the suitcase; I first tried it myself, to make
sure that anyone could fit in that position by himself.
What interests me is how strange an action looks,
while, at the same time, it is so normal.'

The facelessness of his figures is part of what
makes viewing them so uncomfortable. Often the
characters' heads are covered with long, unkempt
black hair. What lies beneath is unclear. 'The viewer
can project anything on to these bodies without faces.
In a recent sculpture, *The Collector*, I give the illusion
of finally presenting a face, but when you look at it,
it is slashed. The form of the slash was taken from
the slashed canvas found in Bacon's studio after his
death. Its interior is a black void, and if you look
with more attention you can see yourself reflected in
a black mirror.' The viewer becomes an active part
of the sculpture. This mirroring happens in an earlier work, *Eye Cast*, where a mirror is placed beneath
a hole in a studio bench. When the viewer looks in
they are confronted with their own eye framed by
a screaming face.

Sendas's work plays with the boundary between
truth and fiction. Reality itself is brought into
question. His lifelike approach has had unexpected
effects. 'I was taken by surprise when one night,
before an opening, I received a call from a curator
saying that the police had tried to arrest one of my
pieces and that they had beaten it up, breaking its
neck, and that some people called an ambulance. To
me, it was like someone reading a book and phoning
the police to arrest the main character.'

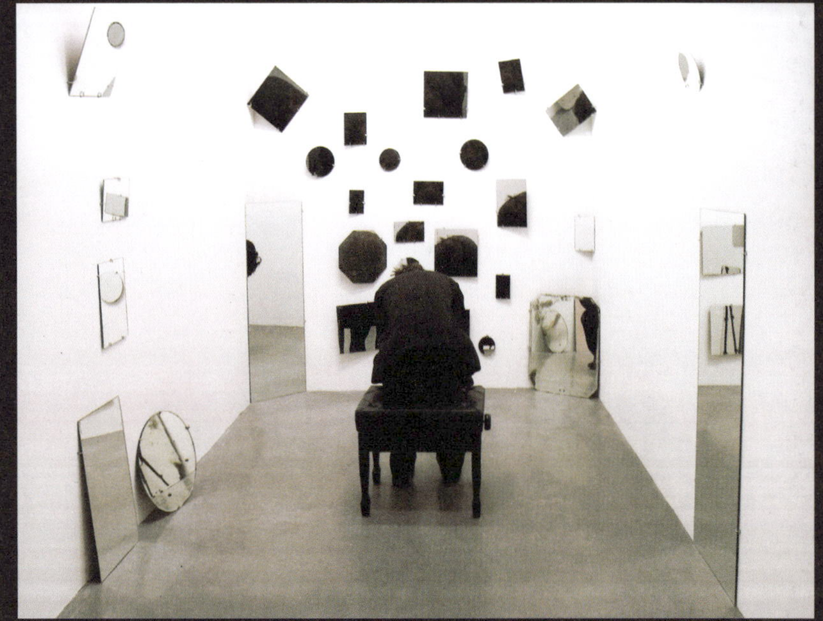

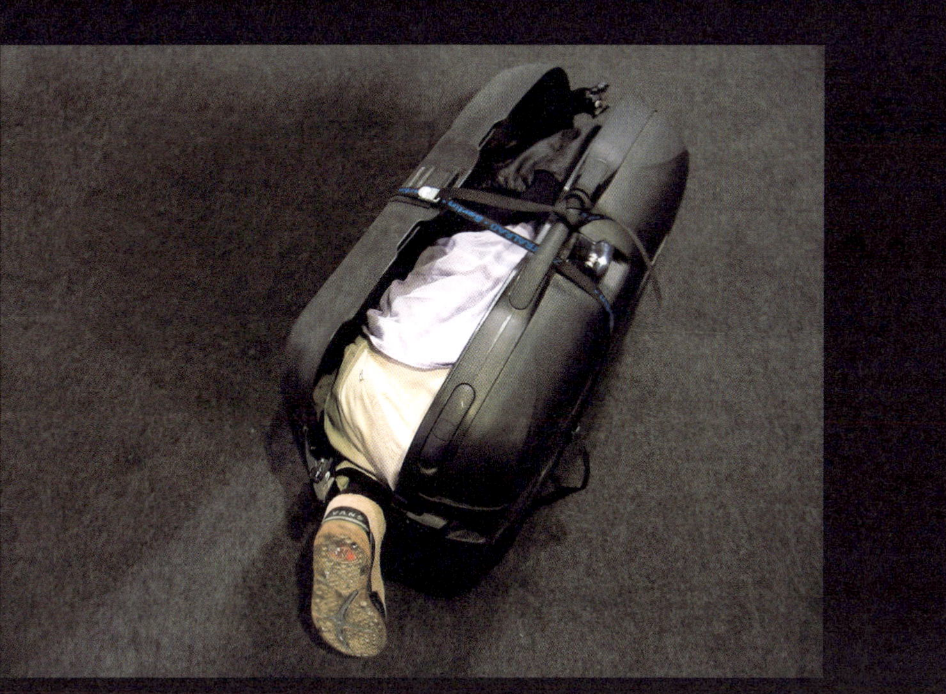

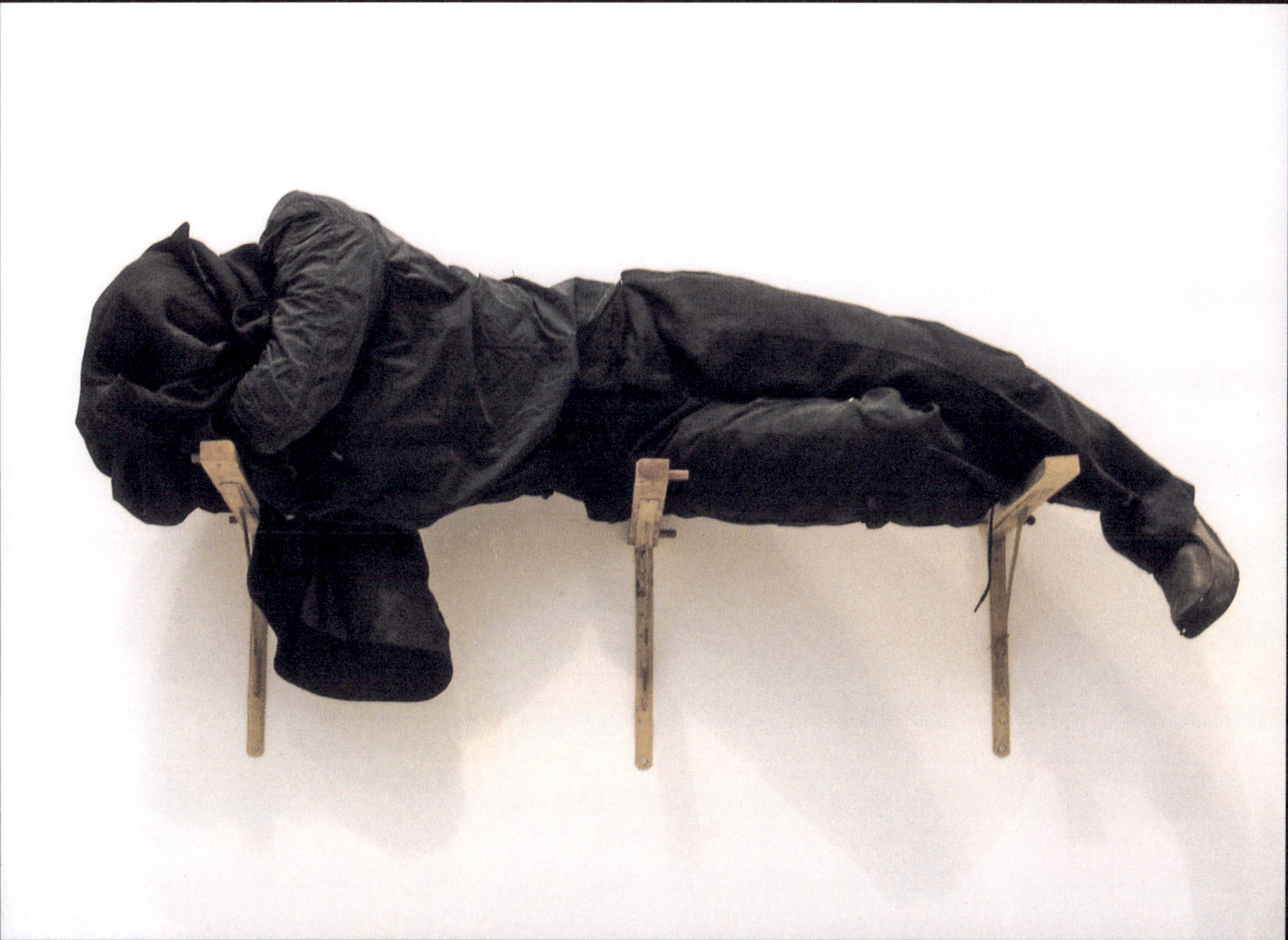

ricky swallow

It is hard to surpass the breadth of Ricky Swallow's technical skill. His work moves fluidly from paint and drawing to intricate, perfectly finished carved wood. 'I like the Adam Phillips notion that "weak obstacles impoverish us". The techniques I employ are tactics to keep myself from becoming an obsolescent medium within the practice. I never studied sculpture or any specific technique. Since art school I've been more of a medium pirate, bootlegging various genres and traditions.'

Swallow taught himself to create his wood pieces. 'Out of a desire to make myself uncomfortable in the studio, I started making the works from wood. It's a moment filled with both anxiety and excitement. It is hilarious to me now, but I found this book, *How to Carve Realistic Birds* by David Tippery. It was something I learnt as it happened. I feel like the way I work was also shaped by the kind of things I was carving.'

He often uses wood to depict bones or dismembered body parts. The connection between wood as a living thing and the human body is made explicit. 'Circulation is an important part of the work, and that's within the grain of the wood itself. Trees are a type of body. They contain limbs, growth rings and other human attributes,' he points out. His sculptures of body parts are detached fragments, existing as independent forms. There is an interesting tension between the dead/alive wood and the dead/alive animals or objects Swallow depicts.

His creatures and body parts are usually sprawled on the ground and dead. Even when they appear to be alive, they have the scent of death. This is clear in Swallow's drawing and sculpture showing a snake sliding through

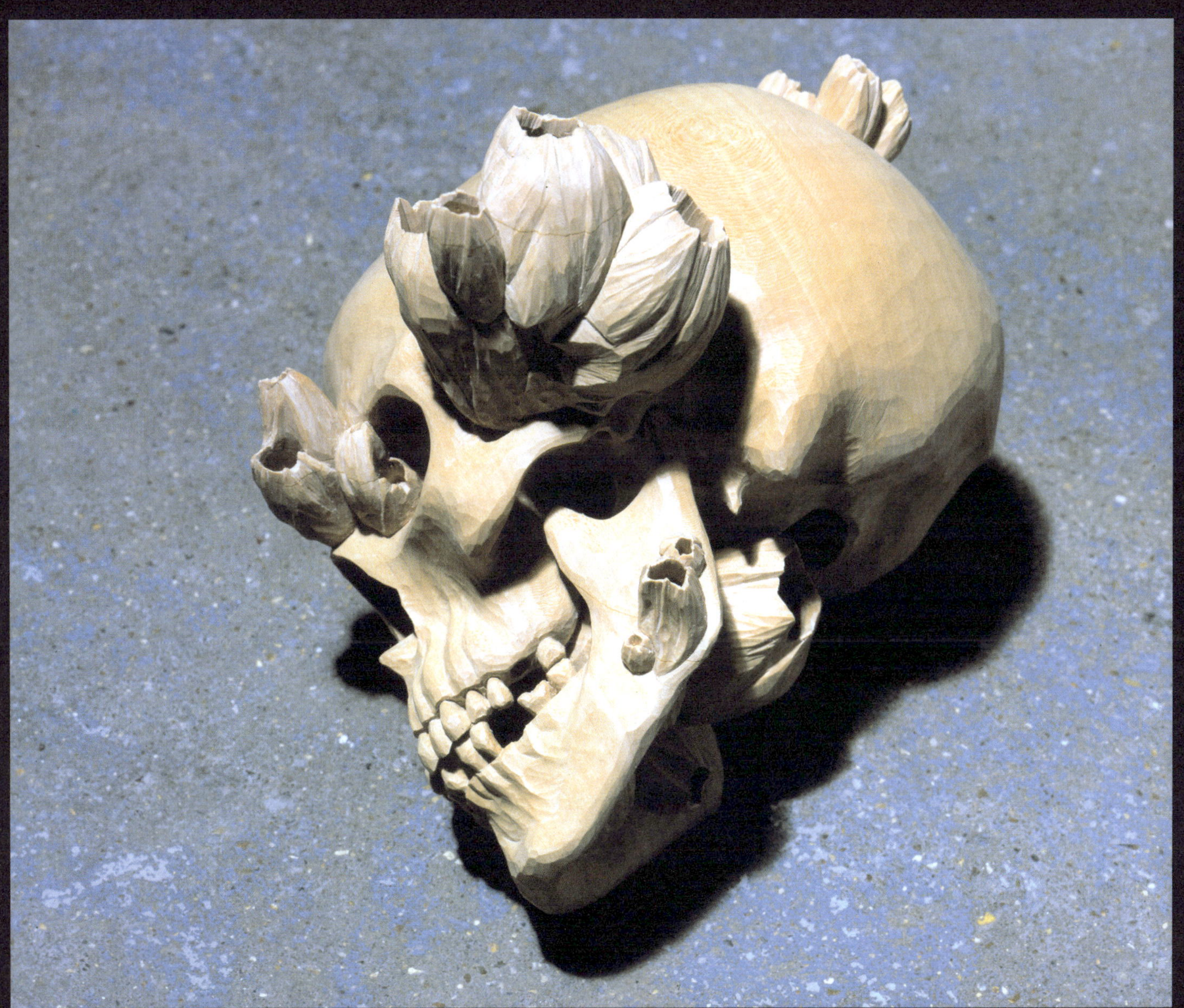

discarded cycling gear. 'The snakes inhabit the cycle helmet as a sculpture and create this third object or organ as a result.' The snake forces a collapse between interior and exterior space.

There is an intentional connection to the Dutch traditions of still lifes and seventeenth-century vanitas paintings in Swallow's work. He explores how still lifes comment on the transience of life and the emptiness of earthly existence – artistic reminders of human mortality. He is fascinated by the contradiction within the *memento mori* tradition. On one hand the works admonish the vanity connected with material and earthly belongings, yet on the other hand these material objects are painted with lavish and obsessive detail. In a similar way to the Dutch paintings of Harmen Steenwyck or Jan Treck, time is the main idea behind Swallow's pieces. When something becomes sculpture, it is fixed against diminishing time. Instead of the finality or darkness of death, Swallow strives for something more flexible.

The aesthetics of death seem to feed into many of his pieces. Skulls and skeletons are central, recurring themes. His sculptures beautifully depict the detritus of death – a lost shoe is thrown from an accident and lodged on to jagged wood, skulls decay until they are covered in barnacles. 'The skull is this tactile full stop, the most universal of death's symbols. Yet it walks and talks – from the Dance of Death to The Grateful Dead. I've made skulls as a way to imply the premature death of previous sculptures, and other times I've carved skeletons and bones there's activity or again "circulation" occurring. There's an empathy in death that I'm trying to reach, something beautiful beyond decay, within a structure both poetic and formal.'

Swallow sees drawing as a more malleable part of his practice, 'akin to a vacation'. He created a group of drawings based on postcards from the Palermo catacombs depicting comically dressed skeletons in officers' uniforms or aristocratic attire. 'The clothes become these plinth-like supports for the precarious skulls. The colouration of the cards is strange, like hand-coloured black and white shots.'

Swallow's aim is to slow down looking. 'The experience of an artwork is a great challenge; just to move someone as a result of your own engagement with a sculpture is an achievement, I think. If some kid sees a sculpture of mine and goes home and starts carving a whale out of his bedhead with a penknife, I think I've done my job.'

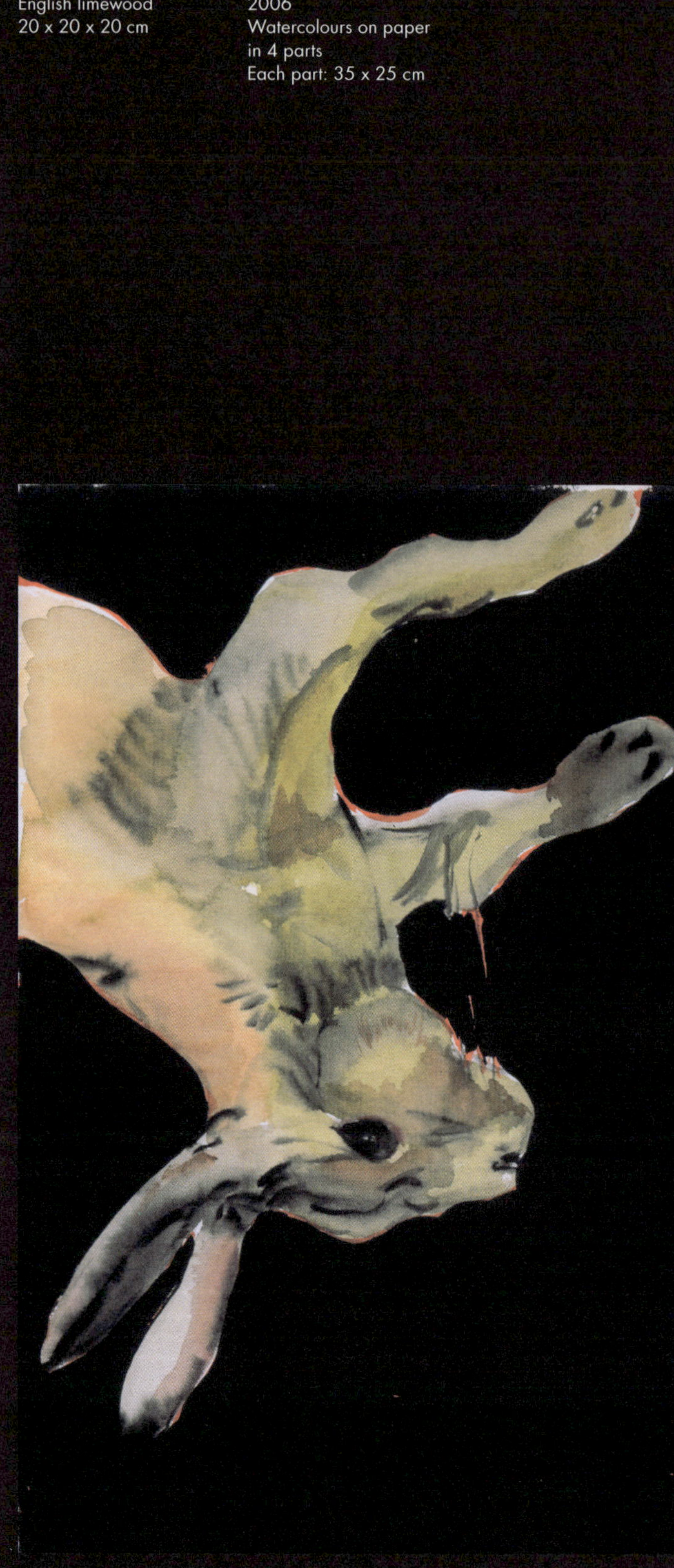

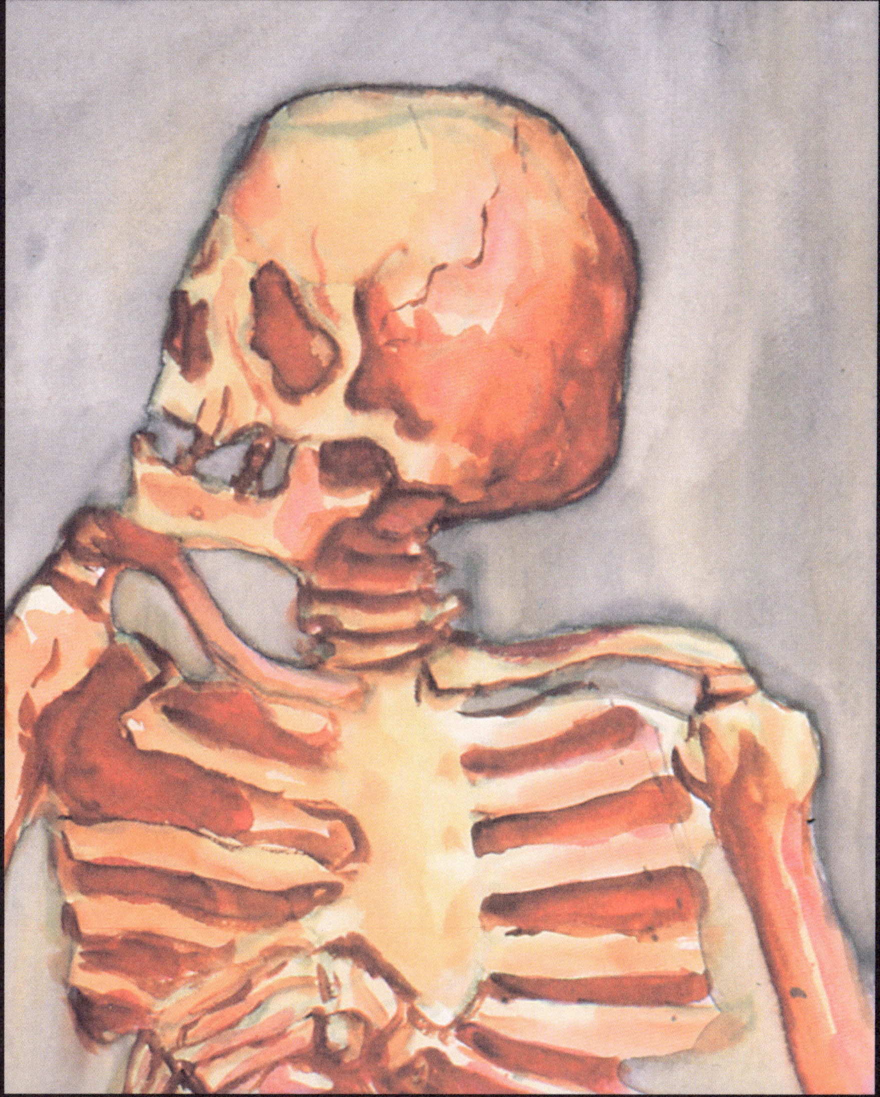

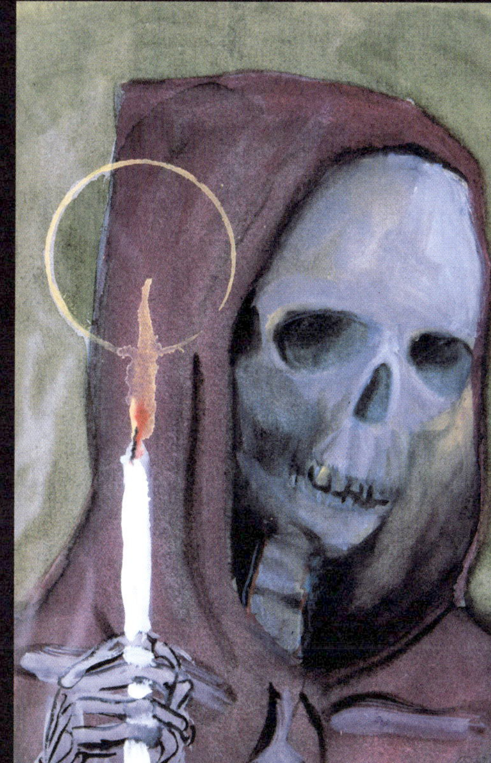

Below (left)
The Arrangement
2004
European limewood
26 x 51 x 46 cm

Below (right)
Snake/Helmut (Green)
2004
Watercolour on paper
38 x 28 cm

Opposite
*The Exact Dimensions of
Staying Behind*
2004–5
Laminated limewood
70 x 10 x 105 cm

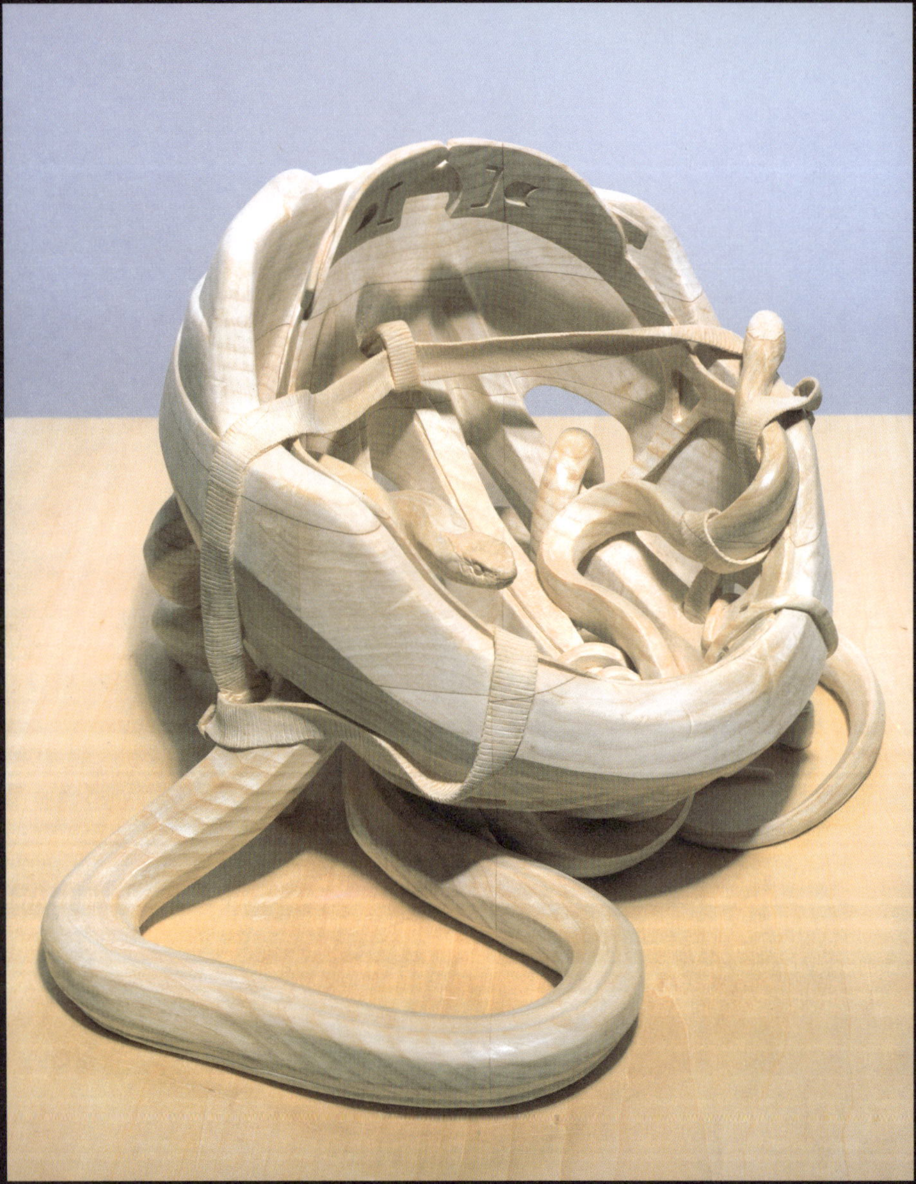

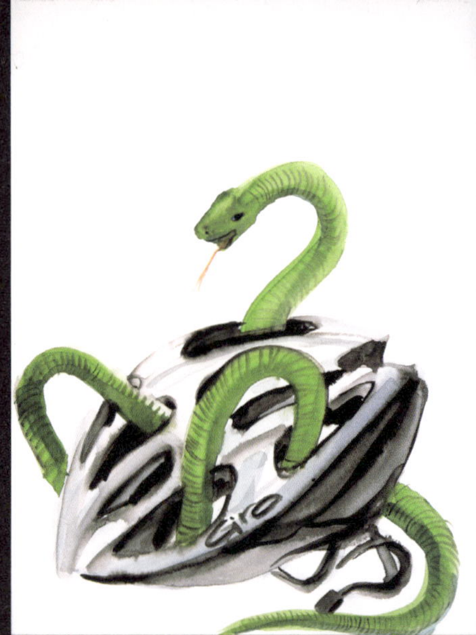

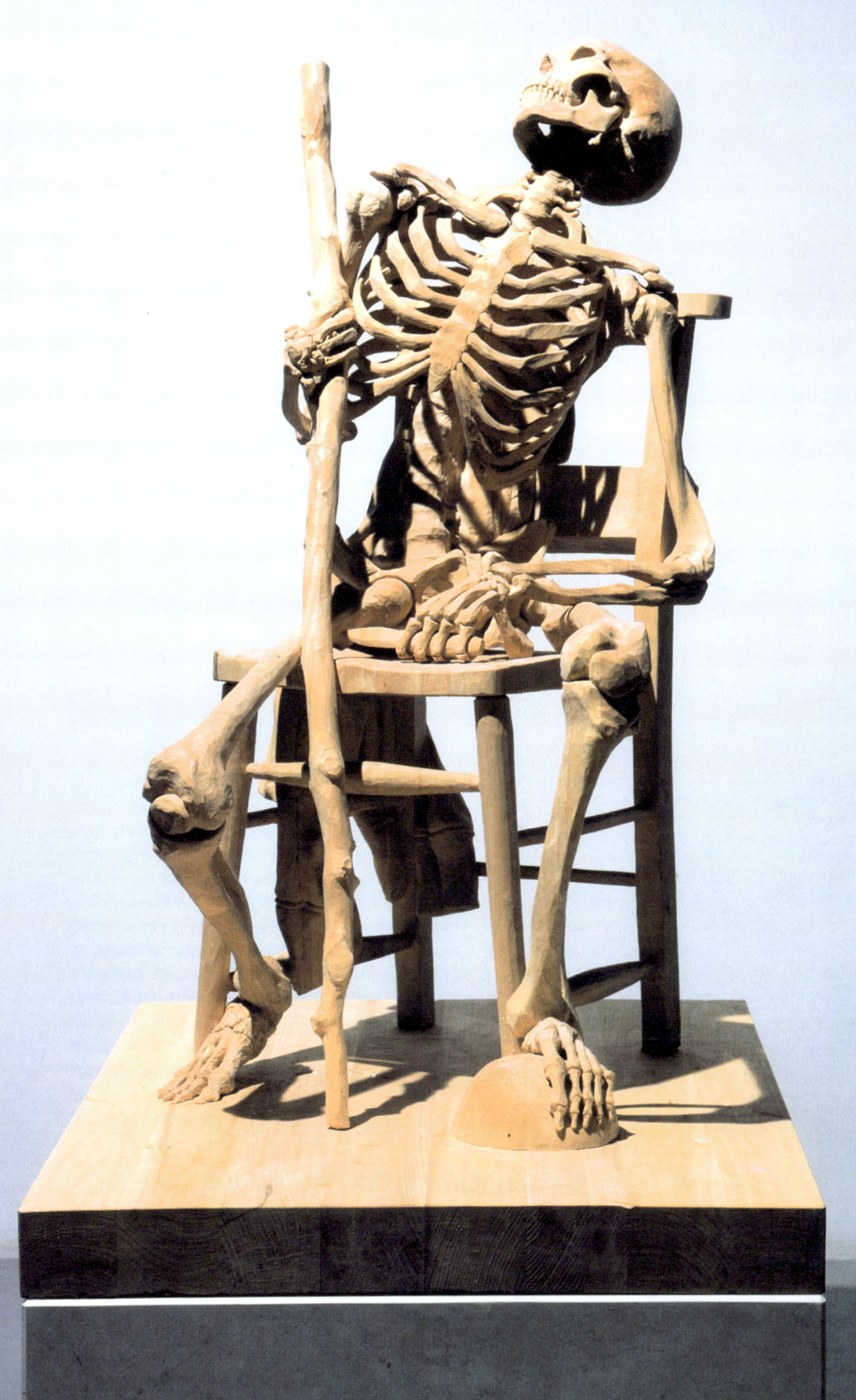

erik tidemann

here is a natural relationship between fear and dark forest landscapes. Erik Tidemann draws on his heritage in the Norwegian woods to create work that ranges from narrative-led performance to prints and paintings to strange installations. What connects his work is a very personal representation of violence. 'I don't intentionally want to make violent work but I guess much aggression is mixed up with personal issues such as isolation, sadness, humour and frustration. Some people might find this funny, but some find my work extremely sad, too.'

He originally came to art through graffiti work as a teenager, though he had been creating war drawings since childhood. 'They worked as a kind of role play, where a battle was played out on an A4 piece of paper. I got into thinking about aesthetics, and creating images that "live on". The war drawings always ended in chaos, after the explosions and flames I drew in.' That sense of chaos comes across in some of his ritual-infused performance works.

Pieces have ranged from group performances using animal skins to solo pieces, such as *Woodchoppin' Chop Chops*. This work captures a lonely ritual of a man melting a group of snowmen in the forest. He wears a dead deer's face while throwing Molotov cocktails, which explode in the snow around him. 'This is a ritual where a real person is somehow resurrecting this dead deer by taking its face and looking through its empty eyes. The character made the ritual for himself and for no one else to see.' There's a sense of risk to these pieces, as Tidemann transforms himself into a character for the scenarios. 'Wearing a bloody skinned

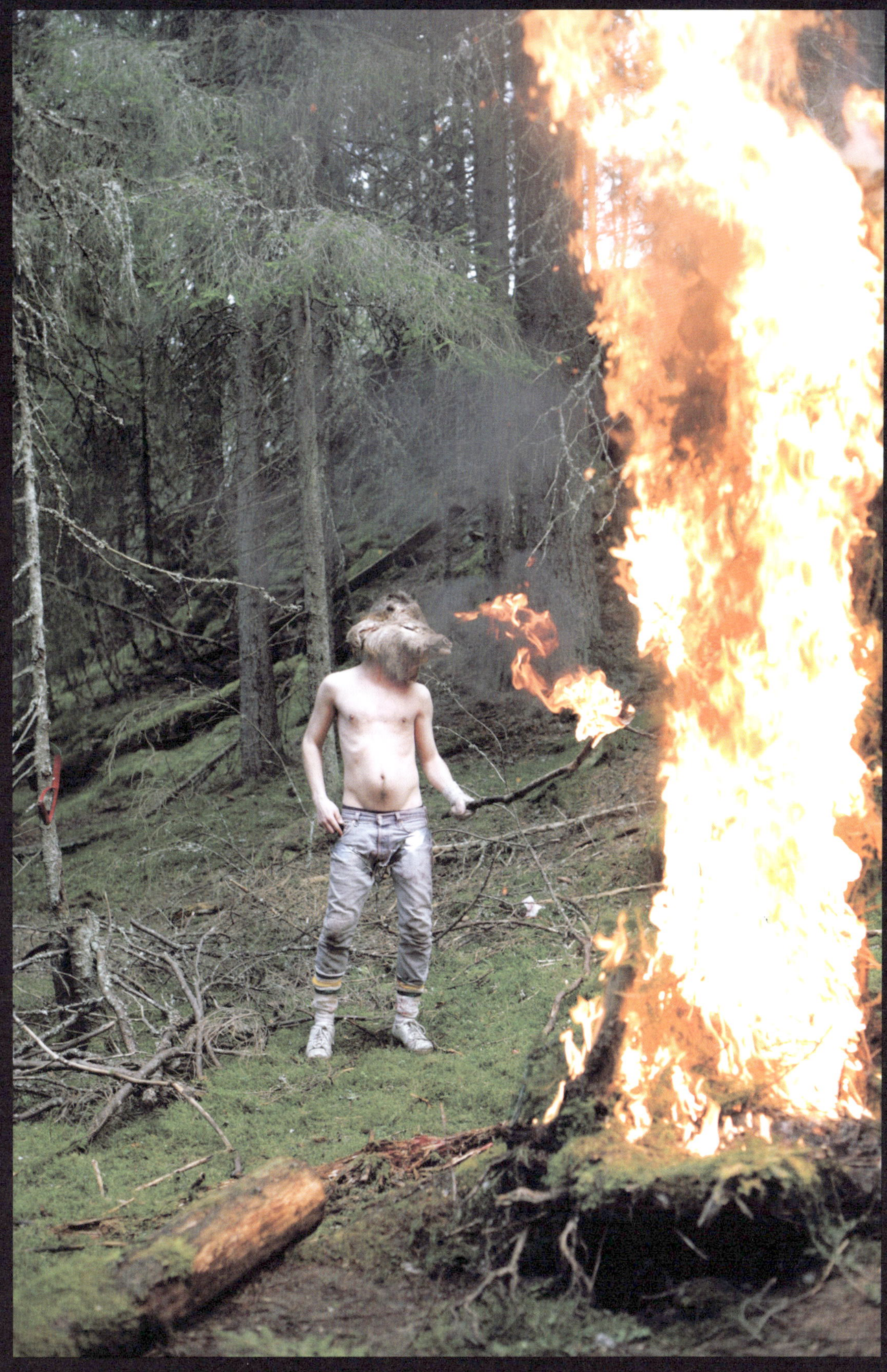

face or part of something dead or any costume, makes you feel as some new character.' It is a way of tasting death without dying.

Dead animals and skins (often taken from road kill) feature in a number of his performances and installations. 'I do deliver carcasses to Satanic black metal concerts, for them to impale on stage. I know it's filthy and does not show much decency and honour for the dead animal. But the kicks, I guess, have come before decency as my work has progressed.' Deer, in particular, are a recurring theme in his art. Tidemann connects the animal to dreams and sees them as a symbol of his father, who died when he was nine. 'I've used sheep based on the Revelations of St. John, and spiders for death and resurrection performances. The spider both creates new spiders by making cocoons, and also keeps its killed prey in cocoons. I feel that both birth and death are very close.' For Tidemann, they come from the same emptiness.

Tidemann's work aims to make the experience as real as possible, to the point of injury. 'I made a piece that was called *Black Botany*. I was inside this large cocoon filled with polystyrene balls. I ended up losing the tube I was breathing through, and got loads of polystyrene in my throat before I was shipped to hospital.' There's a loose sense of narrative to the works but nothing is obvious. 'I like the word "tale" when I make projects. The show becomes some visual ride into a storyline, as you read a book, but with no words and specific explanations.' His inspiration often comes from the media and outsiders. He frequently builds stories around lone individuals isolated from society, characters who invite hatred from the media and the world by following their own path.

His pieces are not entirely serious. 'I like trash, gore, blood, nunchuck catapults, shitty monsters, violence and over-used clichés like that. I like images that punch the viewer in the stomach. But I try to combine these trashy elements with aesthetics and decadence at the same time. It always starts off really grotesque and then, as the process goes on, I filter it out. My exhibitions always end up being very decadent, quite beautiful and maybe a bit too polished. I always question whether they are a bit too nice and friendly. Maybe they should be trashier and more messed up.'

Previous and this spread
Trailer Trash Gear
(4 documentation photographs of performance)
2007
Performance
Courtesy Erik Tidemann.
Photography Thomas Sørgård for *Chief Magazine*, New York

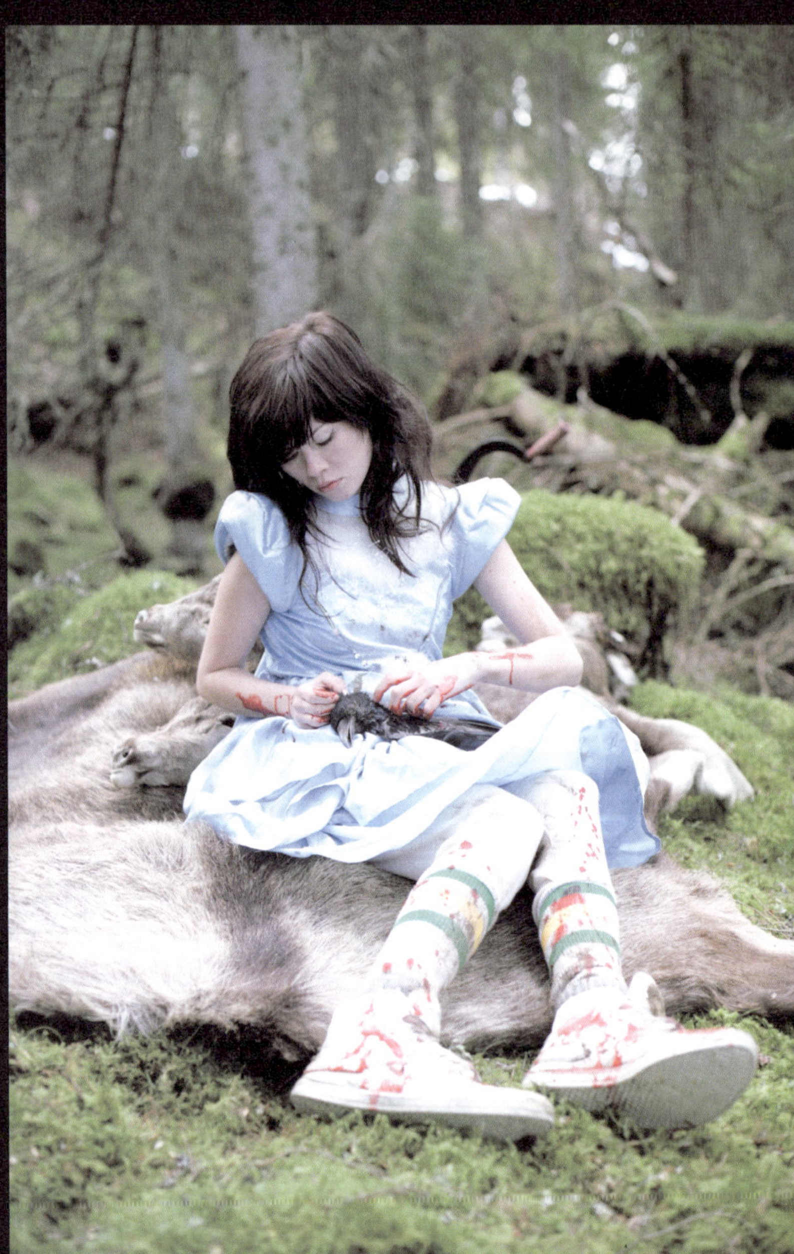

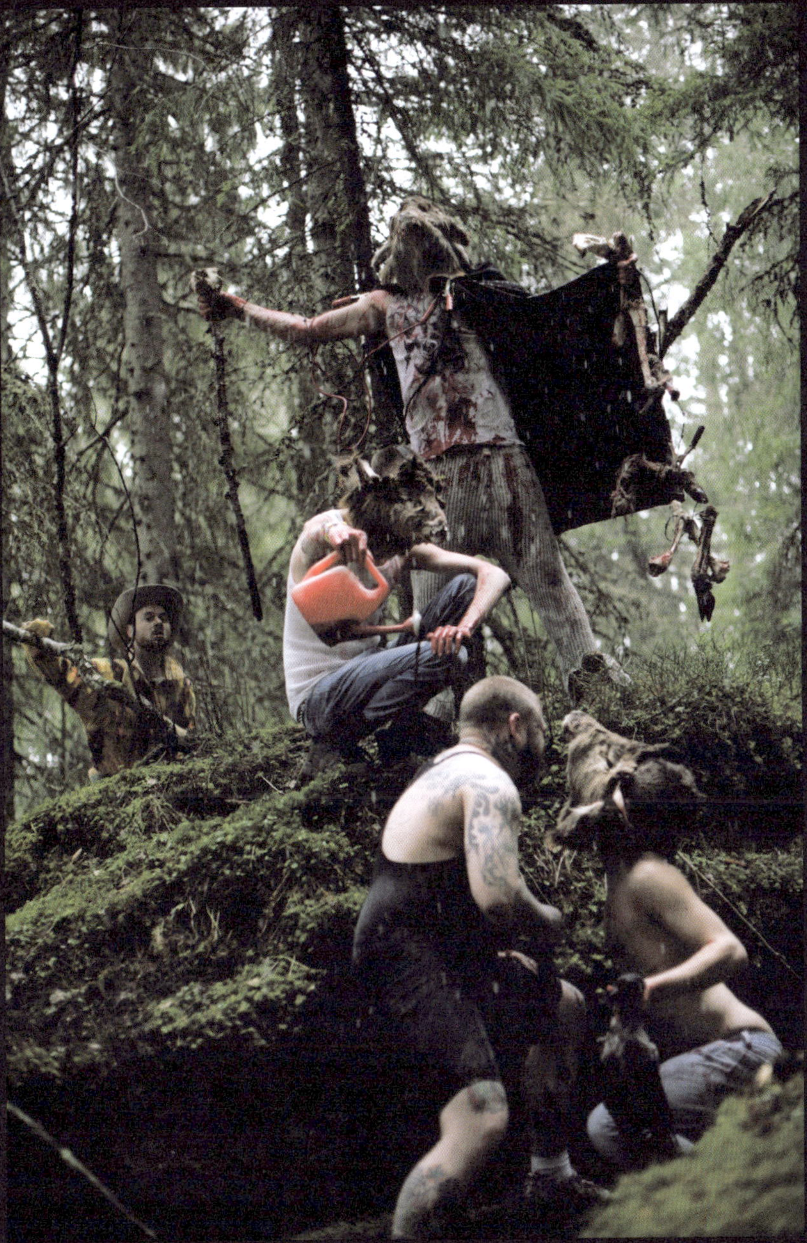

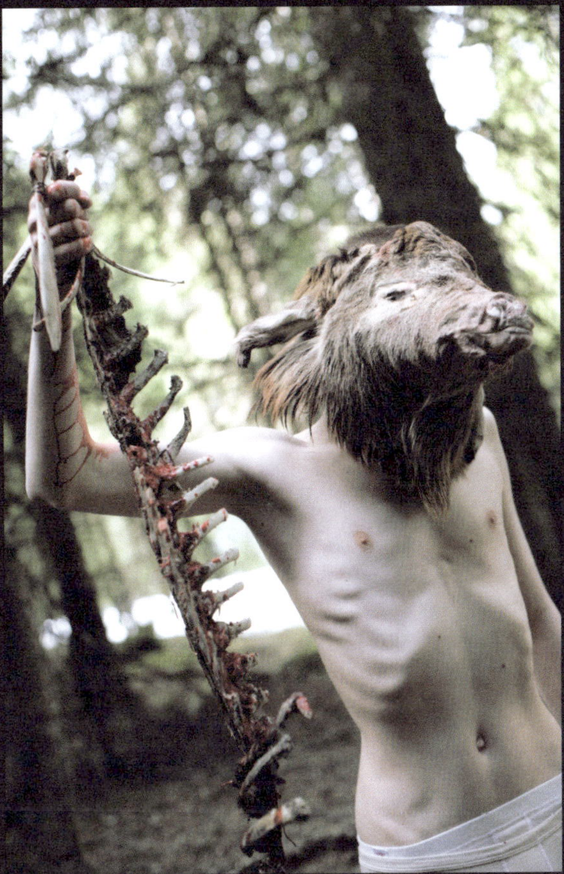

iris van dongen

Iris Van Dongen fuses the melancholic approach of symbolist painting with contemporary subcultures. Many of her paintings focus specifically on teen fandom – young girls are depicted next to band or film posters, hinting at their obsessions. 'I still feel an affinity with many subcultures. I don't know if this is teenage or adult.' Van Dongen has never had a connection to the gothic scene, although her work has been linked to its imagery. 'It looks like everything that refers a bit to darkness or death is called "gothic".' Her work owes an obvious debt to the Pre-Raphaelites and High Renaissance religious works. Her compositions echo paintings by Victorian British artists such as Dante Gabriel Rossetti and John Waterhouse or symbolist painters like Franz von Stuck. She also veers from the soberness of Vermeer and Goya to the beauty and lightness of art nouveau. But there is a modern essence in her work that combines a classically decadent painting style with a bit of punk edge. 'It's like looking around you. You swallow it, filter it and mix it into your own story.'

She is drawn to the throwaway consumerism of heavy-metal, punk and hooligan merchandise. Her pieces quote pop culture references on scarves, posters and other ephemera. The idols of adolescent obsession are raised to something iconic and beautiful. 'I think, at least, they are honest about life.' As with the Pre-Raphaelites, young women are often the protagonists in her pieces. 'I am myself a young woman – in a way it's autobiographical. I can identify easily with these girls.' Her reworking of a symbolist or Victorian melancholic aesthetic has a socio-political edge. 'I'm interested in "rewriting" history by giving

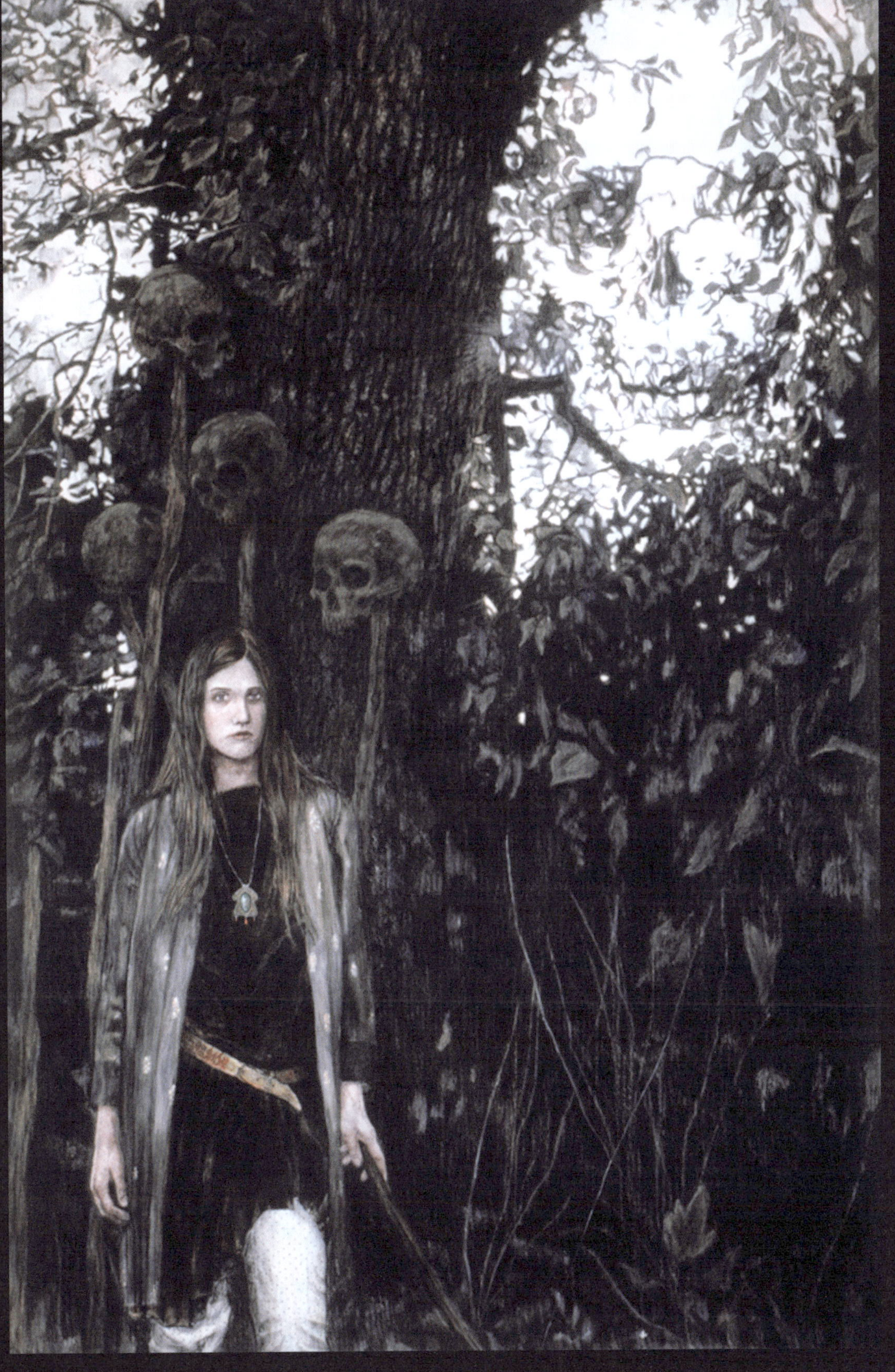

the female a self-assured, strong and "liberated" image, instead of the fragile, half-fainting, helpless ladies depicted in Victorian times.' Sometimes the characters she draws are symbols that suggest mythical, superhuman narratives. Or sometimes a character depicts a symbol 'that imagines the fate of that person, their courage, their fears, their history, what's going on in their mind'.

There is a conscious juxtaposition between the past and present in her work. 'Although the drawings refer to earlier movements in traditional art, there is always a small element, such as the sweatband with the skull on it, which shows that it is from the present day: a symbol from a contemporary subculture and, at the same time, an age-old symbol. This gives extra emphasis to the aspect of mortality or melancholy – or neutralizes it.' The things she juxtaposes – good and evil, past and present, and, literally, the figurative and the abstract – aim to highlight and explore the limits and emptiness of these contradictions.

She doesn't just use paint in her work – charcoal, etching and pastels are all part of her working process. 'I started drawing with charcoal in lines, in a schematic way. Then I became interested in etching. I love the darkness and simplicity of the lines.' Her aim is to try to recreate that darkness on a larger scale. She invented a method of using pastel colours as a base and layering over them with black charcoal. The results helped to create the sombreness she strives for.

Her darkly lit work is often littered with skulls. As Van Dongen puts it, death is a cliché that she has juggled with since childhood. 'I have always used images referring to death, ever since I was little. The contradiction between life and death has always tickled me. I even lived next to an old seventeenth-century graveyard and happily dug up bones. I wanted to be an archaeologist and I put some bones and teeth I found on my window sill. Sometimes I freaked out as I thought their spirit would come and take them back. It fascinated me that you can look at things in a scientific way, and at the same time be very scared and lose yourself.' For the artist, fantasy and curiosity lie side by side.

Van Dongen's work plays with an Ophelia-like depressive yearning for death, consciously prodding at cultural clichés. These women are powerful but despondent. They are lost in fantasy yet hinting at an underlying anger or violence – they wear football scarves implying hooliganism or are surrounded by the imagery of hard-punk bands. They are overtly sexual or unable to express their sexuality.

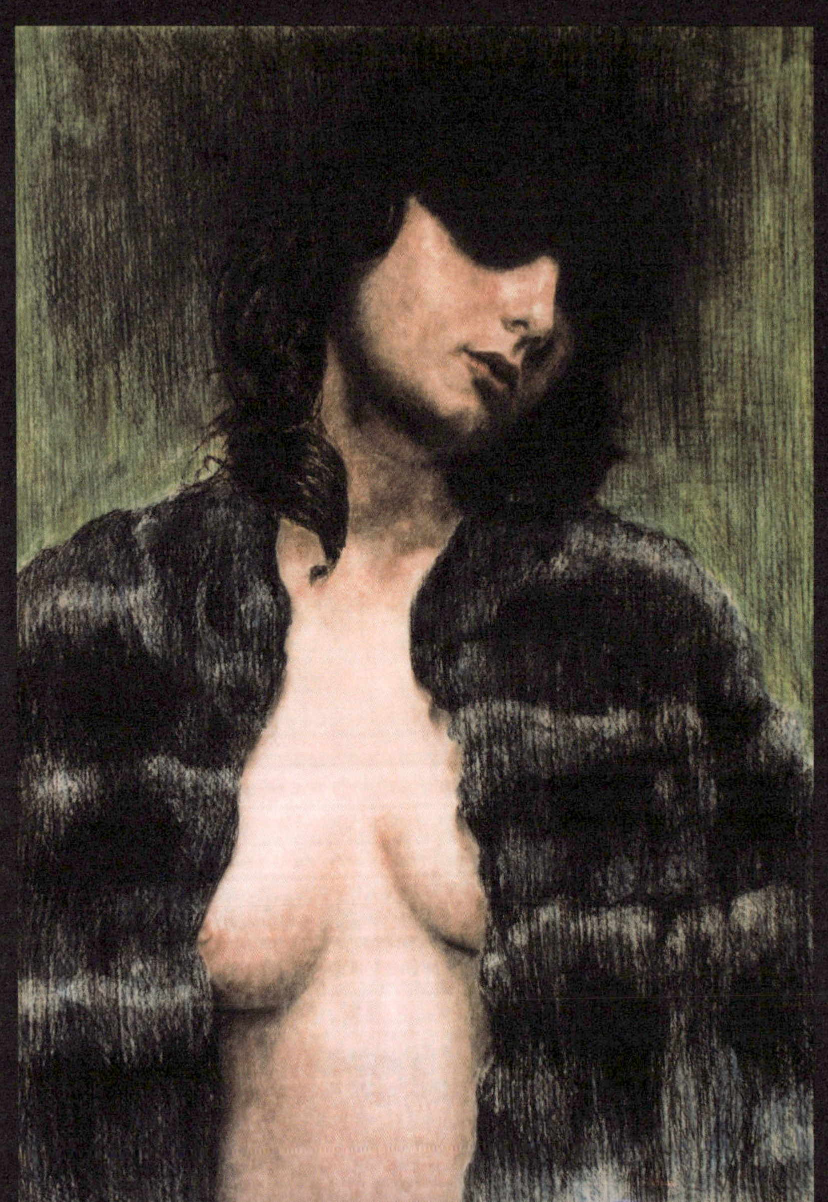

Below
Hooligan II
2004
Pressed charcoal,
soft pastel on paper
273 x 150 cm

Right
Dragon II
2007
Pressed charcoal, soft
pastel on paper
145 x 220 cm

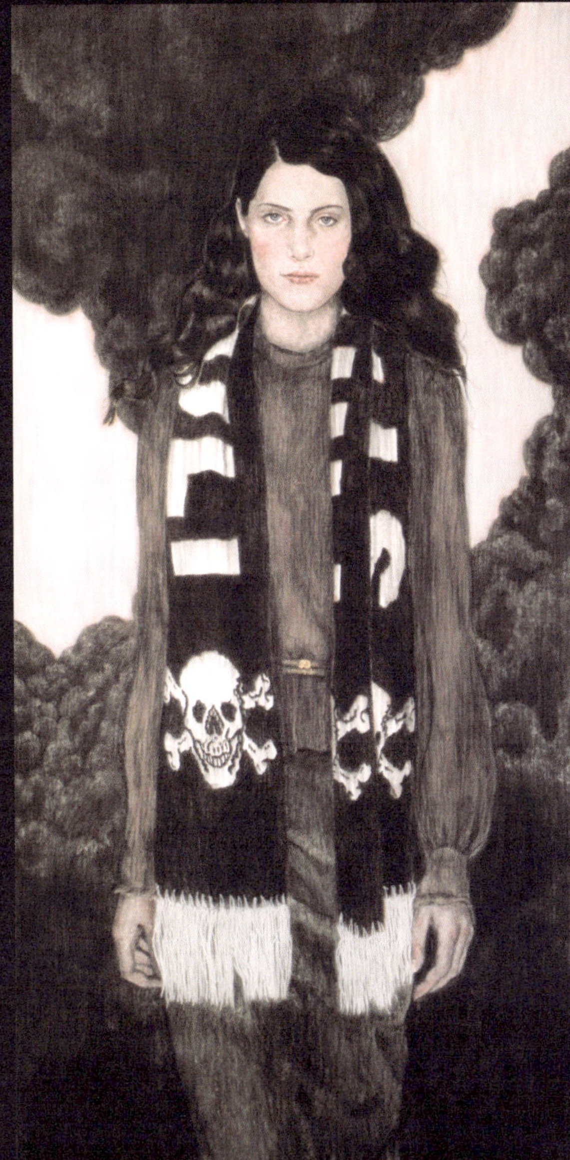

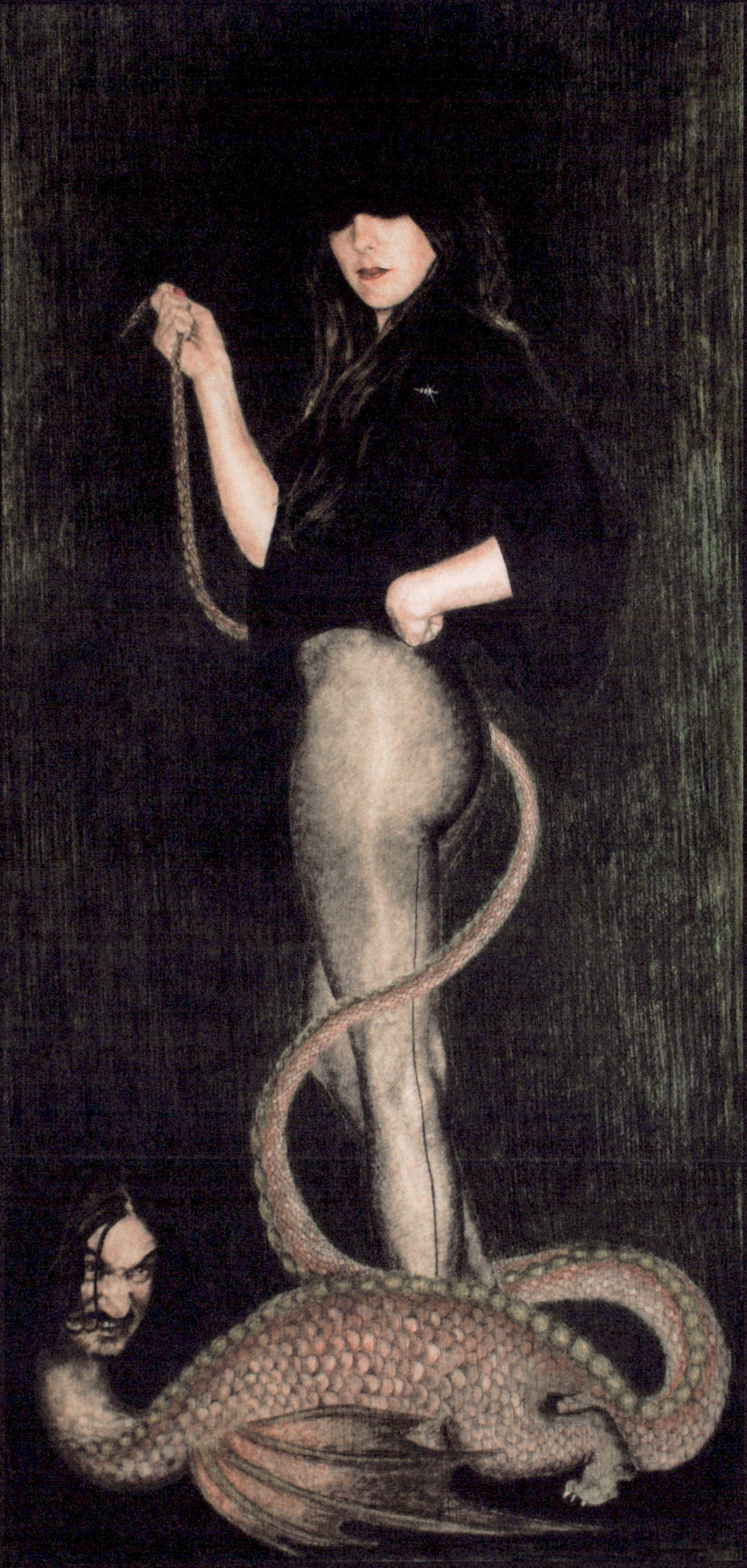

banks violette

Looking at Banks Violette's installations of cast white salt and gleaming black plastic can be uncomfortable. Empty coffins lie with their lids cast open. Stages are set for unseen performances. The imagery of darkness is here, but negativity or evil is not the artist's intention. 'It's not about the morbidity of something. That has never been the point.'

Violette's interest in art grew out of his involvement with subcultures. 'I've always made album covers and T-shirts for artists – always been involved as an active participant in a subculture and investing in that culture rather than waiting for somebody to hand it to you.' This emphasis on the active creation of a creative movement still informs his approach to art. It also feeds into the content – the use of skulls, coffins, stages and sound systems. 'I had this available vocabulary that I had an intimate relationship with, one that I felt was really relevant to the idea of what art should be.'

Violette participated in the hardcore scene in upstate New York, where he grew up. More important than the music was the culture surrounding it. 'There was this very active scene that I was a part of. People I knew were making music or printing records. It was a logical extension. It had its own economy and methods of distribution and promotion. There wasn't a hierarchy between you and the audience. You were active and you had an equal responsibility for making this thing.' There is something wider and poetic about subcultures that interests the artist; a Utopia aware of its own demise. 'Subcultures are often connected to the idea of youth – so there is this idea that they're

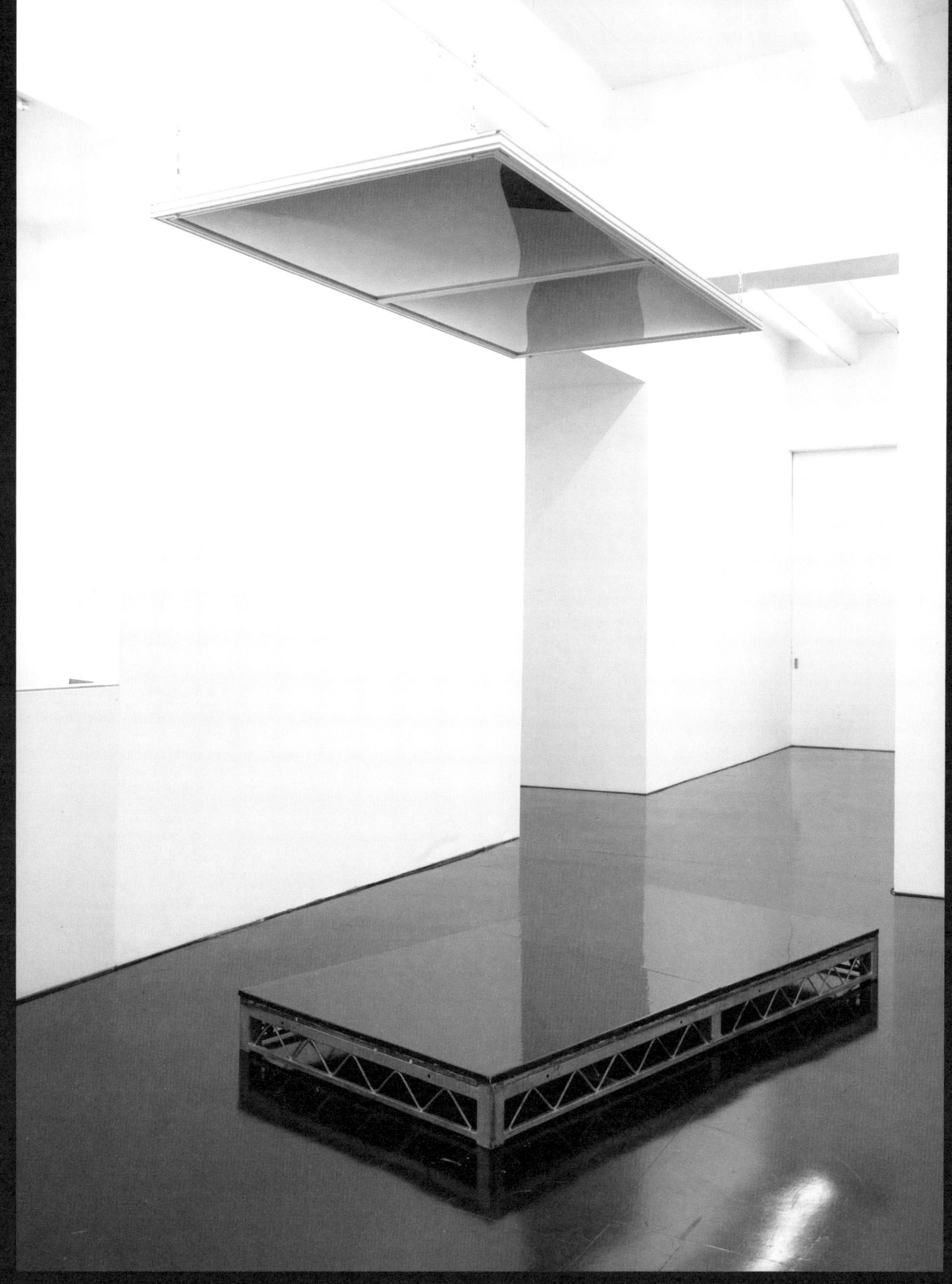

predestined to fail and they are transitory, which is really bizarre because they're such beautiful ideas.'

A refusal to see cultural boundaries – high and low, mainstream and underground – makes his work so effective. He uses minimal forms and abstraction with the language of subcultures and death metal. His work explores how visual language itself is classed. He defies the arrogant notion that abstraction is solely the domain of high culture, 'as if subcultures don't figure these things out on their own and don't manifest them'.

Part of what gives his work so much resonance is its sense of absence. He creates a performance without a performer, stages with no band and primitive drum kits with no musicians. There is a kind of lacking or void.

He has collaborated on interesting installations with cult band Sunn O))). Pronounced 'Sunn', the O))) refers to an amplification system that aimed to create the most massive sound possible. The symbol indicates the pressure of sound radiating out of a speaker. Violette created a sculptural version of a recording studio inside a gallery. The band performed and recorded within the space, working out its acoustics. They created sound frequencies that intersect and create sub-audible harmonics that have a physical effect on the body. The 'ghost' of this audio experience has a kind of conceptual imprint on the space itself. Violette adds a fourth dimension to his sculpture – the absent performance.

Violette's work is largely monochrome, although the binary oppositions are something he finds meaningless. 'I like the idea of exhausted ideas – things that are so blunt and over-determined that they seem incapable of real meaning anymore.' Black versus white is, for Violette, an empty metaphor. The tension between textures in his sculpture has a similar effect – the grain of his speakers made of salt, the gloss of plastic and of black Perspex coffins. 'I just like that they have a tension – contrasts on a really basic level. They are almost ham-fisted declarations of something. Something is so devoid of the potential to contain any kind of meaning, yet people still put a lot of faith in this idea of black versus white, good versus evil and things like that.' Instead of examining what the oppositions are, Violette's work looks at why we have faith in binary oppositions at all.

Faith itself is the question that lies at the bottom of his work. In particular, he is interested in the idea of faith as being transformative, 'that there's an imminent value in that thing – in the wafer or the coffin. You direct your faith towards it, and that makes it something more. And if you have a whole community doing that, then you have a religion or a subculture, or you have art.'

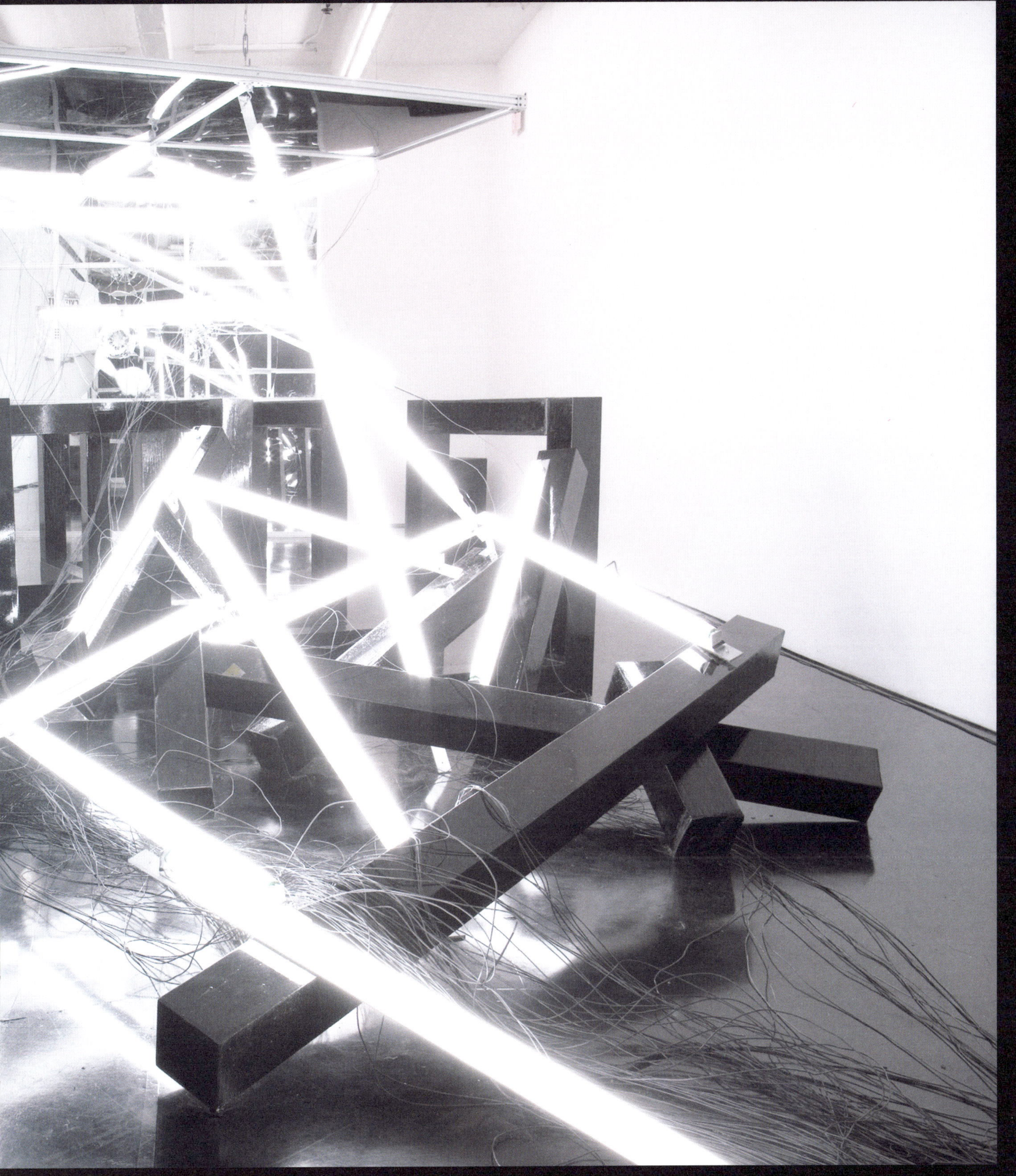

Previous spreads
and below
*Not yet titled
(Light Spill)* (3 views)
2007
Fluorescent light
fixtures, plexiglas,
aluminium, wood
and epoxy
254 x 1036.3 x
426.7 cm
Courtesy Maureen
Paley, London; Team
Gallery, New York
and Gladstone Gallery,
New York

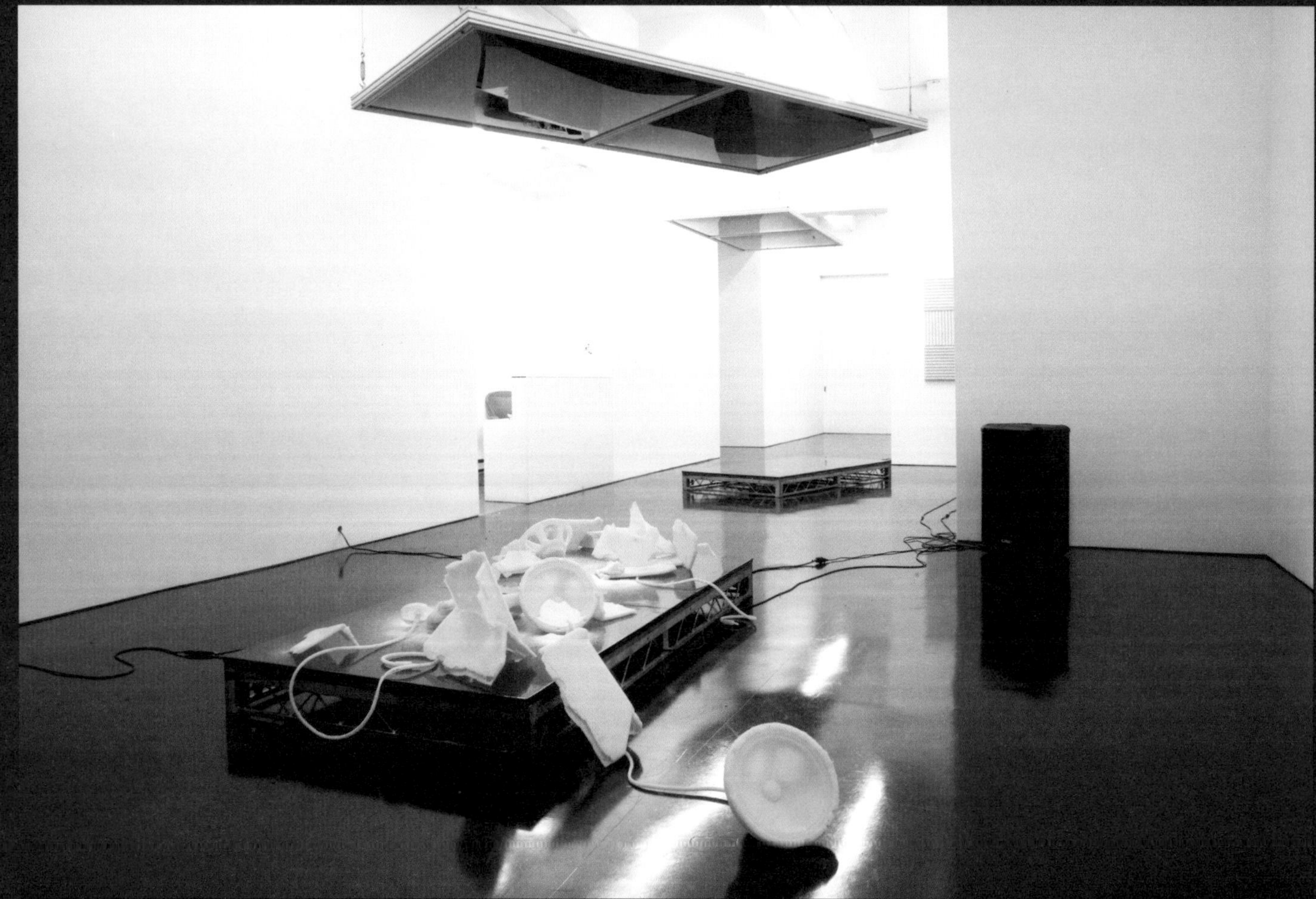

Below
Sunn O))) / (Repeater)
Decay / Coma Mirror
2006
Steel, hardware,
plywood, paint,
fibreglass, tinted epoxy,
salt and resin
Dimensions variable
Courtesy Maureen Paley,
London

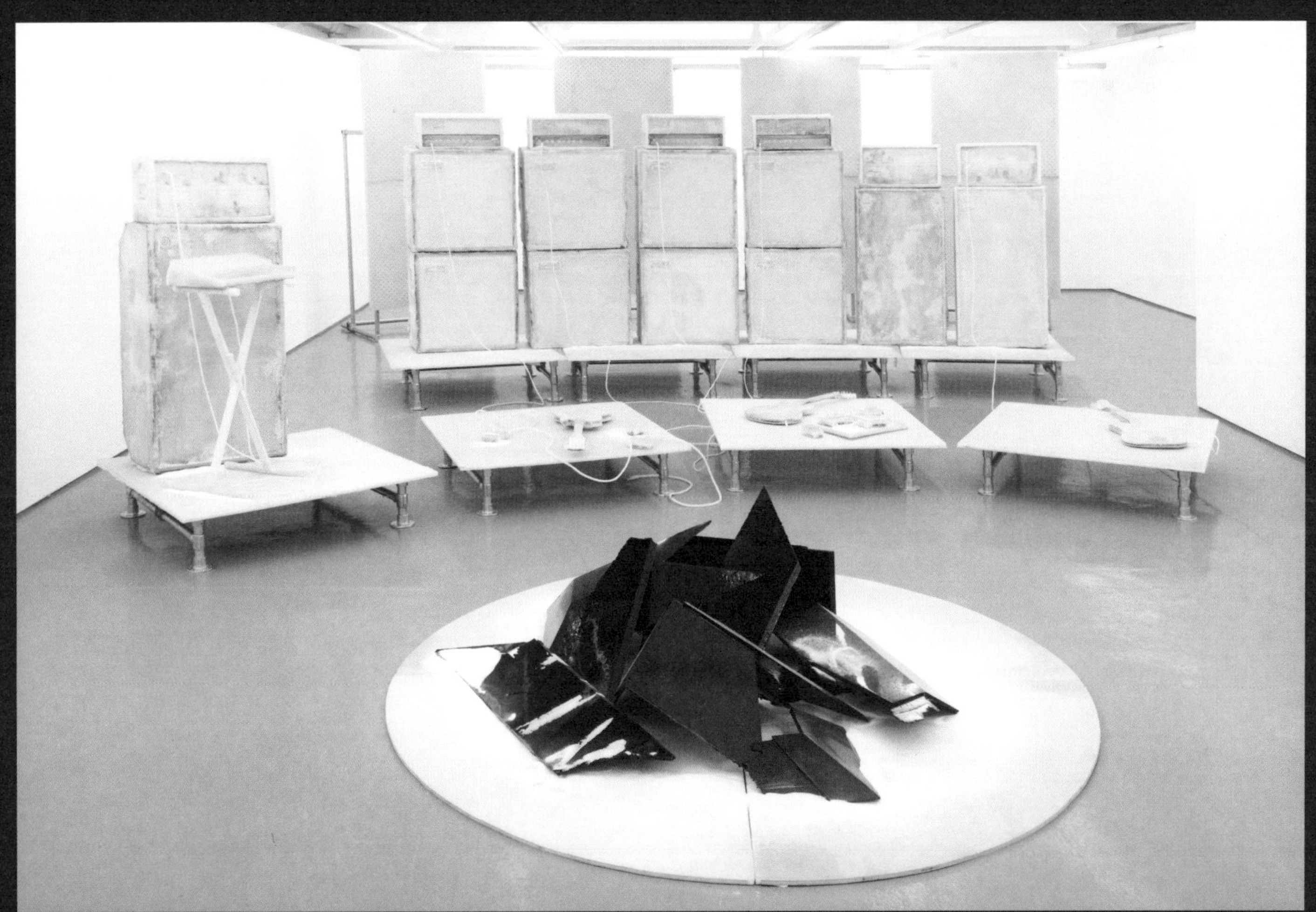

marnie weber

Marnie Weber creates consciously handmade film pieces, brimming with an hysteric sense of haunting. Full of exaggerated colour and accompanied by strange synthesizer soundtracks, her videos focus on The Spirit Girls, a fictional girl rock band who died tragically in the 1970s before they became famous. The group was partly inspired by the theatrical progressive rock bands of Weber's teenage years. 'I had always wanted to do an all-girl band, as I had been playing in bands for years with guys.' The idea was to conceptualize a band as the centre of an art piece, keeping it held together with tight aesthetics.

This ghostly musical group features throughout Weber's work, to eerie effect. The girls all stare out from expressionless, hard white masks. They are dressed in Victorian white nightgowns or tartan country dresses and Mary Jane shoes – like unearthly virginal creatures. Weber creates a fascinating contrast between childlike fantasy and death or darkness. 'I like the extreme emotional contrast. As a child and a young woman every day was an opera of imagination mixed with intense feelings. As a young girl my most vivid moments were elaborate funeral processions for dead animals I had found in the woods. We would all wear costumes, design the coffin, create a lovely burial plot with flowers and send the animal on its way. Death is a natural part of childhood fantasy. It seems that we need to grow with that balance between darkness and light, to grow as complete human beings.' Weber is interested in how death becomes subverted, anaesthetized and hidden in social etiquette,

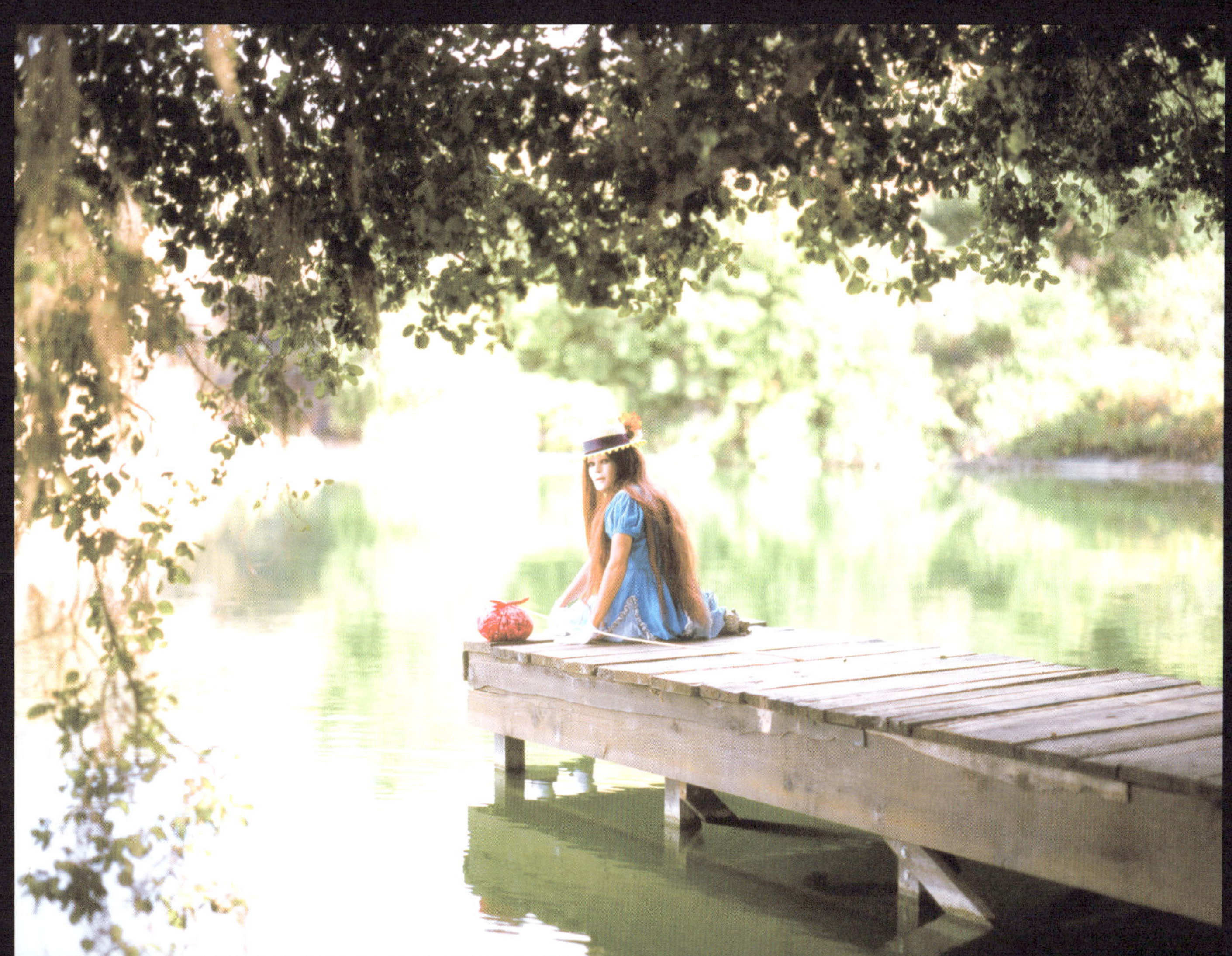

particularly in American culture. The natural role of birth and death gets lost as we become socialized.

Alongside this fascination with death, her work explores metamorphosis. She specifically examines the transformation from a girl into a woman and then into an old lady. 'What interests me is how the core personality and soul remain the same, but the body changes over the years. How people see you is very different.' The representation of women has always been central to Weber's practice. Early collages depicted women's bodies cut out of men's magazines, placed in surreal or bucolic landscapes. 'This was originally from an art historical perspective, looking at how female nudes were represented in paintings as languid limp creatures without strength. I realized most of the poses still occur today in men's soft-core magazines.'

The filmic narratives around the girls are only part of the wider Spirit Girls' world. Weber also creates their music, which has been released. 'The CD has vocals that tell of the girls' journey, hopes and emotions. I like to think I am writing in character when I make music, but obviously it is influenced by me.'

She uses photo stills from her films to create collages. Originally her background landscapes came from travel magazines, but as she began to work on a larger scale, she used production stills from her shoots. She now uses a landscape painter to paint backdrops from photographs, which Weber re-shoots, in combination with a diorama, animal figures and miniatures. It is a complex process. The girls in her collages are usually Weber herself in different clothes, wigs and masks. 'I like the fact that I am creating my own little world and that the pieces are unique. Many people think they are editions, but they are not, they are one of a kind.'

Unlike the more rigidly structured film process, there is more freedom in creating her collage pieces. 'I don't have a clear idea of the narratives in the collages before I start, because the subconscious makes connections between the characters, much like dreams create situations for us. You can go back and figure out what the dreams, or in my case the collages, are trying to say.' There is a sense of unease in looking at Weber's pieces, which is intentional: 'I think from my days in music and performance, I got accustomed to trying to move people emotionally while I was on stage. I carried this into my visual artwork. Sometimes people are uncomfortable with the conflicting emotions they derive from my work; it can open them up or shut them down. It is worth the attempt, because I am not interested in making objects that look good.'

Previous spread
Film production still from
A Western Song
2007
Archival ink jet print
50.8 x 63.5 cm
Edition of 5
Courtesy the artist and
Patrick Painter gallery,
Los Angeles

Below (top)
In the Haystacks
2004
C-print collage
85 x 104 cm
Courtesy the artist and
Emily Tsingou gallery,
London

Below (bottom)
The Spirited Girls
2004
Collage
85 x 104 cm
Courtesy the artist and
Emily Tsingou gallery,
London

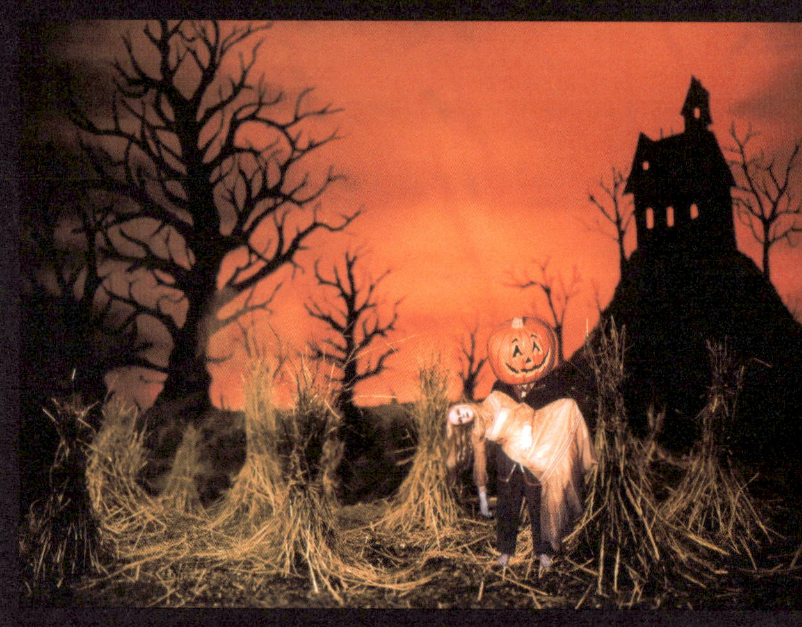

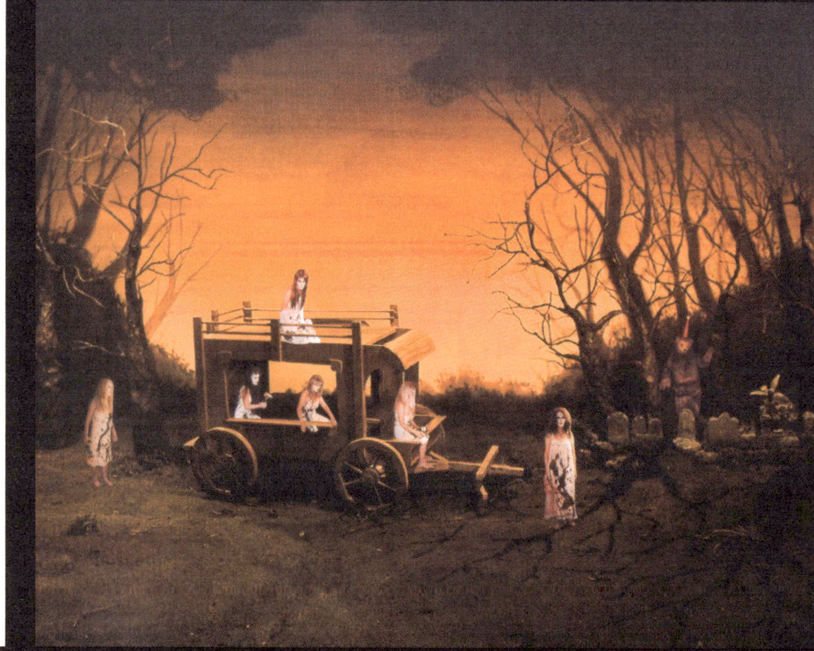

Below
Film production still from
A Western Song
2007
Archival ink jet print
50.8 x 63.5 cm
Edition of 5
Courtesy the artist and
Patrick Painter gallery,
Los Angeles

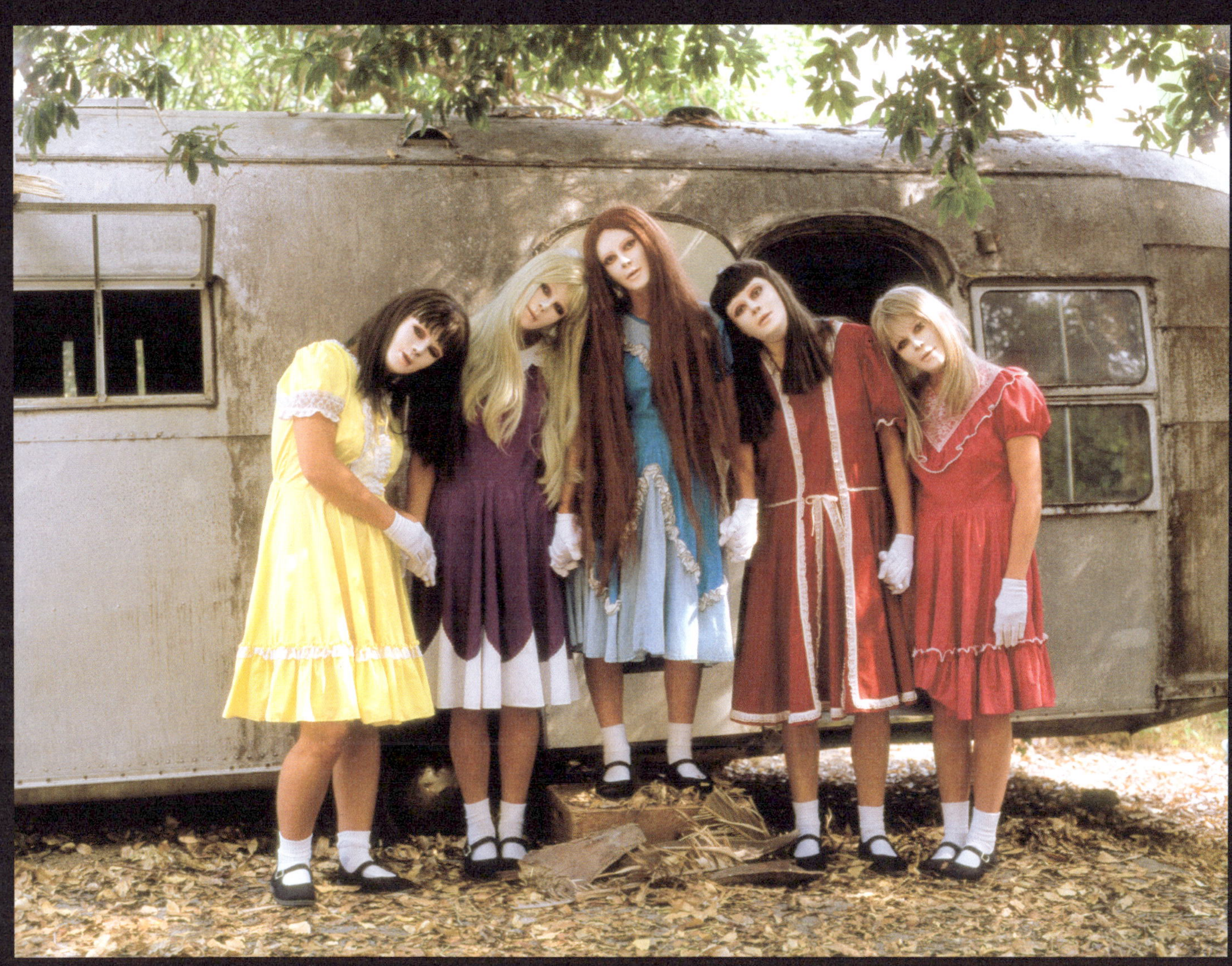

Below
Untitled
2003
C-print collage
76 x 101.7 cm
Courtesy the artist and
Emily Tsingou gallery,
London

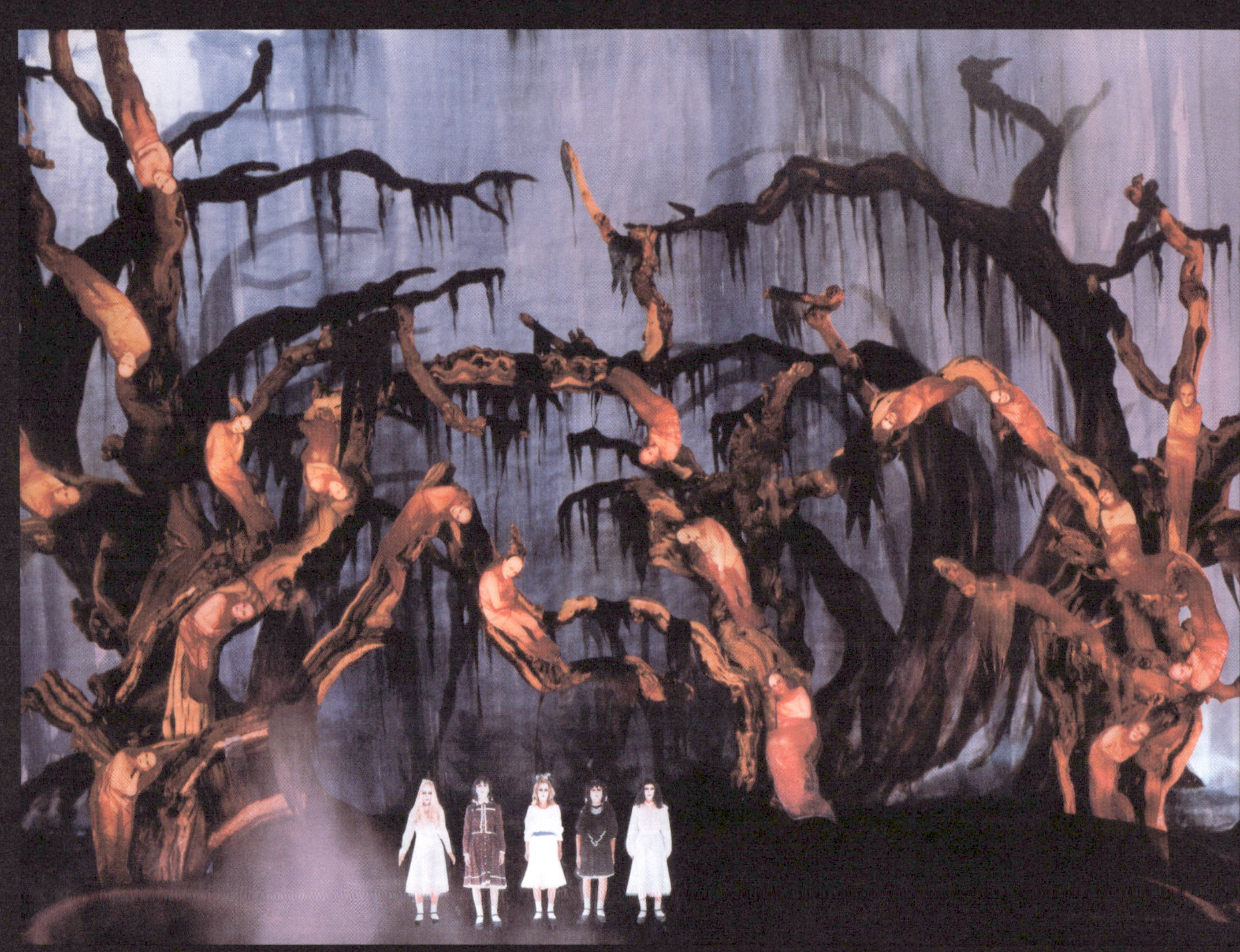

Below
Floating Castle
2004
78 cm x 103.5 cm
C-print collage
Courtesy the artist and
Emily Tsingou gallery,
London

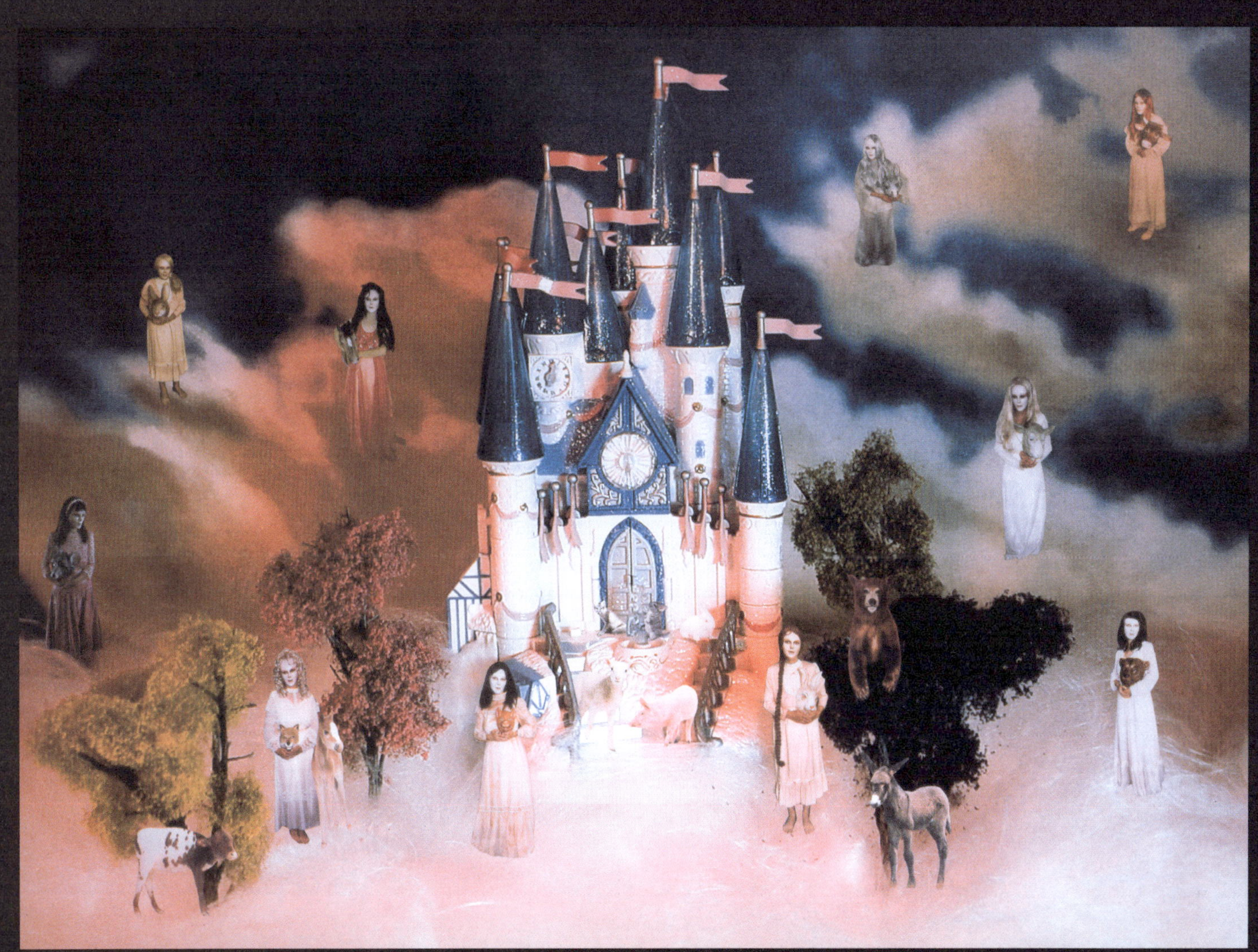

sarah woodfine

arah Woodfine turns drawings into monochrome jewels. The British artist creates storybook, gothic landscapes and places them inside glass containers, like oversized snow domes. 'The drawings in the liquid-filled snow domes are two-dimensional. The images become three-dimensional through the illusory process of viewing through liquid and manoeuvring around the object.' That three-dimensionality is something she strives for – a sense of hyper-reality. 'Whilst presenting themselves as solid representations, they simultaneously seem like facades; almost like stage sets with nothing behind. I started to explore what could be concealed.'

Woodfine has always been drawn to sinister imagery. 'I find gothic imagery both magical and darkly threatening. My work explores the symbiotic relationship of these extremes. I am attracted to its starkness and flamboyance.' In particular, she depicts gothic architectural spaces – a castle lit by moonlight, the image of a classic haunted house. She is fascinated by these buildings' structural forms, their sense of claustrophobia and their excessive detailing. 'There is a real sense of excess and extreme abundance. In gothic architecture, there are places of complete darkness, such as crypts and dungeons. The architecture has a sense of magic and fantasy.'

There is something undeniably childlike about Woodfine's work – something of which the artist is aware. 'I often use recollections from childhood within my work. Even though I may use, for example, Hitchcock's *Psycho* as a visual and contextual trigger for making work,

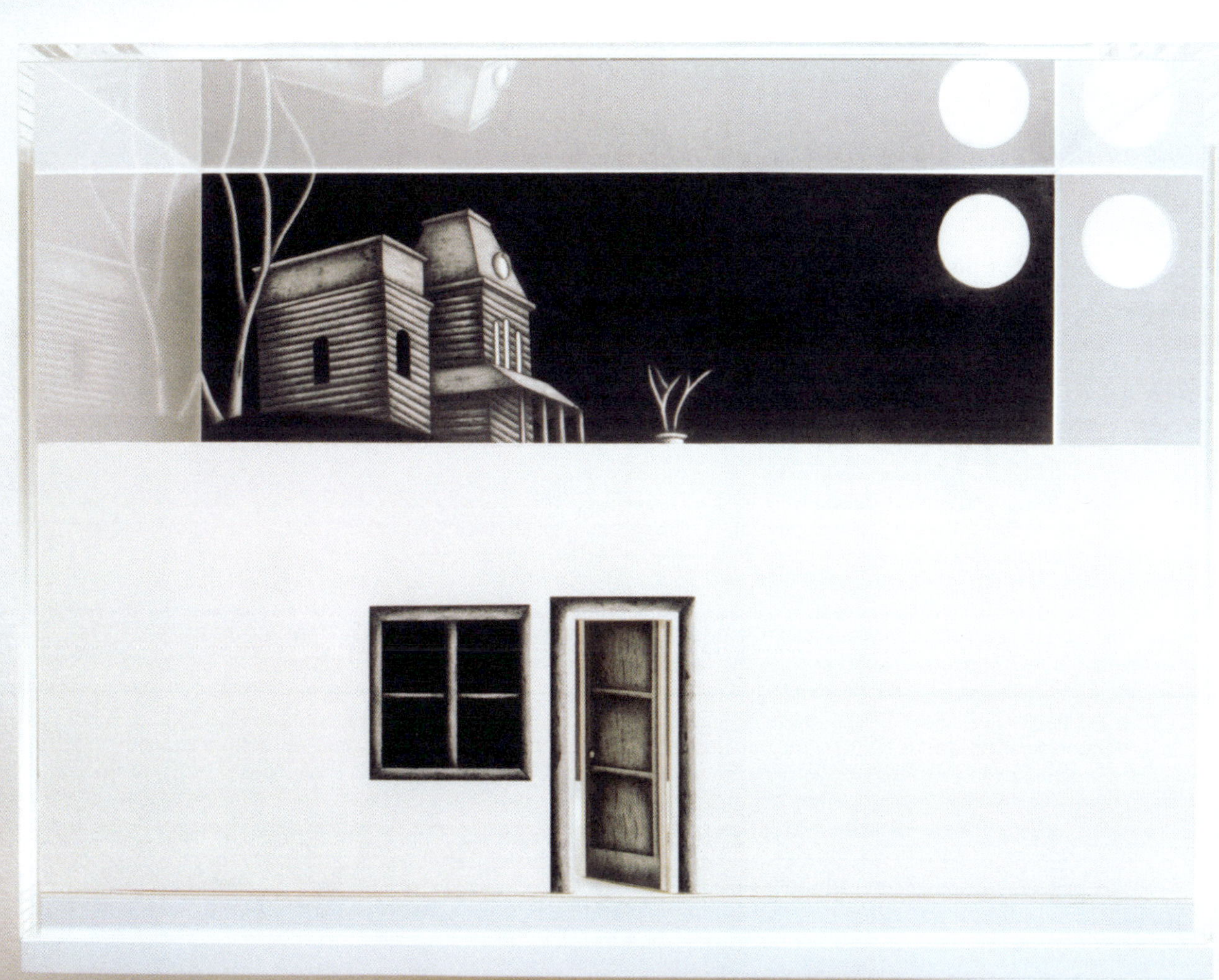

there is always something deeply embedded within the subject that refers to secrets and psychological experiences originating from my childhood.' They resemble dioramas or sets for fairy-tale narratives, but there is nothing linear about her approach. Instead the viewer glimpses stories informed by their own imagination and their own psychology.

Her work is intensely created, almost to the level of obsession. 'My relationship between the tip of the pencil and the surface of paper is intense and very close. I focus on the minute details, microscopically created by the graphite marks. The lead within pencils is a physical object, which becomes embossed into the grain of the paper. This relationship creates an almost mystical alchemy.' That sense of closeness comes out in the perfection of the detail in her work. The artist creates imaginary worlds in perfect, stylized detail.

Many of Woodfine's subjects are depicted at night – caravans or castles lit by extremely bright moonlight, surrounded by deep, black darkness. The moon is used to create an eerie atmosphere. 'The notion of its transformational powers is intriguing. In film, characters such as "The Wolfman" transform in the glare of huge full moons.' Other films have influenced her work more directly. *Alfred's Story* explores Hitchcock's *Psycho*. 'Hitchcock is the master of intensity. I am attracted to the extreme psychological states and sense of foreboding in his films. Characters who have split personalities, or have the ability to transmogrify, interest me. I was particularly drawn to the staging between the Bates's house on the hill and the motel. The work is my interpretation of the fated motel room.' Her black and white sculptural drawing echoes the palette of the film. By looking at the scene, the viewer – like Norman Bates – spies on the architecture. By looking, we become implicated in the violence that will occur within the space.

Her work is also informed by death. 'I wanted to try to find beauty in death. Death has become very concealed within in our society. The body is hidden from our view or sterilized and re-presented in funeral parlours. We are afraid of death more than ever.' The cut-out, children's-activity-book approach she adopts to illustrate coffins highlights how strange and comical our attitudes to death are. 'Coffins have taken on a Hammer Horror persona, becoming ridiculous and scary, which in itself intrigues me.'

Woodfine's work is really about fantasy – between imaginary worlds and so-called reality. 'I am interested in the idea that there is a fine line between these realms. I believe that essentially they are one and the same. I have an affinity with fantasy that is very personal to me. In an exaggerated sense, it expresses realities that you can't experience in the real world.'

Previous spread
Alfred's Story
2006
Pencil on paper in
perspex box
23.5 x 31 x 23.5 cm
Courtesy the artist
and Danielle Arnaud
contemporary art

Below
Untitled (Castle)
2005
Pencil on paper in
snow dome
38 x 38 cm
Courtesy the artist
and Danielle Arnaud
contemporary art

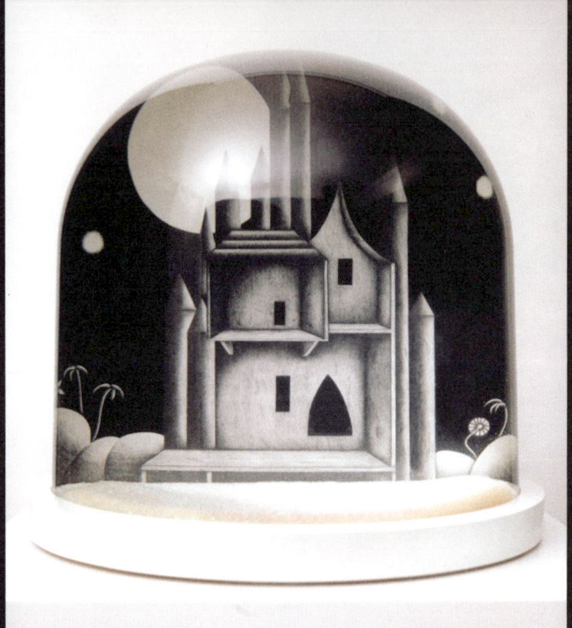

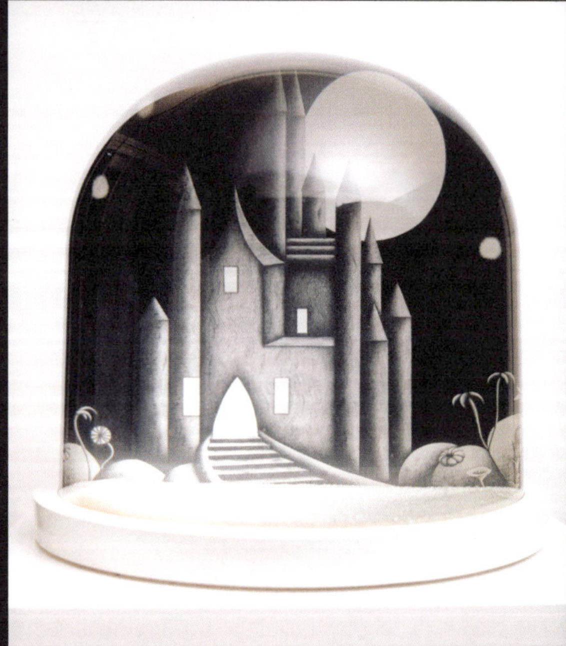

Below
Coffin
2003
Pencil on paper
73 x 93 cm
Courtesy the artist
and Danielle Arnaud
contemporary art

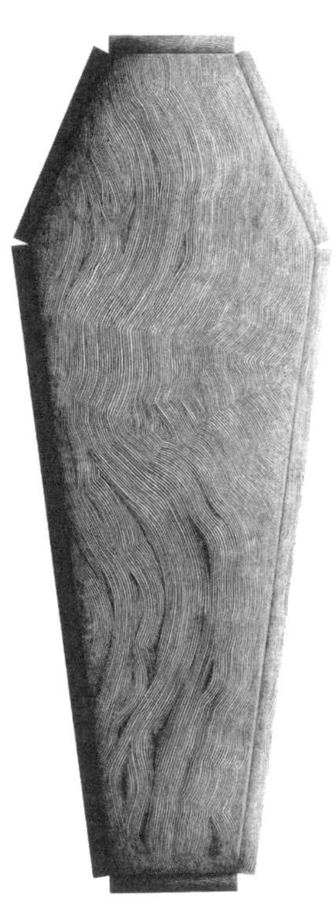

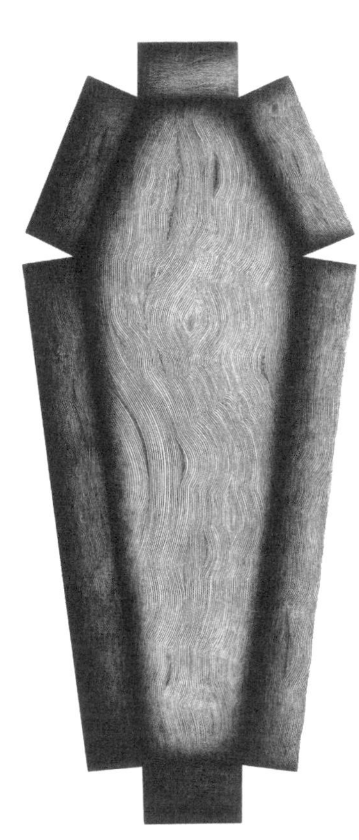

Acknowledgements
I would especially like to thank all the artists who were kind enough to take part in the book. I would also like to thank the following people for their help: Sylvia Farago, David Risley, Ilsa Colsell at Stuart Shave Modern Art, Tiffany Noe and Richard Lidinsky at Peres Projects, Imke Wagener at Contemporary Fine Arts, Kyoko Nitta at Taka Ishii Gallery, Amelia Hinojosa at Kurimanzutto, Justyna Niewiara at Lisson Gallery, Andrew MacLachlan, Honey Luard, Helen Evans and Donald Dinwiddie at Laurence King, Seana and Bianca Gavin, Nicholas Roeg, Bram Stoker, Jack Torrance of the Overlook Hotel, Mr Hyde, Dorian Gray and Paola Gavin for her second brain.